Sisters

BARBARA MORTIMER
In association with the
Royal College of Nursing

arrow books

Published by Arrow Books 2013

2 4 6 8 10 9 7 5 3 1

First published in Great Britain in 2012 by
Hutchinson
Random House, 20 Vauxhall Bridge Road,
London SW1V 2SA

www.randomhouse.co.uk

Addresses for companies within The Random House Group Limited can be
found at: www.randomhouse.co.uk/offices.htm

The Random House Group Limited Reg. No. 954009

A CIP catalogue record for this book
is available from the British Library

ISBN 9780099547747

The Random House Group Limited supports the Forest Stewardship
Council® (FSC®), the leading international forest-certification organisation.
Our books carrying the FSC label are printed on FSC®-certified paper. FSC
is the only forest-certification scheme supported by the leading environmental
organisations, including Greenpeace. Our paper procurement policy can be
found at: www.randomhouse.co.uk/environment

Typeset by carrdesignstudio.com
Printed and bound in Great Britain by CPI Group (UK) Ltd, Croydon, CR0 4YY

This book is dedicated to the nurses who worked at home and abroad during the Second World War in the most difficult conditions supporting the wounded, civilian and military.

CONTENTS

LIST OF ILLUSTRATIONS

THE NURSES' WAR

Home Front and the Channel Islands		Overseas and the War
4 October: 'Battle of Cable Street', British Union of Fascists (BUF) active in East End of London	1936	1936–9: Spanish Civil War
1 September: evacuation of London patients and staff to 'sector hospitals' in Green Line buses Gas masks issued to civilians Call-up of reservists	1939	1 September: Germany invades Poland 3 September: Britain and France declare war on Germany 9 September: British Expeditionary Force (BEF) deployed to France with medical and nursing support
January: food rationing introduced 10 May: Churchill appointed leader of a national government January–June: some London hospitals' staff and patients return to the city June: internment of enemy aliens 30 June: Channel Islands invaded and occupied by Germany July: Regional Blood Transfusion Service to cover the whole country authorised August–October: Battle of Britain September 1940–2: the Blitz. Initially London, later industrial centres. 40,000 civilians killed 14–15 November: bombing of Coventry, 554 killed	1940	May: *Blitzkrieg* in Western Europe; Netherlands, Belgium and France overrun 'Phoney war'; no active hostilities until June 26 May–4 June: Dunkirk, 336,000 Allied troops evacuated, 140,000 remained 10 June: Italy declares war on UK 22 June: surrender of France July: Italian invasion of Egypt October: Italian invasion of Greece and Albania November: Allied troops to Greece

	1941	
13–14 March: Clydebank Blitz, 528 residents killed		February: Rommel and the *Afrika Korps* to North Africa
10 May: full moon, largest raid on London, 1,400 killed		April: German invasion of the Balkans, Allies evacuate
June: clothes rationing introduced, 66 coupons annually		June: German invasion of Soviet Union
20–21 March, 21–3, 28–9 April: Plymouth Blitz		6–7 December: Japan attacks Pearl Harbor. USA enters war
		11 December: Germany declares war on USA

	1942	
January: Control of Engagement Order regulating employment of women 18–40 years of age		15 February: surrender of Singapore. 25,000 Allied prisoners taken
January: Belfast welcomes the first US servicemen to UK		Soviet Union demands a second front
Summer: clothes ration reduced, 'austerity' regulations limit trimmings and design		June: USA wins Battle of Midway, turning point of the war against Japan in the Pacific
June: Channel Islands, diphtheria epidemic		June: North Africa, Rommel captures Tobruk
15 September: Channel Islands, some individuals deported to European prison camps with their families		August: Europe, Dieppe raid, heavy Canadian losses
December: Beveridge Report published, foundation document for the NHS		November: North Africa, Battle of El Alamein, seals victory in North Africa for Allies

	1943	
March: Channel Islands, 1,000 prisoners or 'slave workers' arrive		Allied victory in North Africa confirmed
Channel Islands, Wehrmacht population estimated as 26,800, plus 4,000 'slave workers' on Alderney		May: Allied bombing of the Ruhr dams
March: widespread bombing of UK targets. East and south coast towns, Hull, Grimsby, Sunderland		July: Allied landings in Sicily
November: UNRRA (United Nations Relief and Rehabilitation Administration) established		3 September: Italy surrenders. German invasion of northern Italy
Nurses Act, creating a General Nursing Council (GNC) roll for assistant nurses		

	1944	
V-1 flying bombs and V-2 rockets targeted on south of England, particularly London, from European launch sites		January: Allied landings at Anzio, Italy
		February: fighting at Monte Cassino, Italy
6 June: D-Day, 156,000 Allied troops landed in northern France		5 June: Rome liberated
Channel Islands, increasing numbers of local escapes		June: rapid Soviet advance in eastern Europe. 350,000 German prisoners killed or wounded or imprisoned
31 August: Channel Islands cut off. No further supplies from France with 16,000 German troops now trapped on the Islands		August: Paris liberated
September: Channel Islands, no gas		
October: Channel Islands, German government passed a message from the Bailiff to the Protecting Power. Red Cross ship SS *Vega* with medical supplies and food parcels arrived in Guernsey 27 and in Jersey 30 December		

	1945	
February: Channel Islands, no electricity in hospital at night		January: Soviet liberation of Auschwitz
6 May: VE [Victory in Europe] Day		12 April: death of US President Roosevelt
9 May: liberation of the Channel Islands		28 April: Mussolini shot
		April: Russians reach Berlin
July: general election. Labour government voted in with Clement Attlee as Prime Minister		30 April: Hitler's suicide
		7 May: German unconditional surrender
		6 August: atomic bomb dropped on Hiroshima
		9 August: atomic bomb dropped on Nagasaki
		14 August: unconditional surrender of Japan

29 June 1946: Control of Engagement Order for nurses lifted. Nurses can now seek employment anywhere

PREFACE

The Royal College of Nursing Archives' oral history collection numbers almost 1,000 interviews, recording the lives of nurses from the First World War to the present day. We began collecting these life stories in the 1980s, and overwhelmingly the nurses we interviewed were the generation who had trained in the inter-war years. Through their memories we have been able to capture a way of life and a culture that have vanished. This was the world of pre-National Health Service hospitals, where the nursing culture demanded long hours and harsh discipline, and a hierarchy of matrons, sisters, staff nurses and probationers (student nurses) battled against disease and illness without antibiotics, disposable products or labour-saving equipment. For this generation the Second World War was a life-changing experience. Whether they were part of one of the traditional nursing services of the army, the navy or the air force, or working in one of the many branches of civilian nursing – hospital nursing, district nursing, industrial nursing, midwifery or health visiting – they all played a vital role in the war.

Dr Barbara Mortimer, who has selected and edited the extracts for this book, has been closely involved with the oral history collection held at the RCN Archives for many years. She is a nurse historian with an international reputation, contributing to conferences, journals, books and summer schools for many years. Her knowledge of the collection and its unique strengths is evident in the choice of themes, from the essential introductory chapter 'Nursing in 1939', to the final chapter 'Beginning Again'. In between, the day-to-day life of nurses during the war is described in their own words, jumping from the African desert to the home front and from pioneering work in the treatment of burns to the challenges of rationing and cycling in the blackout. In these extracts Dr Mortimer has captured not only the ebb and flow of the war, but also the emotions of the nurses, their pride in their work, their grief and their joy. At the same time, the reader is given a sense of the nurses' awareness of their part in a major historical event, one of the most devastating wars man has ever seen, and the fact that they were living through a period of profound social change.

Susan McGann
Former Royal College of Nursing archivist

MAKE NURSING YOUR WAR JOB

—it's War Work with a future

FOR FURTHER PARTICULARS APPLY TO
THE NURSING SECTION · COUNTY HALL · WESTMINSTER BRIDGE · S·E

Throughout the Second World War, London County Council were
desperately looking for willing hands.

ONE

NURSING IN 1939

Nursing is a service for the nation because it serves a national need …
the time has come when the public health authorities and the State
should realise that it is a service of outstanding importance.

*The Rt Hon. the Earl of Athlone, chair of Interdepartmental
Committee on Nursing Services, Interim Report (1939)*

When Eileen Willis left her convent school in 1939 at the age of 18, she knew that she wanted to become a nurse. Her middle-class parents were appalled. Forbidden from pursuing professional nurse training, and inspired by the writing of Vera Brittain about her life as a Voluntary Aid Detachment (VAD) in the First World War, Eileen joined the Red Cross, gained certificates in nursing, and volunteered as a mobile VAD. When war broke out, she was immediately called up. For the next six years she worked as a VAD and, later, a student nurse. By the end of the war she was a fully trained nurse and the world was a very different place.

But all that lay in the future. In 1939, almost all nurses were young women, many of them, like Eileen, keen to be involved and ready for anything.

Nursing as a profession had been developing since the mid nineteenth century, when it was one of a very small number of jobs open to respectable women. It was a pioneering career choice for women, but the job was accompanied by a stifling regime of discipline and service. By the time war broke out in 1939, there were many more jobs available to women and the way that schools of nursing and hospitals were organised made nursing look distinctly uninviting.

There was a national shortage of nurses, which seemed to get worse and worse. In 1937, a committee had been appointed 'to advise how recruitment could be improved'. It had only issued an interim report by the time war broke out, and was shelved for the duration.

Thanks to the lobbying of politically minded matrons and their allies, women like Sarah Swift, former matron of Guy's and co-founder of the College of Nursing, the first Nurse Registration Acts had passed into law in 1919. They established the statutory bodies known as the General Nursing Councils, which began to organise the national education, training and regulation of nurses.

In order to train as a nurse, a potential recruit applied to a nursing school attached to a hospital; there she worked as an apprentice in the wards. If she had chosen wisely, the hospital school would have an organised PTS (Preliminary Training School), where she would be taught anatomy, physiology and hygiene, and drilled in basic skills. These included bed-making, damp dusting, scrubbing mackintoshes,* filling hot-water bottles, sluicing foul linen and preparing special diets, all to be done correctly and quickly. Each student had a booklet prepared by the General Nursing Council that listed the skills a student nurse should master. When she had 'done' a skill, her book was signed by the sister or the sister tutor. At the end of her training the nurse took her completed book to her final practical examination, where it was inspected.

Nurses' pay during their three-year training was a pittance, the hours were long and the work was hard and included much exhausting domestic labour. Once PTS was over, there would be some formal lessons in a classroom, normally given by a doctor or a sister tutor, but in all hospitals nursing skills were honed at the bedside. There the student nurse was taught, supervised, almost driven by nurses who were senior to her.

The hospitals looked for a particular sort of recruit. They wanted mature, reliable women who would fit into the culture of the school. The ideal was an educated middle-class girl or, failing that, someone with the manners of a superior sort of domestic servant. But the shortage of nurses was such that nearly everyone who wanted to nurse could find a hospital somewhere to take her.

---

* Patients were nursed in bed for long periods. Mattresses were protected by red rubber sheets which were scrubbed between uses.

Finding a training school

The most prestigious hospitals were much sought after; they offered a becoming uniform, superior accommodation in a nurses' home and eventually a certificate, a hospital badge and, in most cases, preparation for the statutory examination of the General Nursing Councils that would virtually guarantee future employment. In exchange, such hospitals could be demanding. They frequently charged an enrolment fee, and required that the nurse pay for her own uniform.

As maturity was valued, the age of entry could vary between 21 and as old as 30. Broadly there were two sorts of hospital: the large, long-established teaching hospitals like St Bartholomew's and St Thomas' in London, as well as many smaller provincial hospitals, which were voluntary hospitals, funded by contributions collected locally. The second group were municipal hospitals, organised and financed by local government.

Annie Altschul, Jewish refugee, student nurse, Ealing Hospital, London, c.1940

Annie Altschul was one of many young female Jewish refugees who had fled the approaching war and embarked on nurse training as one of the few ways to support themselves. She was mildly amused by the culture she found in her adopted country.

The hospital system was voluntary and municipal. Ealing was a voluntary hospital, smallish, bit toffee-nosed. One was everlastingly looking down one's nose at the other half. Later, I joined a London County Council hospital, and then I looked down my nose at King's College, opposite, which was a voluntary hospital.

Everybody said I wouldn't like it [Ealing] and I didn't. I remember on one occasion, students were asked to come and see something we were never going to see again and we all had to troop in there and there was a foetus, and that was so rare, you weren't ever going to see an abortion again!

Well, once I got to Epsom Municipal Hospital ... I discovered that abortions were two a penny ...

By 1939, the rising cost of health care and the worldwide economic depression had made the financing of voluntary hospitals shaky. The municipal hospitals, on the other hand, were able to turn to local taxes for help. They had more stable funding, offered better conditions, including superannuation schemes, and were usually better equipped. Despite these differences, the high status of voluntary hospitals continued to attract those with social ambitions.

Patricia Lloyd, pupil midwife, Paddington London County Council Hospital, c.1944

After completing general training at St Bartholomew's in London, Patricia Lloyd enrolled as a pupil midwife in a local-authority hospital, where she was horrified by what she found.

I had to take whatever was available and that was Paddington, London County Council. I had heard about bad nursing in my time and didn't actually believe it; I thought, 'Ah well, we're all prejudiced here, you see.' But when I got to Paddington, I saw what they meant. It was dreadful, it really was; standards were so low.

The first thing you do when you join a ward is go and see the sister to sign in, and she would say, 'Right, go and do something or other.' Well, I walked into the ward and found the sister sitting on a patient's bed smoking a cigarette and she said, 'Shut the bloody door after you, nurse.' I thought, 'Good heavens above, where have I come to?' And that was the tone of it.

The London County Council hospitals had lots of wonderful equipment; I mean, for instance, we had to do bedpans with Lysol at Barts. But the London County Council had these terrific bedpan sterilisers that you just pushed them in and brought them out sterile ... hopefully.

Student nurses

Once enrolled as a student, a notorious feature of nurse training, and one of the things that drove many to leave nursing, was the seemingly mindless discipline imposed on students by some of the matrons, sisters and staff nurses who managed the daily life of a hospital.

Afra Leckie, student nurse, Margate Hospital, c.1932

Afra Leckie was a student nurse in Margate; her mother was dead and her father away at sea for long spells.

I was one of a family of three. I had two brothers, and we lived with my grandparents. They were absolutely wonderful but very, very strict, very Edwardian in their outlook.

A great school friend went into nursing at Margate, she told me how marvellous it was. So I decided that's what I wanted to do. I can see myself now, sitting in the hall of the hospital, with my tennis racquet, and my red hat on, waiting to see what it was all going to be like.

I found the training fascinating, and I enjoyed the work enormously. I found some sisters extremely difficult, and some very understanding. I wasn't altogether popular with the matron. She used to rather like her nurses to be ladies. I'm not quite sure that I was lady enough.

There was one time when I got quite fond of a private patient. We went off, and I was seen coming out of a public house. I was not the worse for drink at all. I'd had one drink I think. But the sister saw me. I had to go to the matron, then I had to go before the hospital board. My brothers came over. They thought that it was extraordinary, of course, that anybody could make all this fuss because you'd been seen coming out of a public house, and laughing probably, but doing nothing else.

The board asked where I'd got my money from. I said I have only the money that I am earning here. A lot of my pals would get money from parents, and so forth. But I didn't have anything from anybody. It was a perfectly normal, happy sort of relationship with this young man. Nothing happened, nothing awful or silly. It was built up to such an extent that I was given three months' probation.

Kathleen Raven, student nurse, St Bartholomew's Hospital, 1933–7

Kathleen Raven's brother was a doctor at Barts. He didn't think she would cope with the demands of nursing life.

Six o'clock every morning one was called, then breakfast at half past six, on duty at five to seven. Half an hour for lunch, no break for tea, we had it in the ward. If you were lucky you had two hours off at some point during the day but usually not. Then finish at eight in the evening and dash down for supper, very often you were late and maybe there was no supper left; a hard life.

You were still on probation until you got your first ward report, after three months, and then you had to go before the board and be elected by the governors. If you didn't have a good report or your conduct wasn't right, you were not elected and you went out of another door and were never seen again. You just went home. It was very tough.

Everything was run like clockwork. When the ward sister walked on to read the prayers at eight o'clock, that ward had to be perfect, with all the patients having had their breakfasts and washed, beds made, dusted, all the lockers done, the floor done, everything. There was no question of, haven't had time for this, haven't had time for that. Then the sister came on and did the charts, went round with each chart and spoke to each patient. Each of us in turn went 'home' for about 10 minutes to change our aprons and collect our mail, then came back. We had a cup of tea in the ward kitchen and then the doctor arrived about half past nine to ten o'clock for his ward rounds with all the medical students and the sister went round with him. There hadn't to be a sound.

Doris Carter, Royal Hampshire County Hospital (RHCH), 1939–40

After further training in London, Doris Carter returned to her general training school, RHCH, as a staff nurse.

During PTS we had a day off a month, plus a half-day every other Sunday. It didn't always work out, especially when we were on the wards. If the ward was busy we just didn't get the half-day. It was never made up to us, we just lost it. And I do remember on one occasion, when I had lost six half-days, going in to Matron (which was absolutely unheard of, I still wonder how on earth I had the courage to do it) and complaining to her. I told her that I was entitled to my half-days. She looked me in the eye and said, 'Nurse, you're entitled to nothing but service to your patients, and furthermore, as punishment, you can go on night duty.'

Sue Aylmer, paediatric student nurse, Royal Alexandra Hospital, Brighton, c.1942

Orphaned as a baby, Sue Aylmer longed to work with children. After training as a nursery nurse with Barnardo's, she took children's nurse training (RSCN) in Brighton.

I found the ward sisters difficult. The baby ward sister's attitude was that if a baby died, it was something you had 'done'. I'll tell you a lovely story. We had a child come in frequently; she had some sort of blood disorder. We had her in because she was the eldest of a large family; you know, dad out of work and the family very poor. She didn't like the ward sister shouting at the nurses, and she'd say, 'Never mind, nurse, Jesus loves you.' The ward sister got so exasperated one day, she said, 'I love them too, Maureen, but they need training.' She was a lovely little girl. When she died, the whole hospital was sad.

Grace Howie, registered fever nurse, Glasgow Royal Infirmary, 1939

After fever training at Ruchill hospital in Glasgow, Grace Howie enrolled for general training at GRI.

It was a four-year training, but if you had previously trained as a registered fever nurse or registered sick children's nurse, you did three years. What I couldn't understand was why in that case you were paid first-, second- and third-year salaries instead of second, third and fourth? So she [Miss Husband, Matron of Glasgow Royal Infirmary] investigated everything and it was because a predecessor had done it for economy. She got that one sorted out just as I arrived, so that was fine, I started on second-year salary. Matron was a very able woman, and a very sound woman.

One might ask for what was known as a late pass. Normally on off duty one had to be in by ten thirty, but a late pass was half past one. And [at Glasgow] one asked Matron, 'May I have a late pass, please?' 'Yes, nurse', date, time and what have you, and you got your pass. Not, as happened in many smaller hospitals, which distressed me later, 'Where are you going and with whom are you going and when will you be back?' Well, of course that causes mischief and 'in the windows'. The number of young nurses who have been pushed in the windows by their boyfriends, but we didn't need to, we could ask for a late pass.

Eunice Boorman, student nurse, Oldchurch Hospital, Essex, 1940–3

From a nursing family, Eunice Boorman enrolled for general training in 1940.

We had to lay out trolleys for blood transfusions and pneumothorax. That was very interesting. During the war when people came down from the London hospitals, they couldn't lay out those trolleys and I said to one of the girls, 'Why weren't you taught to lay out that setting?' and she said, 'Well we had a lot of student doctors and they did all the work.' At Oldchurch we had to do it all and get it ready for the doctors.

Matrons

Every hospital had a matron, who was in charge not just of nursing and patient care but also domestic administration such as catering services. The job varied enormously, depending on the size and the nature of the institution. Matron of one of the major hospitals was managing a very large institution indeed and was typically correspondingly efficient, but some of these women were much less competent than, say, Miss Husband at Glasgow Royal Infirmary.

Isobel Balmain, student nurse, Royal Hospital for Sick Children, Edinburgh, c.1939

As the Royal Infirmary of Edinburgh (RIE) did not accept students until they were 21 years old, Isobel Balmain began her nursing career at the Royal Hospital for Sick Children.

Matron was a lovely person to look at. I don't think I have ever seen a lovelier face in any woman. [But when] my first pay was stolen out of my handbag and I went to her ... she said, 'Nurse, go away, any nurse could come and tell me that.' I had no money until I told my father, who gave me some.

When I was home on leave once, we went on holiday to a little cottage my parents used to take up in the Cheviots. I ran down to the burn, which I always did in the morning, and I fell and sprained my ankle. My father wrote to Matron and said I couldn't come back immediately, and when I did come back she asked me to take my stocking off so that she could look at it.

Ivy Scott, matron, Royal Halifax Infirmary, 1934–47

Ivy Scott trained as a general nurse at King's College Hospital in Denmark Hill, London; she then went to study midwifery at the General Lying-In Hospital, in

York Place. Following that, she undertook ward sister and assistant matron posts, finally becoming a matron in 1934 at the age of 34.

I found myself not only responsible for the nursing, but also for the domestics, which I was expecting, and the porters, which I was not. The kitchen, catering, laundry, it all came under the matron in those days. Really, I thought afterwards, I feel I am about 90 per cent a welfare officer and 10 per cent a matron. Of course it took an awful lot of time.

I was allowed to go to the house committee every month, but I only went in to give my report and to listen to any queries there were on the nursing staff, and then I left. I was never allowed to sit through the committee, which I regretted.

There was no nursing committee in those days and I suggested to the secretary 'I feel there should be a nursing committee where I can air more things than I can at the house committee.' Eventually I got them really

These newly qualified staff nurses all began training in 1939. They surround Matron Lucy Duff Grant of Manchester Royal Infirmary. The infirmary took in around twenty new students three times a year.

interested in nurses and nurse training and the problems, and they realised that it was something that they should have known about long ago.

Afra Leckie, night sister, Maidenhead Hospital, c.1941

When Afra Leckie was working as a night sister at Maidenhead Hospital, she had a very unpleasant encounter with Matron.

The climax came, and the matron just went for me. She caught me on night duty ... in those days the night sister had to wear 'strings'* with a bow underneath her chin. That could rub your skin raw behind the ears. She caught me walking about without them on. I think she caught me twice. She was so mad with me. I thought 'to get like that over such a small item', and that was it. I just gave my notice in, just like that. I didn't know where I was going.

---

* This was starched cotton tape tied under the chin with a bow and fixed on top of the head, under the cap, with a comb or kirby grip.

Sisters

Each ward was run by a ward sister, many of whom were respected by medical and nursing colleagues alike. They were powerful figures and frequently had reputations of almost mythical proportions, particularly amongst the junior nurses whose lives they ruled. Many remained in the hospital where they had trained and were very proud of that institution.

Kathleen Raven, student nurse, St Bartholomew's Hospital, London, 1933–7

Kathleen Raven went on to be a sister herself in the course of a long and successful career, but she struggled with the sisters when she was a student nurse.

I did surgical, medical of course; I did everything. We had some harridans of sisters. Some of them were nice, but some … Nurses nowadays wouldn't tolerate it, they would walk out … You couldn't do right, whatever you did was wrong and really I don't want to use the word sadistic, but it almost was.

Looking back on it, most of them I suppose had lost their fiancés in the First World War, there were millions less men than women so there was no chance of them ever getting married, which was all one wanted to do in those days, wasn't it?

They weren't old, they couldn't have been more than 30 or 40, but all us young things coming in to a different era, I can only think it was resentment and jealousy. Their lives were completely blighted, there was nothing for them but this ward sister role, unless they were outstanding and went on to something else, but there was very little choice in those days for nurses.

Elizabeth Weisz, née MacIntosh, student nurse, St Thomas' Hospital, c.1945

After working in the Observer Corps during the war, Elizabeth Weisz enthusiastically began nurse training, where she was shocked by some of the conditions but determined to succeed.

Sisters were mostly remote and unapproachable to us, of course, as juniors; a few were cruel. One in particular had me so terrified that I used to go home weeping and my mother would say, 'You don't have to go back, you know', and of course back I went. In those days there was absolutely no question of even mentioning the fact that she was tormenting me to anybody else. She was so tall that she could look over the top of the screens and she made it her interest to see that Nurse MacIntosh was not doing things properly, and of course I shook so much and was so nervous that in fact I didn't do things well at all. I was extremely glad to get off her ward and on to someone kinder who I could work for happily.

Kathleen Raven, student nurse, St Bartholomew's Hospital, London, 1933–7

To explain the kind of things they did – it's petty but it's so stupid … Every morning the ward had to be perfect and ready for prayers at eight o'clock. So, one day she didn't come up, five past eight, ten past eight. I thought, she's coming up late today, I'll read the prayers. So I did. She eventually came out, stepped to the lectern and I said, 'Oh, Sister, I've read the prayers.'

'You've read the prayers! How dare you read the prayers? What do you mean by reading the prayers?'

So two or three mornings afterwards, eight o'clock came, ten past eight came; I thought, I can't read the prayers. Quarter past eight came and she went straight to her desk and did the charts. I had to go up to her and say, 'Sister, I haven't done the prayers.' Then it was 'Why haven't you read the prayers? It's quarter past eight, you should have read the prayers.' This kind of thing went on throughout everything; it was most odd.

It changed after I had a confrontation with her. I got in with them all because I was older than most; I expect that's why they sent me to all these difficult places.

Sheena Kilminster, née Craig, student nurse, Royal Infirmary of Edinburgh, c.1940

Sheena Kilminster, like her mother before her, trained at the Royal Infirmary of Edinburgh.

Sister Richardson had prayers first thing in the morning when she came on duty at eight o'clock, having received the night report from the outgoing night charge nurse. She thumped an old piano with the nursing staff sat round in a semicircle behind her. We sang a hymn and we knelt at our chairs and said the Lord's Prayer, she in a loud voice, we very much more quietly. On one occasion she finished the Lord's Prayer 'for ever and ever, Amen. Who is the inside probationer? Nurse, this chair has not been dusted!'

She was notorious for saying to every new probationer who came to her ward, 'Nurse, dust is germs, germs are disease, possess yourself of a duster and follow me.' And [on this particular morning] she proceeded to instruct me on what was then known as damp and dry dusting; one hand contained a damp duster which dusted the patient's locker etc. and the other one dried it off.

She really was a notorious character; she ran a very, very efficient ward, but it was hell to work for her.

Margaret Broadley, sister, Harrison Ward, London Hospital, Whitechapel, c.1938

Margaret Broadley trained and followed her entire career at 'the London'. The sisters may have been objects of terror for some nurses, but they were also recognised for their skills by the medical staff.

The medical students were taught by the ward sisters, and the medical college paid a small honorarium to the sisters that did it. So when I became Sister Harrison, I also took over lecturing to the medical students. You did it once every three months, and gave them a two-hour nursing demonstration.

It took a lot of preparation, because they had to be shown packs, and cupping, and enemas, and all the things that you don't very often do. The same demonstration that was given to the medical students was also given to the student nurses.

'Poppy' Bocock, sister tutor, Nightingale School, St Thomas' Hospital, 1940

As a former ward sister, now a tutor, 'Poppy' Bocock was well placed to recognise the skills of the ward sisters.

It was remarkable, the co-operation between the ward sister and the consultants and the registrar. The registrar was responsible for the medical students; he was responsible to the ward sister for their conduct and their teaching. And the ward sister was responsible for teaching them how to give injections, or anything else that they might be required to do for a patient.

Of course, in the women's wards, no patient was ever examined without a nurse being present. The student had to come and fetch a nurse, and she chaperoned.

Isobel Balmain, ward sister, Royal Infirmary of Edinburgh, c.1939

Sisters were in many ways both the embodiment of and the victims of the quintessential view of nurses as being wedded to the job. One aspect of their lives that illustrated this particularly clearly was their accommodation.

I slept in a bedroom just off the female ward. If the nurses got into difficulties they came to my room and called me and asked me to come and help, so I used to put on my dressing gown and pop over to either one ward or the other. With the result that you were constantly on call.

Another thing, which nobody would tolerate now and I don't think I would either, was my bathroom was the outside bathroom in the male ward, where all the dirty linen had been. The night nurse would put a big heavy screen around the bath, and there was I, [bathing with] people behind the screen going in and out. I think they tried not to when I was there but inevitably they had to. The smell in that place wasn't very pleasant at times, you know.

You got your meals [breakfast and lunch] sent up; the ward maid collected your food. You went down at night for set dinner with all the other sisters. All in uniform, all in certain places depending on seniority.

It was one night when I was at dinner that I must have been in a very thoughtful mood. I looked around and saw all that collection of very wonderful people, some of them were my colleagues, some a lot older than me, some by this time maybe a bit younger, and I thought, you're all marvellous but you're all far too old and sedate-looking for your age and I'm not going to get to that stage. By this time I'd been nine years as ward sister and I decided to go up and write my resignation ... The chief [senior consultant] was very kind about it, he said he wasn't going to stand in my way.

It wasn't a good thing sleeping on the ward and eating on the ward. It was like living in a little world on its own, you didn't know what was really happening in the big wide world.

Win Gordon, née Logan, student nurse, Royal Infirmary of Edinburgh, 1945–8

Win Gordon knew she wanted to be a nurse, but her parents were keen for her to study for a degree. After gaining her degree, she still wanted to train as a nurse. Her parents then encouraged her.

As far as I can recollect, the sisters without exception lived on the wards. It was an old building and had quite large rooms with high ceilings. A number of the sisters at the Royal had a private income and didn't have a salary at all. They had beautiful sitting rooms with antiques and beautiful things, and they had proper 'down to dinner' every evening with silver service and all the rest of it. It was, I suppose, gracious living, but very restricted.

Margaret Thomson, ward sister, Royal Infirmary of Edinburgh, c.1945

Margaret Thomson trained as a nurse despite her mother's worry about this sort of job. After general and midwifery training she was appointed a sister in her training hospital.

You had to sleep in but I had a room over in the Florence Nightingale [nurses' home]. I had a sitting room on the ward; but it was only certain wards that had the sister's bedroom on the ward. I was fortunate, I was one of the first sisters that got permission to sleep out. It wasn't easy, mind you, getting on duty in the morning, because you had to be on at half past seven. There was a lot of struggle to get the right to sleep out. That was in 1953.

Staff nurses

Sisters were supported by staff nurses, younger women who had completed their training.

Winifred Hector, student nurse, St Bartholomew's Hospital, London, c.1935

The daughter of an engine driver and an enthusiastic socialist mother, Winifred Hector enrolled for nurse training at Barts, after seeking the advice of her GP.

My role models were the staff nurses, sisters were too far out of sight and too harsh and cranky anyway. I can recall one surgical ward sister who wouldn't allow her night nurses into the clean sink room at night because

Winifred Hector, fourth from the left in the back row, was one of the sisters who remained at Bart's throughout the Blitz.

she used to wash her smalls there. When I say smalls, they were rather long, combinations and things like that. You used to have to get out packets of dressings and so forth ready to use. But the staff nurses were just a few years ahead of you, glorious in belts and buckles, very accomplished women. I still rather look up to them now when I see them at the Barts League meetings, the women who to me represented Barts nurses.

Nursing work, 'good nursing'

✚

Most of the labour of nursing was done by student nurses; their work was embedded in 'routines' which everyone knew. As far as illness was concerned, there were few effective medicines to fight disease and in many cases doctors prescribed supportive measures, 'rest and a good diet'. Patients were routinely kept in bed for long periods; this could amount to a year or more in the case of tuberculosis. At the time of the outbreak of war, the most effective therapy available to the doctor was often 'good nursing'. The classic situation where the nurses' skills were prized particularly highly was in nursing pneumonia, the 'captain of the men of death'.

Janet Crawley, student nurse, Royal Infirmary of Edinburgh, 1935–9

Janet Crawley was the only daughter of a seaman's widow, who tried to discourage her desire to nurse. After a commercial course, Janet enrolled for general nurse training at the RIE just before war broke out.

The first three months of the year, you sort of looked forward to getting pneumonias in. They were real nursing from the time they came in. There was usually someone 'specialing' them; they had to be sponged down every two hours. You were always giving them sips of water to try and keep their temperatures down. You were just with them all the time; you were not allowed to leave them at all. I would say that was real nursing … you do not get that now. Watching their backs for bedsores and their heels as well; taking their temperatures.

Some did get better and some didn't. But you felt that you achieved something, if you saw that they were getting better. If you saw them go walking out the ward, you used to think it was wonderful.

Lisbeth Hockey, Jewish refugee, student nurse, London, c.1945

Lisbeth Hockey left Austria where she was studying medicine just before war broke out. In London she trained as a nurse.

I was impressed by the quality of the nursing. Patients had a blanket bath every day – in those days we blanket-bathed patients – it doesn't happen any more. Patients were looked after as people. But there were lots of rigidities which one wouldn't tolerate now … you have to move with the times. But I think the quality of care that the patients got was amazingly good.

Anna Brocklesbury-Davis, student nurse, St Thomas' Hospital, London, c.1936–40

The daughter of missionary parents, Anna Brocklesbury-Davis undertook general training at St Thomas' just before war broke out.

There were thirty beds in a ward, fifteen each side, and the probationers were called day-side, which were all the fifteen beds on the left, and night-side, which were all the fifteen beds on the right, and thirds. Thirds used to have to look after all the equipment, and also help with food and serve from the trolleys, which went round with all the meals.

'Poppy' Bocock, sister tutor, Nightingale School, St Thomas' Hospital, 1940

We had these lovely long wards with high windows, and the light was beautiful. But of course the patients, although you would think they weren't, they were much more isolated than in the hospitals where you had small wards with four beds in, because they couldn't hear each other. When I was first there we had to carry two screens for each bed. You never, ever, did anything for a patient without screens.

The night nurses did a bedpan round before we came on, and then we had a bedpan round at midday, before the midday meal, and we had a bedpan round in the evening. And on those occasions we put the screens across the door of the ward, and nobody was allowed in as long as that was going on. And then when you'd finished and all the bedpans had been cleared away, then you took the screen down. Even the consultants were not allowed in when the patients were having their bedpan round.

Doris Carter, staff nurse, Royal Hampshire County Hospital, 1939–40

Both as a student and as a staff nurse, Doris Carter recalled preparing dressings and packing drums for surgery.

We had to make all the dressings including the gauze swabs. They were ... given to us in 100-yard rolls and we had to cut it off and fold it to the size required. In fact any sort of dressings we had to make ourselves; they had to be packed into the drums and put at the door so that the porter could take them up. They were sterilised in autoclaves on the premises.

The other thing about the sterilising was the fish kettles; big oval things, in which we boiled up everything: enamel dishes, kidney dishes. It was perched on two small gas rings. It always surprised me that no one knocked it over and we didn't get ourselves scalded. These enamel dishes were an absolute nightmare, they used to get so filthy and we had to keep them clean with some strong stuff, which I believe was called 'general acid' or some such name. I know it was very, very toxic. It was the only thing that would clean these enamel bowls. Later it was really marvellous having 'stay bright' [stainless-steel] dishes after the awful enamel things.

The other thing that I remember distinctly was the bedpan washer. When I first went there, there was no such thing. You just took the bedpans into the sluice room and cleaned them out with a mop, best you could; real messy job. But while I was there they introduced a bedpan washer, which was really heaven. You just slipped it in and turned on the tap and the bedpan was washed out.

But the thing that used to really get us down was the urinal washer because we used to forget which tap to turn and, if you turned on the wrong tap, a fountain would go to the ceiling and ruin your cap. That happened to dozens of us heaps of times. You were always turning on the wrong tap and you got drowned with the fountain from the urinal washer.

We also had to do the urine testing every day; that was a major job for the pro [probationer]. You usually spent an hour in the sluice room every morning testing the urines and it wasn't a matter of sticking in a paper, it was all very complicated and every urine had to be tested for everything; it was a wonder we weren't in there longer; you reckoned to spend an hour in the sluice room testing the urine in the morning if you were a junior pro.

The giving of drugs was quite a performance; I think it took at least ten minutes to give a quarter grain of morphia. We first had to get the glass syringe out of the spirit, where it was kept at the end of the ward on a trolley, we had to rinse it out in cold water and then we took the morphia from a minute vial, having counted it to make sure that the right amount of drug was there as recorded in the drug book. We took out one of the minute pills, like a little saccharine pill, and put it into a teaspoon with water. That was then boiled up over a spirit lamp and drawn up into the syringe.

Having done that, we then got a kidney dish from the steriliser and took it to the bed and we were taught that the person who drew it up must go with the person giving it, so that it was given to the right patient. We asked the patient their name, checked it with the board and administered it. Then coming back, we'd dismantle the syringe, wash it and put it back into the steriliser where it had to boil. Quite often it got broken while it was in there; you forgot all about it in your other many duties or somebody came and put something on top of it. If it was broken, you had to pay for it. We had to pay ninepence for a syringe; we also had to pay ninepence if we broke a thermometer; if we broke anything in the kitchen we had to pay threepence; so out of our meagre salary that was quite a consideration.

Having given the drug, we then had to enter it into the drug book and sign up with our two names. I would say it was probably ten minutes to give an injection of morphine, or anything else for that matter.

Survival

Nursing was so demanding and the conditions of service so challenging that it was common to discover that 50 per cent of a student intake failed to complete their training.

Eunice Boorman, student nurse, Oldchurch Hospital, Essex, 1940–3

Only about six of us completed the course, of the twenty-six that went in. I was the only one out of my class that went through and trained as a midwife; some of them did their first part and didn't go any further.

Rose Telfer, née Hall, student nurse, Royal Infirmary of Edinburgh, 1935–9

Sixteen of us started together in 1935 and only six of us finished the course. Some of them just could not cope, couldn't take it at all.

Kathleen Raven, student nurse, St Bartholomew's Hospital, 1933–7

A lot did leave, because in those days it was a very hard life. I can understand the wastage, although I don't think it was any higher than it is now. It was a very tough life but one got a great deal of satisfaction out of it.

Staff sickness

Working hard, permanently tired and exposed to all sorts of disorders, it was not surprising that some nurses succumbed to the same illnesses as their patients. In the days before antibiotics, septic fingers were particularly common and it was impossible to work with them.

Janet Crawley, student nurse, Royal Infirmary of Edinburgh, 1935–9

I was actually the only one that finished up to time, you might say, because I had no sick leave. Most of the others had a spell, but I had none. Four years was quite good with no sick leave at all.

Margaret Broadley, sister, later tutor, London Hospital, Whitechapel, c.1938

The health of the nursing staff was very carefully monitored. A home sister was in the dining room at meals and she really knew that the nurses did eat. There was a home sister who went round at night, so that she knew that the nurses' lights were out by half past ten. And if someone wasn't well enough to be on duty they were promptly put in the nurses' sick room – there was no such thing as being poorly and in your room until tomorrow.

The nurses' sick room had eighteen beds, six surgical and twelve medical. There were almost always nurses with infected fingers off duty and I would have said that there were always six or eight at least off sick with minor ailments.

Sheena Kilminster, née Craig, sister, Princess Mary's Royal Air Force Nursing Service, 1944

Sheena Kilminster had a break in training after developing a throat infection. She finally completed her training during the war.

I had a streptococcal throat, which was very common in those days, and no antibiotics of course. You got rid of the throat condition, and it was followed six weeks later by acute rheumatism – rheumatic fever it was called then. Mercifully I was a fairly mild case but the niggly rheumatism followed me through life.

Anyhow, having been accepted on my professional qualifications, I then had a very stringent medical to undergo, and I thought I'd better confess about the rheumatic fever because it was sure to come out in the wash. And so I confessed and they went over me with a small-tooth comb, and they couldn't fault me. I was accepted as being A1 fit for service in any part of the world. So I was a very fit young woman.

Afra Leckie, night sister, Maidenhead Hospital, c.1941

I did enjoy it, but I always remember once, I had a carbuncle here on my arm, and in those days you didn't have any antibiotics. And I was a night sister, don't forget. I had to put my arm in this great bath, and sit up in bed and keep it in the bath. They had forgotten all about me, and I couldn't get it out, my arm was swollen up like anything. Somebody came up and took it out eventually. I was made to go on duty that night with my arm in a sling. There was no question of going off duty. This matron, she just insisted. I didn't have a single minute off for that arm and it was agonisingly painful as well.

Grace Howie, student nurse, Ruchill Fever Hospital, Glasgow, 1934–7

When she began her fever training, Grace Howie was aware of the precautions taken on behalf of the nurses.

We weren't allowed to nurse diphtheria until we'd been inoculated, and before we started we had to have a vaccination against smallpox. As far as possible we were protected and of course we had to be careful with our techniques in the ward, what we did or didn't do.

It was hard work. I would say the risks were in the tuberculosis wards because one spent six months in these wards, day duty and night duty. And the coughing and the spitting … And of course a nurse occasionally started to spit blood and you knew she had tuberculosis and she was off.

Doreen Norton, student nurse, London County Council, 1941–5

Determined to take up nursing, Doreen Norton enrolled in a municipal hospital, where she found herself nursing severely ill TB patients.

My most vivid memory of nursing at the time is on D2, a ward of twenty-eight women, fourteen beds each side and they were nearly all under thirty and all with advanced TB. Some had the miliary* type, it was terrible.

Some had the larynx affected and they had a silence card above their bed to discourage talking – as if it mattered, you know, they didn't have much time left to talk. Also fatal haemoptysis was not unusual and that was absolutely terrible; all you could do was hold the person in your arms. You're supposed to wear a mask in close contact but I could never bring myself to put a mask between a dying patient and myself. This, well, it was a heartbreaking situation; it was of course before the [discovery of] streptomycin and the allied drugs.

These people had all been sent back from sanatoriums, nothing could be done for them, and they were all brought back to be with their families. There was no hope for them. I think most of the London County Council hospitals had wards of this kind; we had two.

Then my world fell apart. I was found to have a shadow on one lung and I spent the next year in hospital in Sidcup in Kent in a ward especially for nurses who'd contracted TB. As I say, it happened to a lot of nurses at that time and it's not really surprising.

---

* A particularly virulent form of the disease.

The patients: children

Lotte Heymann, Jewish refugee, student nurse, Birmingham Children's Hospital, 1941–3

Once she had decided to nurse, Lotte Heymann found it easier to secure a training position in a children's hospital than a general one.

No parent visiting was allowed at all and we had terrible scenes, because in those days children were of course longer in hospital. We had situations like cleft palate, we had a whole ward because Birmingham was a central district; we had children from Wales, from all over the place. A whole ward with only children with mastoid infections and mastoidectomies. They were a long time in hospital and got used to the nurses.

Come the moment when they were going home, there you were, you handed the young child over to a complete stranger and there were cries all round, the mothers cried, the children cried, it was heartbreaking.

Annie Altschul, Jewish refugee, student nurse, Epsom Hospital, 1941–2

Once enrolled in the municipal hospital in Epsom, Annie Altschul was amused by some of the social habits she observed.

We also had a lot of gypsies around in Epsom, gypsies always accompanied race-grounds, and there were certainly totally different rules about how you nursed them. The assumption was that gypsies couldn't be controlled and therefore if they all wanted to sit around the ward visiting, well, poor things, they didn't know any better, they had to be tolerated. When you look back, they knew exactly what was right, they never abandoned their children. They stayed put if the child was in hospital.

The patients: young men

✚

One of the unspoken issues for the genteel young woman was the hidden sexuality of nursing, the inevitable association of the nurse with the naked bodies of strangers, something respectable young women were unaccustomed to. This was rarely spoken of openly; it was acknowledged obliquely when an age of entry was imposed. At twenty-one years of age, a student was deemed to be mature and able to cope with these problems.

Elizabeth Halliday, student nurse, Royal Hospital for Sick Children, Edinburgh, c. 1938

Although she was a farmer's daughter, Elizabeth Halliday was taken aback by some of the things she had to do.

And the horrors that you meet … one of the things I shall never forget is a boy. I was eighteen, I had no brothers, I knew about animals, and I knew what a boy looked like, but I was naïve and inexperienced and what have you. There was this poor boy who was scalded right down the front, and he had a great cage over him. He wanted a bottle and I went and got the bottle and I was standing beside the bed wondering what to do and Sister came along and she said to the effect, 'What's your problem?' and I said, 'Well, he wants to use a bottle' and she said, 'Well put it in, put his penis in and let him use it.' I had to lift this poor burned penis and put it in the bottle, that was one of the horrors.

Doris Carter, student nurse, Royal Hampshire County Hospital, 1936–9

My very first blanket bath it happened, what Matron told me, when she interviewed me, could possibly happen. I was told to go blanket-bath somebody behind curtain four and I took all the paraphernalia, as we were taught to in PTS, pulled back the curtains and there lay a young lad, who a fortnight ago I'd been walking out with. His name was Tom Bennett. I don't know who was more surprised, Tom or me. However I remembered what Matron had said, you're sure to meet people you know and you must just ignore it and get on with your nursing duties. So I tried to put that into practice.

Mrs Burley-Wilson, née Wood, student nurse, Tunbridge Wells, c.1937

Although her father was a governor of Barts, Mrs Burley-Wilson chose to train in a local hospital.

We had another sister who said, 'Never leave the men with the bottles in their bed, never, because you'll get a shock.' Of course we used to take these bottles out all covered in white slime. We never knew what it was. I was as innocent as a newborn flea. That's what they did, they used to masturbate themselves into their bottles.

As war became an increasingly likely possibility, a mood of gloom settled over the sector. The position of nursing in Britain had changed little in the twenty years since the Nurses Registration Acts were passed. The Acts had certainly done something to organise and regulate training, but the work of nursing was still hard, the hours long and the pay inadequate. It was becoming increasingly difficult to recruit sufficient nurses.

Preparing for war: all hands set about defending their patients. These nurses inspect sandbags at a London hospital, September 1939.

TWO

WAR CLOUDS GATHER

I still have a slip of paper giving two addresses in the north of England; my family decided that when, not if, but when Hitler invaded the south we would try and meet up again at one of these two addresses in the north.

Norma Batley, Red Cross nurse, Emergency Hospital,
Leatherhead, 1940

Will war really come?

With hindsight, there were obvious signs of an approaching European conflict in the late 1930s, but as long as efforts were being made to preserve peace, many people did not want to countenance the possibility of war. Nurses were of course no exception to this, but sometimes their work brought them into contact with dramatic events that compelled them to consider the worsening political situation. Avis Hutt was a student nurse at Mile End Hospital in London's East End, and found herself tending fascist blackshirts as well as communists injured in the Battle of Cable Street. Monica Baly, whose family had German friends, was horrified by the Germany she observed while on a walking holiday in 1937. Sometimes, though, no amount of proximity was enough to pierce the desperate hope that all would be well. Theodora Turner visited Germany as a student on the Florence Nightingale International course in 1939 and noticed nothing particularly remarkable.

Avis Hutt, née Askey, formerly Clarke, student nurse, Mile End London County Council Hospital, 1935–9

In the run-up to war, Avis was working hard as a student nurse, but she still had time to get involved with the political scene being played out in the East End.

I went to Mile End in 1935. The area then was predominantly Jewish and it was highly political because fascism was making itself heard. Also Stepney was very left and there was a strong Communist Party. The Spanish war hadn't quite begun but it began during my training. I was on casualty during the Cable Street March and we received about twenty patients, the victims of either the police or the British Union of Fascists. They were very vocal about the causes and I'd already become aware of the specialness of the patients who were, as I say, probably 90 per cent Jewish.

I began to feel political and have something to measure against my previous life ... I was a 'young Conservative' because of the good life, you know, young men and tennis and that sort of thing. It wasn't in any sense of the word an ideological decision, it was just that was the place to be and where you met nice chaps.

Well, Matron would have liked us to have been insulated from some of these social conditions, but [that's impossible] if it's going on all around you and you're going down the Mile End Road and patients are in the beds reading the *Daily Worker* or *Action*, which was the fascist paper.

We were all communists and we had a left book group and discussed what we wanted a health service to be. The man I married had been one of the golden boys of Guy's – set up the rugby·football club, all gold medals – he did a locum in Hollywood, came across the New Deal, joined the Communist Party in Hollywood and came back to this country, to Mile End Hospital as a surgeon. So there was no way that I wasn't going to be involved.

Monica Baly, student nurse, Middlesex Hospital, London, 1935–9

Monica Baly's family in Sussex had good friends in Germany.

It was a very interesting time politically, '35, '36. We had German friends at home and ... in '37 I went out to Germany, with a school friend, on a walking holiday; *Jugendherberge*, you know, staying in youth hostels and so forth. I went out all pro–German, because as I say we had German friends, and anyhow I considered myself to be a pacifist, but was horrified to see all these posters about the persecution of the Jews and so forth. I came back a bit ambivalent about the whole thing, and then of course the next year was Munich, and you know the war clouds were looming. I was in the middle of my training. There was a great deal of discussion went on, particularly with the medical students; they were very bright, that lot. Most of them were straight down from Cambridge, and were full of ideas; some of them went out to Spain, of course, and I got hooked up with the Left-Wing Book Club, and was really a little radical at that time.

Theodora Turner, ward sister, St Thomas' Hospital, London, c.1938

Theodora Turner was content with the career she imagined for herself. She had enjoyed her training at St Thomas' and looked forward to working in that illustrious hospital.

I was quite happy being a medical ward sister but Dame Alicia [matron of St Thomas'] sent for me one day and said, I think you ought to apply for this. It was the Florence Nightingale International course; you either took it to prepare you for administration or else for being a tutor. You were considered on your way to more senior positions and you had to get a scholarship. I got a Red Cross scholarship; it was three terms, from '38 to '39. [At] the beginning of the course we lived in Manchester Square. There were twenty-four of us and only four came from Great Britain.

We had lectures in the College of Nursing and at Bedford College, then we took an exam at the end of the year. We also did a tour of hospitals, which we could choose, in Europe or England. I travelled with a Canadian and an American. We went in the spring of '39, started in Germany and went to Latvia, Poland, Sweden, Finland, and, oh, Holland and Denmark; seven countries in five weeks. We started in Dusseldorf and then we went to Berlin. It was planned, you see, where we went. There were all these messages around the place, and there were all these air-raid shelters, completely ready. We couldn't make out what all these advertisements were because none of us spoke German.

[In Germany] we weren't shown any modern hospitals at all, we were shown old hospitals, and we weren't put up in a hospital, as we were in the rest of the tour, we stayed in a hotel and we were taken to see the enormous stadium where Hitler used to [speak] in Berlin. We actually stood for a moment, wherever he stood and did his speech.

Sheena Kilminster, née Craig, former student nurse, recovering from illness in 1939

Sheena Kilminster had a break in training after developing a throat infection. To aid her recovery, she and her brother set off touring in his car. The summer of 1939 was sunny and deceptively beautiful.

The summer of 1939, my brother and I set off on a tour round Britain. Father gave us £25 spending money, and he said, 'Stay in good hotels, the difference in service and quality is maximal and the difference in price is minimal.' We had a fabulous holiday, my brother and I, and of course the occasion never arose again.

We went down the east coast and right across the south coast from Dover to Land's End and back along the north coast of Cornwall, up through the Cotswolds, through the Lakes, over the border.

I think my father always thought that war wouldn't happen; he thought that the politicians would find some way round it. He couldn't believe that Germany would be allowed to start a second world war, but it happened, yes … His philosophy was enjoy yourselves while you're young, it's all too short at the best; and my goodness that was right.

Gertrude Cooper, née Ramsden, assistant matron, Moorfields Eye Hospital, London, 1937–8

Nursing could be a passport to many things. Gertrude Cooper trained at the Middlesex Hospital, London, and seemed to be following a conventional career. However, she found work as an assistant matron a bit tedious. Her new employment put her in a position to observe the build-up to conflict in various parts of the world that would shortly become theatres of war, but Gertrude was largely indifferent to the looming disaster.

I wanted to see the world, and I was fortunate in being appointed to join the P&O Steam Navigation Company as second sister on the biggest liner, SS *Strathnaver*, leaving the Port of London on a Friday night, en route for Australia.

We went via the Mediterranean after collecting mail which had come overland to Marseilles. We proceeded south, going through the canal, calling at Aden, Bombay, Colombo and then nine days at sea until we struck the coast of Western Australia.

We were five weeks going round Australia, after the west coast, going to Adelaide, Melbourne, the port of Sydney, then up to Brisbane, and cruising in the Pacific.

We were the only women officers employed on ships; there were no clerks, as there would be after the war. We were welcomed into the social life of the ship but we were separate and we did not go to their dances. We wore uniform all the time.

On the intermediate runs we occasionally took the Indian Army as they were given more overseas leave and the ships would fit into their pattern. We also offered accommodation to sick servicemen who had contracted tropical diseases and were being repatriated.

We had a cruise to Bombay and were stranded there at the time of the Munich Crisis because the ship was commandeered for taking troops to the Canal Zone, and women were removed from ships of that type. So we came home as passengers on the SS *Bhutan* and the surgeon on that ship asked if I would like to return for the next trip, which was to the Far East, including Christmas in Japan.

Planning for war: evacuees

Ministry planners were well aware of the terrible loss of civilian lives during the Spanish Civil War. The British authorities expected that any new war would see similar hideous casualties at home. It was suggested that people should be removed from danger areas. Planners divided the country into 'evacuation areas', which the non-essential population was encouraged to leave; 'reception areas' that were relatively safe, and where evacuees could be resettled; and 'neutral areas', where the population was probably secure. Families were encouraged to let their children be evacuated, perhaps with their school, to a safer area. Not everyone accepted this offer, but some had no choice.

Afra Leckie, staff nurse, Infants' Hospital, Vincent Square, London, 1939

I remember before I left [London] seeing the children going by with gas masks, all going off to Victoria Station; they were all going away down into the country.

Anna Brocklesbury-Davis, student nurse, St Thomas' Hospital, London, 1939

I went off for my holiday only to find that in Ely, where I lived, my mother was evacuation organiser for hundreds of children to come from London and they had dirty heads – they all had nits and creepy-crawlies – and 'please would I organise a delousing centre for them all'. That's what I had to do in that holiday. I got the vicar's daughter to help me scrub out a ground-floor flat, which we 'requisitioned', that's the word they used to use. And we had to turn this into a delousing centre for all these children.

After bringing up eight children of her own, my mother then took in a German Jewish refugee boy and girl from Hitler, and they were brought up as number nine and ten in our family. When I got home there during that holiday, the boy was acutely ill with very bad tonsillitis, and needing blanket-bathing and all sorts of things at home. So I was 'nursing hands', as part of my holiday duties at home.

Sue Aylmer, nursery staff, Dr Barnardo's homes, Sussex, 1939

I had always been interested in children and I had helped in a local orphanage, and things like that. So when I was twenty-one I applied to Barnardo's, to do 'nursery' training. This was 1938. And they wrote back and said sorry, they had no vacancies. But in July '39 I got a panicked phone call saying, can you come immediately, we are in need of staff. They obviously wanted staff for evacuating children.

I went to Barkingside to the admission place. I was homesick and the children who came in were homesick as well, so we cried together.

Then in August, things were hotting up and they wanted most children out of Barkingside. They sent me to Woodford, which was originally the boys' village home. The children didn't know anything about it; they were only young, four and five. But the sister who was in charge was a very cruel lady, she had very strict rules, and if they disobeyed they were smacked. I didn't like it at all. I had a friend who was in a Barnardo's home in Malden, and I wrote to her and said I was going to leave. I couldn't stand this. And before I knew where I was, the sister was removed from the place and somebody came in her stead; actually she had to resign. I gather they had known about this for a long time, but nobody had ever put it into writing, as it were.

I went to Malden, a girls' school. We had wonderful drills for getting babies down and out and so on. That was great fun. But Malden was not a very safe place to be. So we went to Sussex, and I can remember, we were in a coach, twenty-one babies and all the clutter, with a lorry behind with the cots and everything, and we went from Essex to Sussex, outside Chichester.

There were no signposts when we got into Chichester and the poor man driving the coach was going round and round in circles. Eventually we arrived at this most beautiful house on the Downs outside Chichester. It wasn't suitable as a children's home, they just rented it because of the war coming. Already there were quite a number of older children.

I can remember the lady standing on the doorstep when we got there, saying, 'Before you even come in, I demand that one of your staff help me in the kitchen.' And of course there was nobody to do the work; they hadn't got anybody to do the laundry. You can imagine, twenty-one babies. In the evenings we had to go to the laundry and wash the nappies in the machines and all that sort of thing. They did eventually get it sorted out.

Margaret Thomson, schoolgirl, Edinburgh, c.1940

During the war we were not evacuated as many people were. My mother and father decided that we would be better staying at home and I only have a recollection of one or two air raids where we went under the stair and stayed there until the all-clear went.

Planning for war: hospital services

✚

When war came, the prime target was sure to be London, so the care of Londoners was a priority. An Emergency Medical Service or EMS was proposed.

With huge numbers of casualties in the offing, the planners agreed that all civilian hospitals, both municipal and voluntary, must collaborate in the war effort. To this end central government was given a 'right of direction' over all hospitals, something they had never had before.

London was divided into ten sectors, each based on a major central London hospital. Each sector had a hinterland that spread out into the adjoining countryside, and in each a 'sector matron' and medical officers were appointed.

The plan was that when the bombing began, the city-centre hospitals would operate as 'casualty clearing hospitals'; here bomb victims would receive initial treatment. Once their condition stabilised, they would be evacuated to the comparative safety of 'base hospitals' in the more rural parts of the sector.

This plan was rife with problems. Most of the country hospitals selected as base hospitals had, up to then, been large hospitals for the mentally ill and were not equipped or staffed to care for the victims of war. Equipment and staff would have to be found.

Sector matrons were expected to manage the allocation of nursing staff among all the hospitals of their sector, voluntary and municipal, and generally to supervise everything that affected nurses. Setting up this system would involve the movement of large numbers of staff, patients and much equipment; it was a huge problem for the continued delivery of care and the continued education of nurses and doctors.

Arrangements in the rest of Britain were similar, but it was not until August 1939 that six additional sector matrons were appointed in six provincial centres: Birmingham, Liverpool, Manchester, Leeds, Bristol and Newcastle. These new matrons did what they could to prepare their sector in the single month that remained before war was declared.

Miss Hillyers, matron of Sector 8, with a St Thomas' ward sister in a sector hospital.

Margaret Broadley, nurse tutor, London Hospital, Whitechapel, 1939

I was sent to the Middlesex Hospital to do a course on gas warfare; throughout the course I sat thinking it couldn't possibly happen, the result being that whenever I heard gas lectures afterwards I was confused as to which smelt of hay and which of geraniums.

Eva Cable, assistant matron, Gordon Hospital, London, 1939; assistant matron, Chichester, 1940–6

Eva Cable was assistant matron in a newly built hospital, where the staff received minimal guidance on war preparations.

The main preparation was blackouts. It was rather hurried because nobody thought there would be a war, and so nothing special was done, but then there was a sudden hurry and flurry with sandbags appearing from the army, and we decided we would have to do something and we were inundated with bales of blackout material.

I mustered our sewing party to make these enormous curtains, to protect the hospital of course, and we had to use all sorts of machines, various sorts of sewing machines. I remember I was worried because there were so many people hand-sewing and it was so slow and I remembered that I'd got a sewing machine in my home and I rang up my father and he said yes he would get it and in due course it appeared all done up in sacking and labels of all sorts, 'war emergency', every possible hurried message that he could put on it. And it arrived and we went on and we got the curtains done and we got them up.

For six years, administrators, doctors, nurses and others managed to rub along and make the scheme work, leaving a useful inheritance for the future National Health Service.

Call-up chaos

✚

On Sunday 3 September 1939, Prime Minister Neville Chamberlain made his famous radio broadcast to the nation announcing that Britain and Germany were once again at war. That afternoon Chamberlain told the House of Commons, 'Everything that I have worked for, everything that I have hoped for, everything that I have believed in during my public life has crashed into ruins.' A war cabinet was established and the armed forces immediately called up their reservists, medical staff as well as combatants. The government was already acutely aware of the shortage of nurses, but now the full potential for chaos became obvious. Every reservist called up removed a staff member from a civilian hospital or clinic.

From 1938 onwards, when planners began to calculate the numbers of nurses that would be needed in the event of war, they became very worried indeed about staffing civilian hospitals. The Royal College of Nursing (RCN), the professional organisation for nurses, urged that a 'Civil Nursing Reserve' be set up.

Administrators in the Ministry of Health were so pressured that in November 1938 the RCN was asked by the government to begin a register of qualified and assistant nurses. Their hope was that trained nurses who were no longer working would be identified; they would then be encouraged to make themselves available for war work. By February 1939, over 3,000 applications had been processed by the college. The Ministry of Health later assumed responsibility for this task; however, the college continued to run an enquiry bureau in the Cowdray Hall, Cavendish Square. From July 1939 until June 1940 (during the 'phoney war'), the RCN administered the London register of the Civil Nursing Reserve, which included interviewing applicants, answering postal enquiries and allocating nurses to London sector matrons. The national organisation of this scheme was so ad hoc that conditions of service and pay differed among nurses whose duties were very similar. The whole project owed its survival to the patriotic good will of many nurses and assistant nurses.

At the outbreak of war, the reservists knew what to do, but those who were in charge of directing them frequently did not. After completing her Florence Nightingale course, Theodora Turner returned to St Thomas' for one night before leaving for Netley military hospital in Hampshire. Eileen Willis arrived in the army hospital on Millbank, and Elvira Thomas, after an extraordinary episode in Cardiff Royal Infirmary, found herself in Folkestone and in the army. Joan Crémieu-Javal was called up to a service which had no official uniform and which did not really know what to do with this group of enthusiastic recruits.

Theodora Turner, sister, Queen Alexandra's Imperial Military Nursing Service (Reserve), 1939–45

You [were] given your position, your destination about two years before the war, and your railway ticket. You were told you had to report to the base. General mobilisation was called, if I'm right, on 1 September 1939.

I got back to St Thomas' the night before, because I was going to be the night sister and ... I stayed one night there and then off I went to Netley [military hospital, near Southampton]. And I was mobilised immediately. You see we had our tickets, we had everything.

Eileen Willis, mobile VAD (Voluntary Aid Detachment), 1939–41

Eileen Willis was a mobile VAD attached to the Queen Alexandra's Imperial Military Nursing Service. When you signed on as a mobile, you agreed to be posted away from home.

I had to report to Millbank [London]; my brother-in-law drove me up there. I arrived at the sisters' place at the Queen Alexandra military hospital and there was absolute mayhem because all the reserve QA sisters from all over the country, and also all the VADs, had had their call-up papers and they were all appearing with their suitcases, reporting for full-time duty. Of course the mess wasn't designed for this influx so they put up camp beds in the attics and we all sat there partly dejected, partly overexcited, and of course at that stage there was no work to do. The first job I did in the army was to prepare fruit salad for fifty people in the sisters' mess for dinner that night ... but anyway you started making friends.

Elvira Thomas, staff nurse, Cardiff Royal Infirmary, 1938–9

Elvira was working contentedly as a recently qualified staff nurse in Cardiff Royal Infirmary when war was declared.

Matron, Miss Beauville, had a notice on the Friday before war was declared on the Sunday; there were vouchers for six nurses to be part of what was called the Civil Hospital Reserve. Three had to go to Colchester and three had to go to Folkestone. Rumours got around the night before that something was happening. The matron wanted to see all trained staff at 8 a.m. in the boardroom on the Saturday morning, so we all trooped down and I can remember one girl from Penarth, she was a very big girl, saying 'Well, I'm getting married, nothing [can] happen to me, I'm getting married.'

But Matron told us there were six vouchers, and she, poor woman, didn't know anything at all about it. Miss Davis [the previous matron] obviously hadn't passed on the information. Miss Davis had been a principal matron in the Territorial Army and as girls qualified she roped them into the Territorial Army, but she'd left ... so we were about the first set that hadn't been roped in.

Nobody was going to go and then Miss Beauville said, 'Well, six have got to go, so you can decide.' So then it was decided that six who could go home and say they were going would be the ones, and we found ourselves on the twelve o'clock train from Cardiff. I was one of the three to Folkestone and one of the others was my friend from my own set. Three from the Rhondda went to Colchester. And that was it, we were in the army.

I was mobilised the day before war was declared. I really didn't want to go and my friend said, 'Oh come on,' she said, 'there's not going to be a war.' We'd never had a summer holiday; she said we'll go to Folkestone, we'll have a holiday; well, on Sunday war was declared. I suppose I had more or less accepted it, but I think she really believed there wasn't going to be a war.

And she nearly broke her heart when she realised what she had done, you know.

Joan Crémieu-Javal, née Manning, formerly Cochrane, staff nurse, Prince of Wales Hospital, Edmonton, c.1938

I was invited to a social evening, purely for getting recruits. This was pre '39 and I'd been a year at the Prince of Wales. When I was at this evening they said: 'We are recruiting for medical staff to man the boats, ambulance boats on the river Thames. Are you interested?' And I said, 'Yes, I'm a great boat lover, I'm a "boaty" person.' So I went on the books … it was run by the Port of London Authority, they were the boss of it all.

We were told that this was sort of a secretive behind-the-scenes thing, not generally advertised, that's why we were invited to this party, you see. They said, one day you will receive a telegram and when you receive it you take it to whoever you are working for and you are immediately released from your duties.

So in 1939, day before war was declared actually, I was working and along came somebody and said, there's a telegram for you. There it was, 'Take this to your head of department and you will immediately be released and report to this address.' I went to see Matron at the Prince of Wales, and said, I've been told that I must give this to you, and she said, yes, you're released from now, you can do whatever they say.

So I thought, this is very exciting; off I went and the address was Cadbury Hall on the Thames at Hammersmith, and it was the rowing club for Cadbury chocolate.

When we got there, there were all these people, medical people, doctors, each boat had two doctors and … four or six trained staff and lots of VADs … so we all were there, I should think we were probably about thirty people, a room full.

The first few days of war

On that fateful weekend of 2–3 September 1939, an Emergency Medical Service did swing into action. In London, the city-centre hospitals in each sector were emptied of most of their patients and staff, who were moved into the country using fleets of specially adapted Green Line buses. Nurses were involved in all these activities, and with their 'can do' attitude they were making rather rickety plans work. Margaret Broadley and 'Poppy' Bocock were tutors shepherding anxious student nurses and helping them to nurse patients with minimal equipment. The day war was declared was extraordinarily emotional and tense. Sue Aylmer walked out of church when the siren sounded; Elizabeth Halliday wept in a linen cupboard in Glasgow.

Anna Brocklesbury-Davis, staff nurse, St Thomas' Hospital, London, 1939

At the end of my life at St Thomas', war broke out and the hospital had to be evacuated of all its patients. I was designated to go in Green Line buses, which had been turned into huge ambulances with lots of room for stretchers, and I had to go up and down the corridors of these buses, seeing to patients who were quite ill. I had various things in my little body belt, such as a kidney dish and anything I needed to attend to patients going to and fro from St Thomas' Hospital and Clapham Junction station. Patients then had to be boarded on to trains at Clapham Junction, to go out into hospitals; some of them were mental hospitals, taken over for the care of all these patients.

Well, when that job was done, and I got back to the hospital again, I was then packed off on a double-decker bus, with my suitcase, to be evacuated myself, and I was sent to Park Prewett Hospital, Basingstoke. It was being converted to a reception hospital for air-raid casualties.

Margaret Broadley, sister tutor, London Hospital, Whitechapel, 1939–45

Margaret Broadley was evacuated with student nurses from the London Hospital.

It wasn't until the Friday night before the war broke out that we really realised that it was inevitable.

That Friday night's dinner was the usual dignified sisters' evening meal, the last such that I ever had. After that, the dining room was cleared and everybody was given their orders as to the evacuation that was to take place on the Saturday morning.

The patients, as far as possible, were being sent home, a skeleton staff would be left at the London to deal with them and to receive casualties, the rest of the staff of the London had been split up into fourteen different areas. They were to go to hospitals scattered throughout Essex, Hertfordshire and into Middlesex.

Similar to the disposal of the schoolchildren, each member of the nursing staff could take what luggage she could carry and there were fourteen different-coloured labels, so that everybody was clearly labelled with their destination. I was one of a biggish group, with about sixty student nurses in it, that was sent to one of the Essex mental hospitals. They had cleared their admission block in readiness for us. The operative word was cleared; they had stripped it completely bare. We arrived about twelve o'clock on the Saturday morning to this empty block.

We were then taken to see the nurses' accommodation. Every one of those girls had been used to a single room. They were to be put into twenty-bedded dormitories in what had been a convalescent patients' wing. And there they were with these big dormitories, bed, chair, bed, chair, all round the room with absolutely no facilities for privacy or accommodation of possessions.

As I have said, the Friday night we'd had the sisters' usual dignified evening meal. By midday Saturday we were drinking tea which had been delivered from the hospital's main kitchens in five-gallon enamelled jugs, ready made with milk and sugar.

The war was a very rude shock for us.

'Poppy' Bocock, sister tutor, Nightingale School, Botley's Park sector hospital, 1939–45

Miss Hillyers [matron of St Thomas' and Sector 8] asked me to go down to Botley's Park. Miss Gould, who was the senior of us tutors, she was appointed first, was going down to Basingstoke with a group of nurses in training and sisters. I was to go to Botley's Park with a group of nurses in training and charge nurses,* because there was a very young matron at Botley's Park who would be in charge of us and she thought it was better not to send the experienced sisters down who might be rather formidable with this poor lady. And there was Dr Paddle, the medical superintendent; he was in charge. In mental 'colonies' in those days, the medical superintendent was in complete charge. So that was the set-up. The matron of the mental colony was our *ipso facto* matron, but our own matron from St Thomas' Hospital visited us very frequently.

I had been to the Army & Navy [Stores] and got a big box of biscuits. Well, we started off at about eleven o'clock. We were supposed to get there for lunch but by lunch time our driver was still trying to find Botley's Park. We went round and round and round for a long time, so many signposts had been removed. So I opened my box of biscuits and we shared them out; our first experience [of war] was hunger!

We were to get ready for the patients. They [the hospital staff] emptied four of the colony units – sixty-four beds I think, thirty-two up and thirty-two down. They emptied four of those ready for us. All we had when we got there were a number of splints from World War I, and a lot of babies' potties, sandbags and sand, and canvas palliasses and straw.

[They were] the big sandbags, that had to be filled to be put outside windows and things where glass was not to be broken. So our first job was to try and fill all these bally things! I can't remember the exact detail of how we did it, but we did it.

And then our second thing was that there was nothing in the wards to nurse the patients with. There were beds, but there were no mattresses,

---

* In St Thomas' parlance, a charge nurse was a senior staff nurse, not the male equivalent of a sister.

In 1939 'Poppy' Bocock was a tutor working with student nurses at Botley's Park sector hospital. This photograph shows her when senior tutor at the Royal Free Hospital.

so we had to fill these straw mattresses. We used orange boxes to make lockers.

The first patients to be evacuated from St Thomas' to Botley's Park were civilian patients of course, because the war hadn't really properly started. And I do remember going round the first day, when they'd arrived, and we'd put them into these terrible wards, and apologising.

We spent the first two or three weeks scouring the countryside, every chemist's shop we raided and got anything we could buy from them in the way of bowls, and porringers, and instruments, and syringes and needles and things. After about, I think about a fortnight, supplies began to come in, gradually. Not very organisedly, but they came in. But we never had enough of the sort of equipment that you expect in a teaching hospital.

Well, we had to make do, I mean it meant that perhaps you could get two trolleys set up and then they had to be reboiled and used for the next person. It meant a lot of extra work, really. I think the theatres got quite well supplied on the whole.

I remember Dr Paddle coming down with Mr Rowley Bristow [orthopaedic surgeon] one day, and Dr Paddle had not been used to nurses with different opinions; he began to find the Nightingales were rather much for him. And he said something like this to Mr Bristow, as he then was, and he said, 'I am sure that Dr Paddle is pleased to have so many intelligent nurses on his staff', or something like that. But Dr Paddle wasn't quite sure that he was!

Elizabeth Halliday, student nurse, Western Infirmary, Glasgow, 1938–41

When war was declared I was in the Western, on Sunday morning, on duty, and I thought, they can't, we can't start another war, people are crazy, and I went into the linen cupboard and howled my eyes out.

Grace Howie, student nurse, Glasgow Royal Infirmary, 1936–40

The night before war was declared, Grace Howie wanted to visit some of her army friends.

I went to the office, and of course they knew more about one than one realised ... I said, 'May I be out after nine o'clock?'

'Yes, Nurse Howie, but you will be careful if [there's] a blackout, the first night of a blackout, you will be careful, be in by eleven, nurse.' I said, 'Thank you.'

They knew perfectly well if somebody was naughty, they knew all about it but they were very kind, very funny people, I had great respect for many of them.

Afra Leckie, staff nurse, Infants' Hospital, Vincent Square, London, c.1939–40

Of course, I remember the first siren going off. One of the nurses just panicked, and we had to console her.

I can also remember going over to the nurses' sitting room with the matron and singing 'Dear Lord and Father of Mankind'. She was a very religious woman, and she read a few prayers and we all sang. That [hymn] always reminds me of the beginning of the war.

Sue Aylmer, nursery staff, Dr Barnardo's homes, Sussex, 1939–42

I was there [Woodford village home] just a few weeks, when on 3 September, war was declared, and I happened to go to church that morning and the sister said, 'If the siren goes you must come back immediately.' So the vicar announced that war had been declared and immediately the siren went, so I leapt out of the pew, up the aisle and back.

The children had to go into a shelter. It was very panicky, I was very frightened and I can remember looking up in the sky, there were all these barrage balloons, which I never remembered seeing before, but there they were. Of course, at that time, you didn't know there was going to be a sort of phoney period. You thought that Hitler was going to arrive any minute.

Marjorie Voss, schoolgirl, 1939

The war started when I was fifteen, I can remember I was at my grandmother's house when war broke out and I can remember walking across the school field and thinking to myself, this is the end now, I shall never grow up, I shall never know what it is to grow up and marry and have a family. My mother had a friend, she was a Frenchwoman, she was very pessimistic and she said this war will end all wars. This stuck in my mind and I was very pessimistic about things and I can remember sort of thinking life wasn't worth – it wasn't worth going on with studying or anything like that if we were all going to be wiped out.

Janet Crawley, student nurse, Royal Infirmary of Edinburgh, 1937–41

I can remember vividly, I was in Ward 3, which was the mental ward in those days, for attempted suicides and ... things like that. I remember on night duty sitting there and hearing the soldiers going away. They all amassed in Forrest Road at the Oddfellows Hall. Then big trucks came out and they were all going away singing. I remember thinking, am I supposed to sing with them and feel happy or cry, what am I supposed to do? I did not have the foggiest idea, I did not know.

Eva Cable, assistant matron, Chichester, 1940–6

Eva Cable trained at Charing Cross Hospital.

Later ... I got an appointment as the assistant matron at Chichester, where I was for six years during the war.

Of course we didn't have any work for some time other than the ordinary general part, because it all went very quiet and there was that period of the phoney war, and I remember then we had a team of [operating] theatre people sent to us for emergency who of course had no work at all, spent their time lying out on the lawn in the sunshine and amongst them was one of the surgeons from Charing Cross which was rather nice, Mr Fitzsimmons. I was wearing my Charing Cross medal and I went into the doctors' dining room, the maids were really rather overworked with extra people and I went to see that they were sort of getting on all right, and he spotted it and said, 'Charing Cross, who are you?'

Gertrude Cooper, née Ramsden, ship's nurse, Sydney, Australia, 1939

I didn't hesitate to take another trip and see another part of the world, so I was still in the employment of the P&O company when we arrived in Sydney prior to the outbreak of war. We heard on the radio the Prime Minister say that we were at war with the Germans, and immediately the Australian government pledged their allegiance to the mother country. We felt very dependent; they were wonderfully kind. We came home having painted the ship battleship grey; it had been white. We arrived in Liverpool, October 1939, to a blacked-out country; we were at war.

The quiet period of the phoney war lasted from 3 September 1939 until May 1940. Once the flurry of planning and preparation died down, the Emergency Medical Service had little to do. In this atmosphere people started to relax and there was a drift of both staff and patients back to the city-centre hospitals. But the calm was short-lived. When France fell and the Allied forces, many of them desperately wounded, had to be lifted in their hundreds of thousands from the beaches of Dunkirk, the war was brought home. Britain's nurses rose to the challenge.

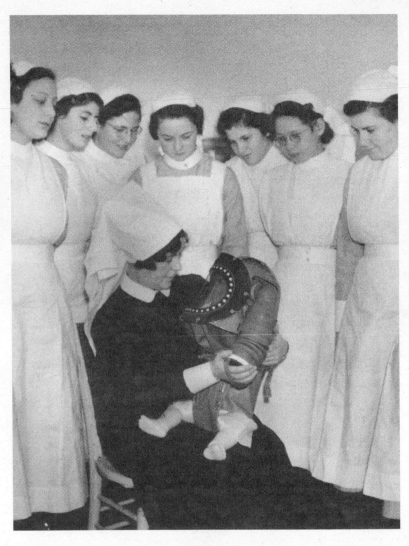

Becoming a nurse of any kind was thought better by many young women than the option of domestic service. Here, a group of refugees from Germany at a training school for nursery nurses, Middlesex.

THREE

REFUGEES
AND NURSES

... eventually a rule came out from the government that people who were not British subjects were not allowed to nurse anybody who might be a prisoner of war or, somebody from another country. So I had to leave the London Hospital in the middle of my training ...

Lisbeth Hockey, Jewish refugee in England from 1939

A particularly poignant strand in the tale of nursing through the war is the part played by Jewish refugees. Throughout the 1930s, when many people in Britain were still convinced that war could be averted and Hitler was not to be taken seriously, numerous Jewish people living in Nazi Germany could see that disaster was inevitable. They went to great lengths to escape, or at least to send their children away from the horrors of mainland Europe. Nurses such as Lisbeth Hockey, Annie Altschul and Charlotte Kratz, whose voices recur throughout the book, were typical of many more.

In order to settle in Britain, most refugees required a visa and had to work, but only in permitted roles. For women that usually meant domestic service or, after a while, nursing, while for many men the only possibility was farm work.

Having fled Europe, often leaving all their close family behind to an almost certain dreadful fate, these refugees found themselves, at the outbreak of war, in an increasingly hostile environment, confronted by the fears and suspicions of both the general public and the press. Some refugees were classed as friendly or neutral aliens and simply required not to live in specific restricted areas. Others, like Lotte Heymann's brother, found themselves interned as enemy aliens perhaps on the Isle of Man or, worse, were sent to Australia or Canada. Around 1,000 of these perished when the ships in which they were being transported to the dominions were sunk by the enemy.

Many of the refugees were very capable people, and a number of them contributed a great deal to nursing in Britain both during the war and afterwards.

Alone in a strange land

Annie Altschul, Jewish refugee, domestic servant, 1938–40

Annie Altschul was born and educated in Vienna. By 1938 she had begun university studies in mathematics, but her family were now certain that they needed to leave Austria.

My sister went first, found me a job. I keep on being highly amused when people talk about the hospitality of the British to refugees. They've always only taken in labourers for the kinds of job that the English didn't want to do. Domestic work and nursing … my sister found a job as a cook and found me a job as a mother's help and then between us we found our mother a job in London.

We were helped by the fact that we had no money and therefore there was no delay … the people who got left behind were people who were worried about their possessions and they didn't want to go away because they didn't want to leave their property.

There was one job in Guildford as a mother's help I enjoyed tremendously, I was sorry to leave there. I certainly learned a bit about British society … It was a huge house, absolutely enormous, in which the grandparents lived with four sets of grandchildren. Each of the sets of grandchildren had a nanny and I was engaged as one of those. We took turns to take time off, to look after each other's lots of grandchildren. But it was almost like running a nursery.

The house was so big that you didn't have to meet anyone else, you hardly ever saw the grandparents, and they were continuing there in a frugal kind of way, dressing for dinner in the evening. I know they dressed for the evening because we had a bomb dropped one night and I had washed my hair and was in pyjamas and when that explosion occurred I dashed into the nursery and grabbed two children and came down with wet hair in pyjamas with two kids under my arms and so did the other various nannies. And the adults emerged from the dining room in evening dress.

Lisbeth Hockey, Jewish refugee, in England from 1939

Born in Graz, in Austria, where her father was an architect, Lisbeth Hockey planned to become a doctor.

I did near-on three years of medicine in Graz. It just began to be very interesting when, you know, the political situation in the country became intolerable and dangerous. So my parents thought it was wiser for me to get away for a bit. Everybody in Austria at that time thought that Hitler wouldn't last very long, so the idea was to send me into safety for a little time and it would all be over. But of course it was never over and I never saw my parents again, they were both killed by the Nazis. Although somewhere in my ancestry there is Judaism, I never practised and I didn't even know about the Jewish component in my family.

The Quakers brought me over to this country. They were very, very helpful. I was met in London ... and they put me on the train to Devon. And this big tall man met me in Seaton and I became governess to their children. I was supposed to teach them German but ... it wasn't easy, obviously.

They were just lovely people and took great care of me. They realised that I had wanted to be a doctor and tried to get [me] into medicine in this country. There was no way, because I was a woman, and in those days it was very rare for women to get into medicine. And secondly I wasn't a British subject at that time and thirdly I had no money. So there were three conditions which just made it totally impossible for me to go into medicine. So meaning well, but probably not terribly sensibly, they thought nursing would be a good thing for me to do.

In 1939, Lisbeth Hockey's hard work to master English gained her a place at the London Hospital training school.

Charlotte Kratz, Jewish refugee, in England from 1937

The Kratz family had relations in Britain, and Charlotte's parents made arrangements for her to complete her education here.

I was born in Dortmund in 1922. I was an only child. There isn't a lot to say about my adolescence. I came to England to go to school in 1937; I was fourteen at the time. I went to boarding school in Westcliff-on-Sea in Essex and took my school certificate a year later.

I think in lots of ways I was very fortunate; it gave me an adequate education and people were interested in me.

I had an uncle who had business connections in London and through him I had some contacts, and of course … there was also the person who originally negotiated the coming to school, whom I actually never met. But no; I wasn't the only one [Jewish refugee in the school]. I think there was a very philanthropic headmistress.

Strange, I remember my mother's concern that we had to have three of everything; she couldn't believe that anyone could manage with three pairs of knickers. With a sort of rotation, this was reasonable. This was the sort of thing she was concerned about. Three pairs of navy knickers, three pairs of under knickers. Very funny liberty bodices, black stockings, green stockings. Once I was in the first team, played netball and hockey for the school, which I had never played before. It wasn't the sort of sports they played in Germany.

I really do not want to say an awful lot about that if you don't mind.

Rosa Sacharin, née Goldschal, Jewish refugee, in England and Scotland from 1938

As the Nazis' treatment of Jews became ever more brutal, people's desperation increased. Between December 1938 and September 1939, unaccompanied Jewish children were entrusted to the care of strangers by their anguished parents or guardians. Twenty thousand children were sent from the Axis countries (Germany, Austria and Czechoslovakia). Britain was prepared to host 10,000 of these, some of whom were admitted without a visa.

The first Kindertransport from Berlin left on 1 December 1938, and Rosa Sacharin was on it. Her father had already been arrested by the Nazis.

I was born in Berlin in 1925, my family were really Orthodox Jewish. My father couldn't see anything wrong with Germany; as far as he was concerned it was an advanced society, and nothing could ever happen. 'I don't know what you are worried about, this is such an intelligent country, they are intelligent people.' My mother said, this will end in tears, but he couldn't see it.

One day the school decided to close and we were told to go home, but we were told, go home two children at a time, at intervals of one or two minutes, and on no account to stop anywhere, in case we were attacked. But being me, I did stop and I looked … because I didn't really understand what had happened at the time. I didn't know that the synagogues had been burned, I didn't know that the shops had been attacked and people had been arrested and killed.

And I stopped at a paper shop, and I then read the poster, what it actually said, and I felt somebody behind me and he touched my shoulder. I froze and he said, 'This cannot last.' To me, it sounded as if he was ashamed … ashamed of what had happened … I lived in an area which was very anti-Nazi, where there were lots of fights between the Nazi groups and the other political groups, and I understood what his feelings were. And there were lots of people who were ashamed of what had happened.

Soon after that, I was told that I would be leaving for England and that was the beginning of the Kindertransport. I was in fact on the first one. We left Berlin on 1 December 1938 and arrived on 2 December.

I was taken to a family in Edinburgh … an elderly couple, and when she opened the door all she said was, well, I really wanted an eighteen-year-old one but you will do. So I became a domestic.

Lotte Heymann, Jewish refugee, in England from 1939

Lotte Heymann and her sister from Freiburg were booked on to the Kindertransport in April 1939 by their parents.

I was born in Hanover, in 1922; neither of my parents was a practising Jew, I don't know if they ever went to a synagogue. My father threw out everything that he had ever been taught about religion the moment he got to university. He became an atheist.

My parents heard of the facilities that might be available to send us out of the country, the so-called Kindertransport. We both got a place in April 1939. We both were offered homes in Oxford, within walking distance of each other, and went to school in Oxford.

I was an 'enemy alien' and until I was sixteen I had to go by regulations. I had a permit to cycle to and from school but I had to get another one if I wanted to go and visit somebody further away.

I can think of one particular day when our gym mistress – I was in the sixth form then – invited … the lower sixth for afternoon tea. She lived outside Oxford, and I had to get a permit. So I went to the police and got my permit.

Edith Bown, née Jacobovitz, Jewish refugee, in Britain from 1939

Edith Bown witnessed the Gestapo come for her parents. Her cousin arranged passage on a Kindertransport for her and her brother.

I was born in Berlin in 1924. I must have been about 11 when the school teacher slapped my face. I got home and my mother said, 'That's it, she goes to a Jewish school.' She was the one that had 'clear eyes'. But my father said, 'Rubbish, I am a *Frontsoldat*,* nobody can do that to my child.' He went and saw the headmaster, who said, 'I'm very sorry, it would be more than my job is worth. I think it would be better if you take your daughter out.'

---

* A member of the Reichsbund Jüdischer Frontsoldaten.

Now, an older lady of about forty used to come to our shop and sell us underwear, and whenever she came she [Mother] used to give her coffee and chocolate cake. One day this lady said, 'My sister is related to the President of the Jewish Community in Belfast and if you want to get the kids out, then write to us, because you have been very kind to me.'

On 5 May 1939, I came home from school in the early afternoon and found two … Gestapo people in the house. The Gestapo told my father and mother to get a few things together. My father blanched and said, 'Surely not my wife when you have got me?' The men just told him to shut up. Until now my mother had been calm. Now she started to sob. She put her coat on sobbing and left with my father and the two men, sobbing. My brother and Aunt Metta and I kissed them and my father said to me, 'Look after the boy, promise', and I promised.

A fortnight before my brother and I left, I had orders to go to Gestapo Headquarters. And I was petrified, but Hugo, my cousin, said, 'You must go, if this helps your parents, it is your duty, no matter what happens.' But nobody was allowed to come with me, so there I was, and I had to have a special passport because it was a part of Berlin that was forbidden to Jews.

I had an interview there with two very polite and kind men. I wasn't fooled by anything, I kept … whatever they asked me … to the barest minimum, always the same.

Ten days later on a Sunday morning at five-thirty, six in the morning, we went to the station with another 150 kids, part of a train which was especially for the 'transport children'. Parents weren't really allowed to say goodbye [in private]. They had to say goodbye and then see their children on the train. My aunt and cousin came from one station to the other by taxi so that they could wave us out of Berlin. When we got to the border there were these SA men, 'everyone out over fourteen' they said.

The ladies who ran these transports, this particular one, were members of the Society of Friends. They went and they got the children back … I mean they must have known by then what was happening.

Building a new life

One of the few occupations open to these refugees was nursing but even if they decided to follow this career there could be complications. None of these 'enemy aliens' were permitted to live or work in sensitive areas and several, including Annie Altschul and Lisbeth Hockey, began their studies only to be forced to discontinue them and start again elsewhere.

Annie Altschul, Jewish refugee, domestic servant, 1938–40; Ealing Hospital, 1940; Epsom Hospital, 1941–3

Annie and her mother and sister were determined to live in the same part of the country. As the Allies suffered setbacks early on in the war, their sense of foreboding grew, and being together became a priority.

I started nursing in Ealing and that didn't last very long because very soon after France fell, there were some new regulations about aliens and in which part of the country they were allowed to live; Ealing was not among the places I was allowed to live.

I shall never forget the day that one knew that Paris had fallen [22 June 1940]. One of my most vivid memories of Ealing was looking out of the window on to lilac and red may bushes which were quite magnificent in the grounds, and being quite sure that I'd never see them again; that was the end of the world as far as I was concerned.

Somehow our only thought at that stage was that we wanted to be in the same part of the country because we took it for granted that there would be an invasion and we felt that we would like to be together, it didn't matter what happened. So I went to Guildford and found another mother's help job in Guildford for about another year after that, not quite a year, until about March '41, and then took up nursing again.

Lisbeth Hockey, Jewish refugee, student nurse: London Hospital, Whitechapel, 1939; Muswell Hill Fever Hospital, 1940–3

Since medicine was not an option and one of the few openings for Lisbeth Hockey was nursing, she embarked upon the training, despite her misgivings.

I would never advise a person who wanted to be a doctor to go into nursing ... However, I did follow that advice and I applied to a variety of hospitals ... The London Hospital had a swimming pool, and although I wasn't the sporty type, I really thought a swimming pool was super and I quite liked swimming.

So I applied to the London Hospital and was told that provided I could learn English by the time of the next intake, which was three months later, they would have me; my English wasn't good enough, but educationally I was OK. So I had to learn English in three months and I was very proud of myself, because I really worked hard at it and eventually got accepted at the London ... so, that's how I got into nursing.

All the lectures in those days were given by doctors, of course; it's all better now, but [at the time] it was just very diluted medicine. I enjoyed the patient contact very much and I was determined to make a go of it. I haven't got much else but I do have stickability. I'm not a person for starting things and dropping them, I feel you get out of anything what you put into it. That's always been my experience and I was determined to have it that way.

But then of course, you see, the war had broken out and at that stage, we [in the London Hospital sector] were all evacuated to seaside sector hospitals. I was evacuated to the Rochford Hospital, Essex, and eventually a rule came out from the government that people who were not British subjects were not allowed to nurse anybody who might be a prisoner of war or somebody from another country. So I had to leave the London Hospital in the middle of my training. [I had a] lovely interview with the matron and everybody, who were themselves very sad for me. It was the second time that my career had been abruptly broken ... without my intention and totally beyond my control.

So I then did my fever training in Muswell Hill; it's now called Coppetts Wood, it's now a geriatric hospital but it was then a fever hospital.

Finally I completed my general, but it took a long time … and then I went into midwifery, you know in those days it was just kind of done. Immediately I realised that I wanted to be a nurse in a patient's home, because I wasn't a good midwife but I liked the idea of being in the family. So I became a district nurse, and then I decided I wanted to be a health visitor, and did that.

Charlotte Kratz, Jewish refugee, student nurse, Nightingale School, evacuated to Royal Infirmary of Edinburgh, 1944

The status of nursing in Germany was lowly. However, Charlotte Kratz's personal experience attracted her to this work.

Nursing in Germany, one thought of it as a non-job … [but] it was fairly obvious that I was outgrowing the school. I was seventeen and I really had to do something. My aunt and uncle didn't mind what I did, but they were not too keen for me to be in London.

I think the thing which persuaded me to train as a nurse was that I was in hospital as I was very ill from April 1941 to January 1942, which was quite a long time. I was evacuated to Park Prewett EMS hospital in Basingstoke. I was in a ward there which had St Mary's doctors but was staffed by St Thomas' nurses. And I thought well yes, perhaps I would become a nurse after all as this was as good a job as any. I [decided that I] had to go to St Thomas' because by then I [had] learned this was the place to go to. But Thomas' was pretty selective in those days. It took me two years to get them to accept me. They wrote and said that I might be better, happier, at another hospital … it was fairly obvious that they didn't think I was the sort of person they normally had. But I eventually managed to find a friend of my aunt and uncle who in turn was friendly with the senior almoner at St Thomas', and she told them that perhaps I might be the right person after all. I would never have dreamt of going anywhere else, I don't know why, partly because I was too ignorant to know anything about it.

So I started in September 1944, which was doodlebug* time, and we were evacuated to Edinburgh Royal Infirmary, where I started my training.

Annie Altschul, Jewish refugee, student nurse: Epsom 1941–3; Mill Hill Emergency Hospital/Maudsley Hospital, 1943–5

Other people probably had different attitudes to war-time work but mine was, some jobs had to be done and if I learnt something in the process all the better.

After being forced to leave Ealing ... I thought I'd start nursing again. Don't know what made me go to Epsom, I think they were advertising that they wanted nursing assistants. I applied and got the job ... [then] somebody there persuaded me to take up training and I said I didn't think I would because I wouldn't be there long enough. But they prevailed ...

People [started to go] into nursing who I think would normally have gone to university or have done other jobs. Women had to do one of the approved jobs. It didn't apply to refugees, we could have stayed in domestic service, but the females who were not conscripted were very strongly urged to go into something [useful].

What happened in Epsom, I think, was that they had never had an intelligent nurse ever before. They had a tutor who dictated notes which you wrote out and handed back for correction and who was totally thrown by the arrival of a few people who were capable of thinking. We fought a kind of war for a bit but it lost its attraction and tutor-baiting isn't particularly interesting after a while. She gave up trying and we gave up being beastly to her. We established some kind of truce in which she dictated notes and we accepted it but we found our information from elsewhere. I trained there for three years. The staff ... well, I must say I appreciated their economy because they were good at discovering what

---

* Colloquial name for the V-1 flying bomb.

Annie Altschul, second from left in the back row, with fellow student nurses from Epsom Hospital. Annie had been forced to leave her first training hospital.

you could do and then they let you do it and it never occurred to them that they ought to teach you anything new, why should they? If you were good at something, why not carry on doing that?

... I always liked old people and I liked the mentally ill. They had a four-bedded psychiatric observation ward, it was really an acute admission for tramps and down-and-outs and they were meant to be there three or four days and then taken to a mental hospital somewhere else. Staffed by about a total of four mental nurses who, after all, had to have days off and sometimes were ill, and I very quickly discovered that I was more than willing to do it.

I spent a lot of my general training looking after the mentally ill in that place. And a lot of my night duty in the geriatric wards, which were enormous, forty or fifty beds in serried ranks, which we had to move in order to be able to make them. There was a very high death rate and an awful business of never knowing who it was who'd died because patients weren't labelled and if they were all lying without their dentures with their mouths wide open and the same kind of heavy breathing and somebody died ... until they were awake and you could ask [them] who they were, you really couldn't tell who [had died]. When you couldn't possibly find out, you called for a doctor and you had no idea whose notes you should look for; it was really an impossible situation ...

Lotte Heymann, Jewish refugee, student nurse: Birmingham Children's Hospital, 1941–4; Addenbrooke's Hospital, 1944–6

The refugees were sponsored until they had finished their school leaving certificate, but Lotte Heymann was typical of their eagerness to become self-supporting.

After leaving school I went straight into hospital. I didn't finish my sixth form because I just felt I needed to stand on my own feet.

Right from an early age I was very fond of playing with dolls. In those days, in Germany, the nursing was mostly done by Red Cross nurses. My mother made me Red Cross uniforms for my dolls. Then, when I was over here in England, there was talk whether I ought to try to stay on for Higher School Certificate, go to university and maybe do medicine. I know this was talked about but I needed not to be a burden to anybody else.

The general hospitals were more difficult to get into as a refugee and so the next best thing was either orthopaedic hospitals, or children's. The bombing by that time was pretty grim in London. I tried the children's hospital in Birmingham and they accepted me after interview ... then, after finishing there, I applied for my general training. In those days, if you had your sick children's registration from the General Nursing Council, you could do your general nursing in two years because the first year and certainly the PTS exams were identical.

I left school in December 1940 and in January 1941 I started my training in Birmingham. In 1944, August, I went to Addenbrooke's Hospital and I was there until 1946.

Do I feel English? Completely and utterly! And I do know, I'm conscious myself at times especially if I have said something on the phone which I have to replay ... to make sure that it has got through to other people. I can hear an accent, and some people say they can't hear anything and others say straight away, 'Well where do you come from?' It varies. Can I still speak German? Yes.

Edith Bown, née Jacobovitz, Jewish refugee, student nurse, Newtownards Hospital, 1942–5

Edith Bown was determined to earn money in case she should ever have the opportunity to support her parents. In the religiously charged atmosphere of Northern Ireland, her Judaism made her a target for evangelical Christians of all denominations.

I had decided that I must get some training because I thought, if by any chance ... and I knew the chances were slim; I still get goose pimples when I think about it ... the parents do survive, I have to be able to look after them and to have money. I knew I didn't have enough education to go to university and nobody would pay for it. All they ever said [was] 'You can marry some man and then you will be all right.'

So we started writing to hospitals including Belfast, but nobody would have a Jew and an enemy alien. But this little hospital in Newtownards, which wasn't that far, would have me; so a fortnight before I was 18, I started [in 1942], and of course it was such a shock.

It wasn't the sort of hospital people applied to. No Protestant would apply there. There was one Protestant nurse there, the others were Catholics. They were at each other's throats the whole time I was there.

And the first thing that happened, I had the ministers of all denominations at me, to convert me. I had a half-day off one Sunday. I went out and one of the ministers stopped me and said, 'You should have come to my church.' I said, 'No, I am a Jew.' 'Oh you'll go to Hell.' And I was so angry by that time that I said, 'All right, it'll be hot there and I won't meet you.'

The only people who were kind were the Salvation Army. There was a major there who had a wife and two toddlers and he asked me to tea without religion. And I went and they gave me tea and biscuits, though everything was rationed, of course, and let me play with the children.

Rosa Sacharin, née Goldschal, Jewish refugee, student nurse, Royal Hospital for Sick Children, Yorkhill, Glasgow, 1943–6

The loneliness and isolation felt by Rosa and her fellow refugees was palpable and exhausting.

I had to make a decision, I was now eighteen [in 1943] and I had to do some work. Everybody had to do war work and it was either going into the ATS, which I couldn't see myself doing, going into munitions, which I wasn't terribly keen on, or going into nursing, which I knew nothing about. However, Mrs M, a minister's wife, suggested that I should maybe go and do the sick children's nursing course and she spoke to the matron ...

I wasn't very keen to go into nursing ... for some reason I was frightened, so I went, I filled in the form and I hoped I wouldn't be accepted. I went to the interview and Miss Clarkson, a very stately person, she was really one of the old matrons, at the end of the interview she said, 'Is there any question you would like to ask?' And I said, 'Yes, how long would I have to stay before I could leave?' She smiled and said, 'Well, Miss Goldschal, if we don't like you or you don't like us then you can leave after three months.' I was accepted.

Nursing refugees

The Jewish refugees who fled from central Europe to Allied countries were not the only tragic refugees washed up by this war. Throughout the war communities were disrupted, populations fled, family members were separated and many found themselves in unknown countries where they did not understand what was happening to them.

Esta Lefton, née Guttman, Jewish refugee from Poland, Auxiliary Territorial Service, Sarafand, Palestine, 1941

Esta Lefton was born in Poland. Thanks to her brother's clear understanding of the political situation and his vigorous lobbying, her whole immediate family were able to emigrate to Palestine before war broke out. Esta was keen to support the war effort. She enrolled as a student nurse, but in 1939, just before qualifying, she was badly wounded by a bomb. In 1941 she joined the ATS.

A very memorable experience in her war-time career was caring for women refugees who had escaped from the advancing Axis forces in the Balkans.

I went to Sarafand and there I joined the services. You go and you are trained; because we joined the army attached to the British hospitals, we were called the ATS (Auxiliary Territorial Service). And after two months or three months we went to Egypt.

The first hospital we joined was … in a place called Kassassin. The front line was then in the desert, they were still in El Alamein, in Tobruk, but, as you know, El Alamein, Tobruk changed hands a few times. On two occasions we had to pack up the hospitals because the Germans came quite near so we packed up, and then of course our troops advanced so we unpacked the hospital. And we stayed on there, I stayed, I think until it was the end of 1942, maybe the beginning of '43 …

When the war really was going, while I was in Suez we had quite a

Esta Lefton, herself a refugee and student nurse in Palestine, joined the ATS to care for the military and civilians.

lot of big problems arising because we had a lot of refugees, particularly women and children. They were refugees that ran away as the Germans took over Yugoslavia and Bosnia, all those countries. We had refugees from Romania, from Yugoslavia, from all the Balkan countries.

Outside our hospital, this was in Suez, our compound, they bought a very old building ... it was a very large building which was taken over by the British and it was made into a very, very large ward and there the children were accommodated that came from Europe and they built a Nissen hut for the women in the same sort of area which is just outside the compound of our hospital and where we lived.

Now when the children were brought in, it was mainly during the day, I could understand what the children were saying, not only from Polish but from Yugoslav because a lot of words are very similar and the children came with kalazar [leishmaniasis], with typhoid, with all different things, and they were screaming all the time, their hair were full of nits, lice, and in the beginning it took quite a few days before they trusted us to take bread; we used to bring bread on a tray and ask them to help themselves but they wouldn't, they shied away, and eventually they used to put their hands out, that makes me cry it really does [Esta has a shaky voice here, sounds as though she is crying], used to put their hands out to take a slice of bread and then take their hand back because, eventually we found, because the Germans used to taunt them by giving them and taking back the food. But eventually they trusted us and they used to take the bread and used to take drinks but they used to hide the bread underneath the mattresses but the mattresses, by then, they were full of lice, full of bugs that they brought in but we couldn't do everything in one go unless they trust you.

So slowly, slowly we start shaving their hair off and washing them and cleaning them, I was working with Sister Kirkland at night-time and these poor children used to die in our arms because with kalazar in the old days and all the diseases they had, I mean starvation, a lot of them couldn't take food and they just died.

Then we had this Nissen hut, for the women, now they used to die really like flies. And in this ward was a German doctor, German-Jewish man, he was a general practitioner and we had an English doctor, Dr Gould, tall and blond and very concerned. And once I heard somebody saying, you mustn't, don't touch this child, and I thought to myself what can this be? Perhaps they are pregnant, perhaps they've been raped, but anyway I thought to myself, the only thing I can do is tell Dr Gould.

And I told him and very gently he was trying to see. They were all Roman Catholics and they were all, they were all afraid and ashamed to tell us, even through an interpreter, that they are pregnant, that they were raped. Obviously they didn't know whether they were pregnant, but they were raped, if [you] don't know what sex or things is, which they didn't, and how many people did know anyway? So Dr Gould actually investigated and found they were pregnant and what's happened while they were running away they aborted and they were rotting inside and they died. So soon after this happened they got injections whether they wanted it or not but they got injections and they got cleared out.

I just tell you, going back again to the children's ward, there was one little girl called Mara, she was at the oldest eleven and she had long black hair and you could see lice crawling in the light and the only thing she did, she was screaming, nothing else, until she was hoarse. She stopped and then she started screaming again. I heard her say *mama, mama, mamushka, mamushka, svier*, that is pigs, and that the pigs are running, *tadeski, tadeski*, the Germans are there, the Germans came and they raped the women, they burned the farm and the animals ran out and she witnessed that and so she was running with the *svier*, with the pigs, and that's how she came.

Once we knew again what's the matter, she was delirious and slowly, slowly I decided not to cut her hair, I washed her hair with paraffin, got all the nits out and everything, and she got some medicine, and she calmed down, and she also had high temperature with this deliriousness and she was so beautiful with this beautiful hair, when I went to Cairo I bought her skirt, I bought her blouse, big ribbons and took her to, I got permission, took her to Suez and bought her some shoes and everything.

Also at the same time the women, and there were some men as well, they went to the Sinai desert, the path which was called El Shad, you had to go across the Suez Canal to the Sinai part of the desert, to El Shad, and there in the beginning of the war there was UNRRA [United Nations Relief and Rehabilitation Administration], was the United Nations, and they put up tents there and housed the refugees there. We used to go over after we finished duty in the hospital, go over there. We used to teach again the women and help them there and teach them how to grow vegetables in the sand, we used to grow flowers out of our tents.

And that's how we worked there in Suez and with the women and teaching them English, teaching them all sorts of things, they were all traumatised.

At the same time I must emphasise we had dances, we had meetings, we organised the troops whether they were Royal Engineers or whether they were all different. They used to come to our camp and we used to have parties, we used to have dances at the same time, because you have to have all this, we had lots of music, otherwise you couldn't survive, you have to survive for the people you treat, for the people you want to give courage to live.

As the war progressed, the populations of more countries were disturbed until finally, when the Allied troops arrived in Germany itself, the horrors of the death camps were revealed.

The refugee nurses were remarkable people, with stories of suffering and courage. Many of them remained in the profession in Britain, and in the post-war years they built careers and new lives. But the traumatic legacy of their losses remained with them. Many nurtured the hope that perhaps they could be reunited with their family. Only one, Rosa Sacharin, did indeed find her mother alive in Germany after the war. The intervening years were an agony of uncertainty for all of them.

From the moment they left everything they knew, there had been no room for complacency for these women. When the uneasy calm of the phoney war was shattered by the fall of France, their British-born colleagues too lost any illusions that the war might somehow remain at a distance.

Hospital's were not spared: the day after a heavy bombing raid over London.

FOUR

DUNKIRK
TO THE BLITZ

You were glad of that tin hat because very often there was a big ack-ack,
anti-aircraft gun, in Hyde Park and it boomed away and you could see
the tracer bullets going up and of course you could hear all the shrapnel
coming down ... I used to sit in the bath with that tin hat on because I
had a horror of a brain injury.

Eileen Willis, mobile VAD attached to Millbank Military Hospital,
1939–41

On 26 May 1940, Winston Churchill, who had replaced Neville Chamberlain as prime minister some two weeks previously, made a speech to the House of Commons describing the 'colossal military disaster' that had engulfed the British Expeditionary Force.

The BEF had been dispatched to France a week after war was declared in September of the previous year. The Allies rapidly found themselves in worsening difficulties. The French defensive plans failed; their inflexible Maginot Line was bypassed by the immensely effective German army, the Wehrmacht, which rolled over one European country after another. Each in turn collapsed in the face of this formidable fighting machine. By late May 1940 the Allies were corralled around the beaches of Dunkirk, and on the 26th, Operation Dynamo was launched with the simple aim of bringing as many Allied troops as possible back to Britain. Ultimately, 226,000 British and 110,000 French troops were rescued from Dunkirk between 26 May and 4 June; 140,000 British troops were left behind in Europe. Though Churchill warned the people that 'wars are not won by evacuations', the 'miracle of Dunkirk' nevertheless passed almost immediately into British folklore as an exceptional act of collective courage and determination.

Many of the returned troops were exhausted, suffering from shock and hypothermia, having stood in cold water for hours as they awaited rescue. Some were seriously injured after being exposed to Luftwaffe bombing; others had gas gangrene as a result of lying on the beaches with untreated wounds. On return to Britain, the most severely wounded were allocated to hospitals close to the south coast. As a student nurse in Northwood, Barbara Greenwood was shocked by the suffering of these soldiers. Other troops were transported by train to more distant hospitals, some as far away as Halifax, which had been prepared to receive them.

Following the BEF's ejection from Europe and the collapse of France, many people in Britain were convinced of an imminent invasion. This did not materialise; instead the RAF and the Luftwaffe engaged in the Battle of Britain, fought largely in the skies over southern England. Monica Baly, visiting her parents in Bexhill and walking their dog, watched Heinkels flying below the promenade.

When the Luftwaffe conceded this struggle, Germany turned its attention to a sustained bombing campaign. Ports and industrial cities were targeted across the country, and London was bombed for fifty-seven consecutive nights. The Emergency Medical Service came into its own.

Dunkirk

Eileen Willis, mobile VAD attached to Millbank Military Hospital, London, 1939–41

Only 19 years old, Eileen Willis heard of the Dunkirk debacle from her patients.

I remember when Dunkirk happened, the ward was full of hernias or appendix cases, normal sort of things that young people get. I remember they all had their earphones on and we were dashing round and dusting, serving meals and they all went terribly serious and we said, 'What is it, what is it?' They motioned [us] to shut up and then at the end of the bulletin there was dead silence and we said, 'What is it?' and they said that France had fallen. Of course that was tremendous for us because there was nothing really between the Germans and the English coast and possibly over the Channel and into us. I remember that very well.

... [They] mobilised every little ship that could keep up in the water and they brought back so many of our troops [though] of course a lot had perished along the way. We had cleared the hospital for casualties and there were all these empty beds and we just kept on replenishing hot-water bottles. Then the door opened and the first ones came in.

I was nineteen years old, just coming up to twenty, and I'd never seen anything like it. Of course they were in an awful state, filthy dirty, exhausted. A lot of them had been lying on stretchers on the beaches for twenty-four hours and there had been an abnormally high tide so a lot of them had been washed out to sea. They had been bombed and starved and they were wounded.

I remember we got them all into bed and they had the first dressings. But they just slept and slept, they woke up and had some food then went back to sleep again. There was a young chap, he'd got white hair and I looked on his notes and he was twenty-one. I said to one of the auxiliary sisters, 'Why has he got all this white hair?' She said, 'It's what he's been through.' But within about six weeks it had all grown through in his own colour which I found extraordinary at the time, but a lot of us found things like that.

Elvira Thomas, Queen Alexandra's Imperial Military Nursing Service (Reserve), 1939–45

When war was declared in 1939, Elvira found herself with little choice but to enrol with the QAIMNS(R) and report to Folkestone. From there her unit was sent to France with the British Expeditionary Force and was caught up in the unfolding catastrophe.

We were based at Le Tréport which was on the coast, not very far from Dieppe. I was on night duty when the Germans almost overran us, they captured the hospital actually, but we got all the patients away. I don't think anybody was left, some of the very ill ones may have been, but they went by train somewhere.

I was in an ambulance with the patients. All the nursing staff went down to Cherbourg, and from Cherbourg we came across [to England] and directly to our own homes, waiting for further news as it were.

Barbara Greenwood, student nurse, Middlesex Hospital, 1939–43

Evacuated from the Middlesex to one of the sector hospitals, Barbara Greenwood was horrified by the wounds she saw.

It was the end of my first year, the beginning of my second year and I was sent down to Northwood [sector hospital] for the last month of my night duty. My name was called out to go on to a ward where there was one army sister, one third-year Middlesex nurse and myself. And we took twenty-five to thirty, a batch of the worst of the [wounded] … when they evacuated Dunkirk. Some of them had lost two limbs, some two legs and one arm. It was horrific. Really was terrible. There were only the three of us. But goodness, we didn't stop all night. We really didn't stop all night.

These poor men were marvellously brave and wonderful in every way. I remember one night, one chappie called me over and said, 'Oh nurse, I have got such irritation in my arm.' He had had an amputation and I said, 'Well let me have a quick look at your dressing.' And I looked at his dressing and it was crawling with maggots, and my hair, I thought my hair had actually stood on end. But I said, 'Don't worry, it's perfectly all right', put his dressing back and went as fast as I could, without running, to the sister, and I said, 'oh Sister, he is covered in maggots', and she said, 'That's

Barbara Greenwood, centre, nursed Dunkirk veterans. She later joined QARNNS where she worked alongside VADs like those pictured here.

absolutely fine.' Apparently they wanted the maggots to eat the dead tissue
and the maggots were left, incredible.

People round about were so good ... there was a great table in the
middle of the ward and it was literally covered with biscuits and cakes
and champagne and everything that people could get. They were all so
sorry for these chaps who were absolutely marvellous.

I thought we worked hard in London sometimes, but my goodness me,
that three months ... It eased off because obviously when they were first
operated on they needed a lot of nursing when they came out, and as they
got better it wasn't quite so bad. I remember one night, Sister saying, 'Now
you can go and sit down for half an hour on the veranda' ... it was summer
time. I said, 'You will have to come and wake me up!'

Doris Carter, staff nurse, Royal Hampshire County Hospital, 1940

Waiting for casualties to arrive could be a strain on the nerves, and once they
arrived the workload was ferocious. Once stabilised, the wounded were moved
on, typically to military hospitals, so the ward could be returned to civilian use.

I was persuaded into going to open Ward 5 for war casualties. At that time
Ward 5 was hardly completed, there were still men there with paintbrushes
and various bits of finishing work to do. But I went down there with two
nursing colleagues. Barbara Turner was one of them, and she and I and
another nurse got the ward beds prepared, and ordered all the equipment
and spent a lot of time changing hot-water bottles in the beds, to keep the
beds aired for when the casualties arrived. I suppose some of the high-ups
knew when they would be coming but I certainly didn't, and suddenly,
one day when I was having lunch, I was called out and told to go back to
the ward because casualties were arriving.

We got down to Ward 5, which was the very last ward on 'the slope', as
we used to call it, and there were twenty or twenty-five men lying on the
floor; they all had bandages on their heads or their arms or their legs. They

also had labels on their arms, on their wrists, saying what was the matter with them. And the housemen were there working on them and told us; they also wrote on the labels what had to be done. So we got them into bed, the ones that were to receive nursing treatment, and gave them what treatment we could. Some of them were to be prepared for immediate surgery. And one or two were sent back to other wards, if they were fairly well able to walk. But most of them had to have some immediate treatment. I stayed on that ward, not a very long time; men were soon dispersed to various hospitals and wards and Ward 5 was taken over as an ordinary ward.

Norma Batley, Red Cross nurse, Emergency Medical Services Hospital, Leatherhead, c.1940–2

After only the simplest preparation, Norma Batley found herself dealing with the arrival of the Dunkirk wounded.

I joined the Red Cross and I did my first aid certificate, my incendiary bomb certificate and my nursing certificate, and eventually I was equipped to go to serve in an emergency hospital at Leatherhead.

There I did a little bit of general nursing, which of course was my first sight of a hospital at all, and then we had the Dunkirk soldiers.

They came back from the front in a very dishevelled condition and very depressed and some of them took a long time to recover in hospital because of course we had no penicillin in those days, which would have made such a difference.

Eunice Boorman, student nurse, Oldchurch Hospital, 1940–3

In Oldchurch, one of the memorable events was the sight of piles of weapons on the lawns outside the hospital.

All the ground-floor wards were empty for casualties. When the soldiers came in, they disarmed them of their rifles, and they were all admitted into the ground-floor wards. All the people that were 'seriously' injured were left at the coast at hospitals like that, but those that were 'badly' injured were brought inland.

They all came with their weapons and things ... to Oldchurch, because they were told to bring anything back with them ... they dumped them on the lawn outside Matron's office. There were two big lawns when you went up to the nurses' home. They were her pride and joy along there but they were terribly big piles of [weapons] that they put there. But the army cleared all that; of course they soon moved all the soldiers out, they didn't stop there for long, they were moved out as fast as they could to army places.

Ivy Scott, matron, Royal Halifax Infirmary, 1939–45

As part of its contribution to the Emergency Medical Service, the Royal Halifax Infirmary had to be prepared to allocate sixty beds for use in war-time emergencies. The first big test of their readiness involved the troops evacuated from Dunkirk. In this situation Matron kept her cool.

The senior surgeon came to see me and he said, 'I've just had a message from the barracks to say that we have got to be ready to receive sixty patients within the next twelve hours or more. What do we do about it?' I said, 'I understood that all orders were to come from the Medical Officer of Health.' He said, 'Oh, of course, I hadn't discussed it with him.' So we had to get hold of him and then they called a medical committee which they did ask me to attend! But we were too busy getting the wards ready for these patients. We planned it in the nursing committee. How it could be done by pushing extra beds into the ward and more beds on to the balconies and so on.

You see there [had been] this phoney war and all that time we had one ward empty and ready to receive [casualties]. The committee, quite wisely I think, felt that this was a waste of time, so they set out to redecorate that ward. And they were in the middle of redecorating when the senior surgeon came and told me that we had got to be prepared to take sixty.

I said, 'Well just come up and look at the ward that they are supposed to go in', and there were the painters' ladders and no blackout curtains and all the linen in the laundry; couldn't have been worse.

So he said, 'How soon can you have it ready?'

I said, 'We will get it ready tonight.'

But he said, 'I don't want you to tell [them about] this, this isn't public knowledge yet.'

So I said, 'Well I am going to tell the sister who will run the ward and she can go and look and be planning in her own mind the way she wants to go about it.' So I took her into my confidence and once we were given the free-for-all everybody came forward and I've never known them work so well. Within six hours we had got that place spotless. Even the painters sat down and stitched the hooks on to the blackout curtains for us!

Gertrude Cooper, née Ramsden, sister tutor attached to St Mary's Hospital student nurses, Park Prewett sector hospital, Basingstoke, c.1939–40

Returning from her work on P&O cruise liners at the outbreak of war, Gertrude Cooper wrote to the Royal College of Nursing to offer her services to the war effort. She soon found herself working as a tutor with evacuated student nurses.

I joined St Mary's unit in November 1939. There were 800 trainee nurses from St Mary's, Paddington, St Thomas' Hospital, Westminster and the West London, and some other hospitals. I was one of four tutors and we had to organise nurse training with very few patients during that first winter.

I remember well the last trainload of wounded [from Dunkirk] being loaded at Dover and coming to Basingstoke where they filled the wards and immediate surgery was performed. The striking cases I remember were those of gas gangrene. Soldiers who had been stranded on the beach, some up to three weeks, with neglected wounds. And from that day onwards, Park Prewett flourished as an acute hospital, providing excellent surgical, medical and nursing care for the services and civilians.

Battle of Britain

Despite heavy losses, the evacuation from Dunkirk had preserved the core of the British army, and the audacity and bravery shown by everyone involved massively boosted morale. But although invasion did not immediately follow, the population were still apprehensive, and those living in the south of England soon found themselves spectators at the Battle of Britain that followed.

Sue Aylmer, nursery staff, Dr Barnardo's homes, Sussex, 1939–42

Gossip and rumour spread like wildfire as planes were shot down and pilots baled out.

I can remember planes coming over and sometimes the phone would ring and they would say, 'There's an enemy plane come down' and 'There's pilots meandering on the Downs' and 'Keep the doors locked' and things like that. But we never ever saw anybody.

[I remember] waiting for the bus to leave Chichester for the village that we went to, and lying on the floor because the planes were coming over machine-gunning. Oh it didn't happen very often, but a few times.

Once a plane came down in Dyke Road, I suppose it was a fighter plane, German, and the wild, wild stories there were. The pilot was in his dressing gown and pyjamas; he'd got boxes of poisoned chocolates in his plane, which he was going to distribute!

Monica Baly, staff nurse, Middlesex Hospital, London, c.1939

Monica Baly was anxious about her parents' proximity to the coast, but found the exploits of the Battle of Britain she witnessed when visiting them exciting.

At this stage my parents had moved to Bexhill, on the coast, and that was a bit traumatic because it was a restricted area. They'd moved there just before the war, when it was lovely to be living in Bexhill, and now all of a sudden there were concrete blocks all along the beach and they were being bombed.

I was with my mother ... we watched the Battle of Britain from the cliffs of Hastings. And I actually saw Heinkels flying below the level of the promenade, you know, there I was walking the dog and watching a Heinkel! A sudden burst ... thinking, you know, 'That's not one of ours', and then hearing a burst of fire, and then hearing about it on the radio when one got home.

Eunice Boorman, student nurse, Oldchurch Hospital, Essex, 1940–3

At this early stage of the war, watching dogfights still held its share of excitement, especially for the younger nurses. Eunice recalled being warned about the hazards of shrapnel by some of the wounded servicemen she was nursing.

When I was on C6 [Oldchurch Hospital], I hadn't been there very long working on the men's surgery when there was a dogfight going on over the hospital. Some of us were standing on the balcony and the forces that we had in – it wasn't a military hospital but we had some – they called to us and told us we'd better come in, in case we got hit with shrapnel. And as we were coming in we saw all these parachutes come out of the planes and ... that was the Battle of Britain. These men, some were English, some were German, landed in the farms at Hornchurch and the farmers all set about them with pitchforks. The English people were shouting out, 'Don't pitchfork us!'

About two or three hours afterwards we had some Germans in that got fractured legs and they were all put on E6, up the top. While they were up there, we had soldiers come and guard them outside their door and down the corridors, so they couldn't get away. I had to ask them to take their hobnailed boots off and put plimsolls on, because they were making so much noise with their boots when they changed guard or whatever they did.

Joan Crémieu-Javal, River Emergency Service, c.1940

After a shaky start, the River Emergency Service was remobilised. The nurses were issued with a smart uniform rather like the WRNS, and they began their patrols on the Thames.

The River Emergency Service had bases from Hammersmith right the way down the river to Gravesend. I was given the job of being a mobile sister on the boats, so I was permanently going up and down, filling in, relieving people. We went to twenty-four hours on duty, twenty-four off. And we did anything on the river that was needed, the boats did little beats, started at Chelsea Bridge, Lambeth Palace, opposite the Houses of Parliament.

I was once on duty at Lambeth Pier, on board, when I looked up and there was a dogfight in the sky, right over the Houses of Parliament. I was giving them [the crew] tea at the time on deck, it was teatime. I said, 'Oh look, the Royal Air Force are having manoeuvres.' But not a bit of it, it was the start of the Blitz, about September, the dreadful bombing. One plane was shot down, and out came a parachute, German pilot, he went right over us, over the river, because we were on the pier at Lambeth, and he went into Lambeth Park or somewhere; we lost him.

The Blitz

September 1940 saw the beginning of a blitz on British targets that continued with great ferocity until the middle of 1942. The Luftwaffe's primary targets were military and industrial sites, but these were often located close to centres of population, and there was immense collateral damage. Young nurses, sometimes students, cared for civilians whose lives were shattered by the bombs. There were attacks on industrial centres like Coventry and all the major ports such as London, Plymouth, Clydebank and Belfast.

The Emergency Medical Service was now fully engaged and the evacuation of bomb victims became almost a routine event in the London sectors and other major urban centres. Medical and nursing staff remained working in the city hospitals; Lotte Heymann was amazed by her ability to sleep through raids in Birmingham. Joan Crémieu-Javal watched and felt the ferocity of the fires in the Port of London from the river; Dora Williams had to manage the evacuation of her Plymouth maternity home patients in the total absence of effective communication; and Fannie Storr, as a child, watched Coventry burning from her home in Leicester.

Eileen Willis, mobile VAD attached to Millbank Military Hospital, London, 1939–41

Initially the army continued to use their main hospital at Millbank; however, the ferocity of the Blitz led them to evacuate to Watford.

When the Blitz started, the place [Millbank Hospital] was bombed, we had a bomb on the officers' ward which killed a Queen Alexandra sister and I think some of the patients.

… Everyone was issued with a service respirator and a tin hat, and it was a very strict rule that you never went anywhere without it; if you went out for a day off, if you went on leave, wherever you went you had to take it with you and so you just put on your tin hat and slung your respirator on your shoulder ...

Norma Batley, VAD, Emergency Medical Services Hospital, Leatherhead, 1940

Working in sector hospitals was exhausting, but a routine quickly fell into place.

Soon after the Dunkirk evacuation, we had a spate of air-raid casualties and they used to come down to us from London in, as far as I can remember, converted Green Line buses, on stretchers. Each morning it seemed that a new convoy was coming in.

This experience I found, in a way, more disturbing than nursing the soldiers who after all were in a sense necessarily part of the war effort. But when one saw the mothers with small children maybe missing a hand or with a badly cut head or whatever or their whole faces peppered with glass from the shattered windows of their own homes, then somehow or other the war seemed to hit me very much harder.

Joan Savage, student nurse, Woolwich War Memorial Hospital, 1937–40

The earliest raids were deeply distressing to Joan Savage. Organisation was confused and young nurses sometimes felt they were facing an impossible task.

It was badly organised in the beginning. All the casualties would go to number one [hospital] [the first night], then number two the next night. We were inundated. I remember one time I was so annoyed because an accident case came in, a man on a motorcycle, and he wasn't a war wound. You know, he wasn't an air–raid casualty.

There were more casualties coming in than we had facilities. We'd take a case to the theatre and [they] couldn't take [the patient] because it was full and you had to take them back and sometimes they died. Well, no hospital was equipped for the numbers coming in; I mean we got 40 admissions in one night. We had mattresses on the floors to put them on.

I remember they wanted volunteers to take four Green Line buses. So I volunteered. This was to take those that were able to sit up into the country so that they made room for new casualties. I remember very well, I had a little baby, whose head [was] bandaged and I carried it in my arms.

There was an air-raid warning [while we were out in the country] and they asked us to stay; we said, 'No.' Sister Watkins said, 'Oh we must get back!' [To Woolwich.] We came back in one coach and the driver and his mate had their tin helmets on, but of course we didn't, so they said, 'I think you should go to the shelter.' Still the sister said, 'No, we must get back!' So we lay on the floor with pillows, not that a pillow would have done much to help us. But I wasn't frightened.

Winifred Hector, ward sister, St Bartholomew's Hospital, London, c.1940

Winifred Hector completed her tutor's course just before the war and went to Manchester Royal Infirmary to run their Preliminary Training School. She felt that her teaching was adversely affected by her lack of clinical experience and contacted the Barts matron, Miss Dey, in London, asking for an appointment to a clinical post.

…This was a marvellous year because all the patients were acute. That is we only did acute admissions. They were bomb victims, the buzz bombs were falling all round us all the year. All of a sudden the place would be full of people covered in chalk dust and blood, you know.

But in between, when times were quiet we used to admit acute surgery … acute surgical emergencies like perforated ulcers, of which there were many, of course, during the war, and that kind of thing. So that I had a great deal of acute surgical emergency experience.

The house surgeons were usually senior students, the others were whisked off to war as soon as possible, so that any experienced nurse had plenty of opportunity for using her initiative, deciding this and that. For instance if a bomb fell near at hand we got a lot of people in, the surgeons would be in the theatre and I would go round and decide who needed urgent surgery and who didn't.

Eileen Willis, student nurse, Westminster Hospital, London, 1942–6

Eileen Willis had now begun her student nurse training and was adjusting to the unsettling reality of nursing during war-time. She remembered her particularly inspiring matron.

When there was an air-raid warning, walking people went down to the basement and bed patients were pushed to the [underground corridor that linked the medical school with the hospital] and, of course, when the warning went you had to push them down and when the all-clear went you had to push them back and then sometimes there would be another warning and they went again.

Every time there was an air-raid warning everyone was either taken down to the basement or pushed down to the corridor and every morning, it didn't matter if it was day or night, off duty or anything, Matron Smith was there, in her black dress with her starched white cap, and she stayed on duty long after the all-clear had gone, comforting people, encouraging the nurses. You know she was absolutely wonderful but very strict, she wasn't handy with the bouquets but we just couldn't help admiring her, she was so dedicated.

Sue Aylmer, student nurse, Royal Alexandra Hospital, Brighton, c.1942

There were plans for every eventuality.

If we were anywhere in the town, off duty, and the siren went, we had to get back to the hospital. And if you were in the cinema, a notice went up on the screen, saying, you know, the siren was now going and that was telling you where to go for shelter, but of course if you were a nurse you had to run ... all the way up East Street and up Dyke Road. So lots of nights I spent sitting on the stairs of the children's hospital waiting for the all-clear to go.

Lisbeth Hockey, Jewish refugee, student nurse, Muswell Hill Fever Hospital, 1940–3

Lisbeth Hockey was nursing children in London during the Blitz.

I remember to this day the kids screaming and the bombs dropping and the parents being killed and kids being left in the hospital because there was nobody to take them home and their home had been bombed.

It was just awful times.

Mrs Burley-Wilson, née Wood, night superintendent, Tunbridge Wells Hospital, 1939

Nurses had to think on their feet about how to respond to a disaster that could happen at any moment.

I was there when [the hospital] was bombed, when the incendiaries fell on the roof.

All the people in the laundry ... they were all terrified and they rushed off and left their irons on. So I had to think of that, well, what's happening down there, it might be that if they left any of the equipment on there would be a fire, so I had to think of that as well.

Lotte Heymann, Jewish refugee, student nurse, Birmingham Children's Hospital, 1941–4

There was an evacuation plan for major urban centres, but the raids were unpredictable and very, very noisy.

There was a lot of bombing in Birmingham, and as soon as any of the children were fit enough to be transported in an ambulance, they were moved. We had various outlying hospitals in and around the Midlands.

You know it is amazing what one sleeps through. We all had a mattress, just a mattress, and every evening when we came off duty, we went to our rooms in the nurses' home, picked up a pillow, our blankets and one very small case with whatever we felt we needed near us, and went across to the main hospital and down the stairs to the basement where we found our mattress, lay on it, and went to sleep, and most of us, after a few nights we never heard any bombing, any noises. It's quite extraordinary what one gets used to. As you do to food and rationing and everything else …

Joan Crémieu-Javal, River Emergency Service, 1939–42

The Blitz created such powerful images that the memories remained vivid for decades.

The docks were on fire and the boat I was on, *Cliveden* I think it was … well, we went right down and then suddenly all the flames shot straight up and we were in this wall of heat and the skipper said, 'It's too hot, can't take the boat. I am not being responsible for it any longer, I'm turning back.' The heat these docks were creating; everything was burning, there was all sorts of stuff that was highly inflammable you see and so we had to turn the little boat round and we went back.

But I do remember the Thames looked scarlet, it wasn't like water at all, it was like scarlet water, red both sides, it went straight up to the dark sky. Quite extraordinary, that period.

Anybody who was hurt was taken on a boat; sometimes they couldn't move up by road. Boats were wonderful, they could take anybody up or down.

Joan Crémieu-Javal in the uniform of the River Emergency Service.

Anna Brocklesbury-Davis, midwifery sister, Radcliffe Infirmary, Oxford, c.1942

With incendiary bombs a particular hazard, members of staff waited during raids on the roof of their hospital with sandbags and stirrup pumps.

I was put in charge of the air-raid precautions on the roof of the maternity department of the Radcliffe. If there was an air raid, I had to organise stirrup pumps and all the anti-air-raid equipment [as well as staff to] watch on the roof, in tin hats, if there was a siren. I always had to have a rota on the notice board, of who was on call.

Georgina Henderson, student nurse, Shieldhall Fever Hospital, Glasgow, March 1941

The Clydebank Blitz lasted two long nights.

I was on a pneumonia ward and it was all children and in one ward the windows had blocks, up in the windows for the glass. We were told that if there was an air raid we were to take all the cots and we had to put some mattresses down and put the bairns underneath. [One night] the siren went, we'd just gone on night duty, there were alarms before but, oh dear, the guns started now.

There was only one other [nurse] and me; I think she was only a year started. What a job we had feeding ... bottles and things, and the air-raid wardens were coming round with milk and the doctors coming round. Everybody was coming round to see it was all right. This went on till six o'clock in the morning; we were never out of that place. [Normally] we used to go for our dinner through the night for a break but we couldn't leave; just carried on till six in the morning.

Our windows were blown out by a bomb that dropped round the back. Shieldhall was beside the docks. The first night the ships weren't prepared for it, but the second night was worse; the ships and guns, and the shrapnel on the roof – it was really alarming, but never mind, we got over it.

Clydebank got it worse; it was across the river from us.

Grace Howie, pupil midwife, Rottenrow, Glasgow, 1941

We were at a lecture one night when, just at the end of the lecture, the sister tutor was trying to demonstrate and get into our heads the mechanism of labour. And this tall nurse, she was one of the two-yearlies* and unafraid to speak up, she said: 'Sister, that's not one of ours.'

So we all went to our wards and this other Irish girl with me, she was a great lass, and we went into the great big sluice room where all the bedpans were and we could hear the alarm bells going, you know, the siren was roaring and she said to me, 'What'll we do, Howie?' (It was surnames there.)

I said, 'Well I think maybe we'd better just give them bedpans.' And it was the wisest thing we ever did because we went into the wards and these panic-stricken women with babies in their cots beside them and sirens roaring and the bombs beginning to fall, it was the Clydebank Blitz that night [13–14 March 1941]. And we arrived with bedpans, well what's more down to earth? I said, 'Well if we don't then they'll all wet their beds.'

So we gave them the bedpans and then we had to do the Heath Robinson thing [improvise]; the staff midwife took the babies into the hoist and down to the basement. The women, the mothers, we got them up and the mattress on to the floor below the bed, made them up in a bed down there and then put the bedspread over the bed so no flying glass would strike them. But by the time the nurses came on in the morning everything was back to normal.

We could see the fires and we got chased for our lives for looking out of the window. Of course when we went down for supper we looked out, then the night sister came in and said to the patients, 'It's Clydebank, not to worry.' She had forgotten that some of the women came from near there. What I said to Hitler wasn't printable.

The other sad thing was, there was a nurses' home with the hospital. They were bombed and one of them [was] killed. I remember that; she was a Highland girl, a very nice person.

---

* Midwifery students who did not have a nursing qualification and who were required to complete two years of midwifery training.

Fannie Storr, schoolgirl, daughter of a nurse, Leicester, November 1940

I remember we had a shelter at the bottom of the garden, one of these Anderson shelters. My mother actually woke me up to come and see the flames of Coventry burning. She said there is something here that I think you should remember all your life ... and I have. I remember her waking me up and looking across and [seeing] Coventry ... from where we were [Leicester] ... terrifying really.

Dora Williams, superintendent midwife in charge of a maternity home on the outskirts of Plymouth, April 1941

Responsibility for mothers and infants was felt very acutely.

Now that was a very difficult time because we were in a very dangerous zone. We had no men at all on the staff, we had to fire-watch our place which meant the nurses had helmets like wardens because we had to go out at night, we had the proper helmets and we had fire-watchers. I had to organise all that.

We were never hit. The [main] hospital was hit in Plymouth, there were a terrible lot of casualties, but we were never hit; but we had to evacuate one night. The fires were raging, Plymouth was burnt more than blitzed, we had more incendiaries than anything else.

My committee had told me, 'In any trouble ring up this, that and the other and you will be told what to do.' Of course, there were no telephones working. So I ran across to the Royal Marines and they said you must evacuate all those mothers and babies, which was a very difficult thing to do because we had no ambulances or anything.

Girls were driving vans, ordinary grocery vans, and we put our mothers and babies in two lots and I sent my best staff off and said, 'You are supposed to go to the Eye Infirmary, see if you can get there.'

Well, the girls were so frightened at the driving, so absolutely terrified when they got to the end of Durnford Street which was a great crater; they drove to the nearest place, which was the naval hospital. [The staff] were horrified at seeing a carload of newly born babies and mothers because they had just been hit: nurses killed, doctors killed, patients killed, but they took them.

The girls were terrified, the drivers, they took half the mothers there and the other half did get to the Eye Infirmary.

I stayed behind, because we still had domiciliary midwifery cases to attend to whatever raid was on.

In the morning the husbands all came along and said, 'Where are our wives?' I had to say I had no idea, I felt simply dreadful.

Eunice Boorman, student nurse, Oldchurch Hospital, Essex, 1940–3

The Luftwaffe pilots used landmarks to find their targets.

One sunny morning, the German planes followed [the railway] up from Southend, machine-gunning people all the way up. It was about seven in the morning, and they machine-gunned all us nurses going on duty. The nurses' home was quite a way in the grounds from the hospital. Some of [the nurses] went back into the home and some laid flat; in fact two people were killed on the bridge here at Newby Park.

'Poppy' Bocock, sister tutor, Nightingale School, Botley's Park sector hospital, 1939–45

The work of nurses at all levels was exhausting, and for some the strain eventually proved too much.

Miss Hillyers [sector matron] wore herself out. She died soon after the end of the war of heart failure. She was a very imaginative lady, she kept us together. She gave us all a little brooch, which I've still got, a little St Thomas' badge. Not the Nightingale School badge, but a tiny badge; even student nurses in training had it, so they all felt they still belonged to St Thomas'. And furthermore she came and she saw them all; any student who wanted to see her could, and any student that I wanted her to see, she would see. She had about five or six big hospitals in her sector, all with St Thomas' nurses in as a kind of nucleus, and she had to get round them all. And she did. Nights of bombing, days of rushing round the countryside. Fortunately she had a driver so that she could relax a little bit in the back of the car.

Joan Crémieu-Javal, River Emergency Service, September 1940

The city-centre hospitals continued to operate despite the dangers.

We were living in billets in St Thomas' Hospital, they gave us rooms ... they thought we were 'their' river service, you know, they said 'our' river service, because we were stationed at Lambeth Bridge and we did the beat from Lambeth down the river to the next bridge. And that night I was in St Thomas' and we had a direct hit ... the operating theatre was destroyed. All the nurses were eating in the dining hall, and it was glass all round, they all got glass in their backs, they had to be brought over to the home, where I was, laid flat on their tummies on mattresses, we had to drag mattresses out for them.

And then, hours later, we heard a dreadful noise and lots of fires starting and my four VADs and myself rushed up on the roof to put sandbags on all the fire bombs ... incendiary bombs, that was our work; took us quite a long time to put out all the bombs ... but we did, we got them all out, all these young girls, they didn't flinch ... Tin helmets on, I can see us now, rushing up these floors and at the top, opening and going on the roof and these wretched bombs ... and how they didn't hit us I don't know, raining down, but there were already sandbags up there to throw on them, they had prepared for that.

That was a terrible night.

Kathleen Raven, ward sister, St Bartholomew's Hospital, 1940

The stoicism of the nurses was dogged, but they were constantly surrounded by danger and distress.

They left me and five others at Barts, so there were six of us to deal with the casualties. Our matron Miss Dey was also the sector matron, so she came to Barts just sometimes.

We were bombed six times, direct hits, but nobody was killed. We had emptied all the blocks fortunately and we just kept certain wards open. We sent to Hill End [St Albans] as many as we could; they converted the Green Line buses into ambulances and convoys delivered every day to Hill End Hospital.

We [would] wait for the next blitz; the victims came in with some terrible things. For instance, a bomb went right into the Bank station and it carried with it all the tar from the road, the tarmac, hundreds of people were burnt terribly and they came to us. One just had to get on with it. Many times I was blown across the ward ...

The following morning [people arrived] to see if their relatives were there. Sometimes they used to go around and see [for themselves] because we had no idea; [people's] discs had been blown off, if they wore discs. Sometimes they found them and it was marvellous, but five times out of ten they didn't. Dreadful.

The determination and resilience that characterised Dunkirk, the Battle of Britain and the public's resistance to the Blitz have passed into legend.

For the Emergency Medical Service, the war's arrival on British territory presented an enormous and ongoing challenge, but it was a challenge that they rose to. Nurses such as Winifred Hector at Barts relished the opportunity to throw themselves into challenging work, and all across the country, nurses simply got on with their extra responsibilities, even when those responsibilities included fire-watching on the hospital roof, as they did for Anna Brocklesbury-Davis in Oxford. All nurses remembered moments of great stress interspersed with constant tension, but they also recalled comradeship and support.

The Blitz continued throughout 1942, but the worst was over by the end of the year. There were many tough times to come, and a shocked and grieving community to nurse.

Most war-time births were at home. This local midwife and district nurse wears her Queen's nurse insignia on her hat and on a ribbon around her neck.

FIVE

THE HOME FRONT

Neighbours would come in with their only egg, rationed, for the mother who had just given birth and they didn't have much to give, a lot of these patients, but they were so nice.

Patricia Lloyd, pupil midwife, Paddington London County Council Hospital, c.1943

Away from the drama of hospital nursing for wounded soldiers and civilians, a small army of dedicated nurses continued to provide support for the community. The fact that there was a war on didn't relieve district nurses and midwives of their duties. In fact, with patients being moved around the country as evacuees, and the worsening shortage of nurses caused by recruitment to the armed services, the pressure on those nurses working in the community grew intense. But life had to go on, even as rationing was introduced and travelling became difficult.

A network of district nurses organised and funded locally by philanthropically minded citizens worked alongside independent local doctors or general practitioners. There were also health visitors and midwives who were linked to the local Medical Officer of Health. Lurking in the background were some 'handy women' who had no qualifications whatsoever. They were simply believed in by their clients, who turned to this cheaper source of help in many family emergencies.

In hospitals most nursing care was given by student nurses, whereas most of the care in the community was given by qualified nurses, but since there was no national health-care body, there were no hard and fast rules. District nursing associations could employ anyone they chose. Some employed the 'Queen's nurses', the most highly qualified and the most expensive. These women had completed both general training in a hospital and district nurse training with the Queen's Nursing Institute. But there was no legal requirement for a nurse working in the district to be a Queen's nurse, or even that she should be a state registered nurse.

Most midwives were doubly qualified. Many nurses felt they were not fully trained until they had added 'State Certified Midwife' (SCM) to their qualifications, and virtually all midwives were also qualified nurses.

At the outbreak of war there was considerable anxiety that recruitment of qualified nurses by the armed services would lead to a collapse in both the district nursing and maternity services. The president of the Queen's Nursing

Institute was the Earl of Athlone, a public-spirited man who before long was appointed Governor General of Canada. Athlone was very aware of the shortage of district nurses and was worried by the prospect of these women being recruited into a more glamorous life looking after wounded soldiers. One of his last acts as president before going to Canada was to send a letter to every Queen's nurse urging her that 'in a national emergency, you will best serve your country by remaining at your post'.

Thousands of nurses, midwives and others from across the country responded to the challenge of this terrible shortage of nurses: women like Kathleen Raven and her colleagues who stayed at their posts at Barts throughout the Blitz. For Anna Brocklesbury-Davis and her fellow nurses, the responsible work of conducting thirteen deliveries in one day for women who had been evacuated was cause for celebration. For everyone who remained at work in the towns and cities – hospital nurses, district nurses and midwives alike – blackout, bombing and rationing added to the difficulties caused by poverty and staff shortages.

Not enough nurses

One strategy deployed to combat the nursing shortages was the introduction of new grades of staff, such as orderlies and assistant nurses, people who could relieve the student or qualified nurse of 'non-nursing duties'.

Ivy Scott, matron, Royal Halifax Infirmary, 1939–45

Ivy Scott was appointed matron of the Royal Halifax Infirmary at the age of thirty-four. She was to prove an able leader of nurses.

I sometimes wonder how we did [cope]. The sisters were really marvellous because as soon as you had trained a nurse in those days, [you weren't] allowed to keep her. She had to go into the forces, which meant that senior nurses were doing staff nurses' duties half the time. It was very rare that I was able to keep a staff nurse. And the wards were overcrowded. We got a tremendous lot of outside help; that was when I appointed what you would call orderlies today. We called them ward helps and they were rather what I would call the better-class domestic. And I put them into their own uniform and told the sisters, each ward got one and they were to relieve the nurses of the really non-nursing duties.

I must say the sisters didn't approve of it to begin with, but before long they would not have done without their 'Green Ladies'. What were, and were not, nursing duties? I left it to the ward sister mainly, they were all very sensible.

Georgina Henderson, pupil midwife, Motherwell, c.1944

Regulations controlling the employment of qualified nurses and midwives were imposed with varying severity. It was common for newly qualified midwives, for example, to be told they must remain in post as a staff midwife for a year.

At that time there was an awful scarcity of midwives. We applied to go into the Q[ueen] A[lexandra]s, Nurse Sinclair and I, in the army, but they said we were short of midwives and we had to do a compulsory year. So we stayed on as staff nurses in that hospital and we did our year and then we went back to this place in Glasgow, and we said we'd done our year and we wanted to join up and they wouldn't let us. We're still short of midwives, you've to carry on doing midwifery. We were mad, we weren't going to do it, so we went, we said let's go and do district. And that's how we did our district.

Janet Crawley, midwife, Edinburgh, c. 1942

I was quite sorry to leave [the Royal] actually. I had tried [to be accepted to work for] all the services. I tried each one during the war. They all turned me down because I had my midwifery.

Yes, I was of more use amongst the population than I would be amongst the services.

I tried, in the Queen Mary, I was doing midwifery there. I asked the matron if she would put me over in the general side, which she did, she very kindly moved me over there. I applied again. But they wanted to know what the matron had done with her midwife. You could not move anywhere, because they had you taped everywhere.

Lisbeth Hockey, Jewish refugee, pupil midwife, c. 1944

There was good reason to worry about the quality of maternity care. Lisbeth Hockey was particularly distressed by her experience in Part I of her two-part midwifery training.

The first part of midwifery was taken in hospital, [it lasted] six months. I did it at the North Middlesex Hospital in Edmonton in London and we had a gastroenteritis epidemic. This was a horrific experience because we lost 11 babies in three weeks. Perfectly healthy babies ... and I thought I would never continue into my second [part].

I chose a place in Essex where you could do your six months on the district for Part 2, because I just couldn't do hospital midwifery any more after this. I decided I would continue and do Part 2 because I didn't want to be half a midwife, so I decided that I would just finish it. I really loved Part 2, where you could really sit with your patients. I was never a good midwife but I loved just being a friend to a woman in labour.

Midwifery training
in war-time

*Joan Savage, pupil midwife, Simpson Memorial Maternity Pavilion,
Edinburgh, 1943–4*

After completing her general training in London, Joan Savage went to Simpson's in
Edinburgh to train to be a midwife.

I set off for Edinburgh on my own, and when I arrived at Waverley [station]
it was early morning because I had travelled overnight. There were soldiers
on the train. I was far too early so I walked up and had some breakfast and
then I went to the Simpson's.

It was a year's training. We had to provide our own uniform, so I took
my 'general' uniform. We had the uniforms of all the hospitals. Barts,
Thomas', Birmingham; that was a very pretty uniform.

I think there were twelve in our [set] with Mrs Myles, who was the
tutor. The sisters varied in character; you might get one who was very
kindly. I remember I was shattered when I went back from a day off and
she asked me if I had enjoyed my day off. I had never been asked that
before. We soon learnt that if you were told that you could have the
afternoon off, you did not stay in, you immediately put your coat on
and went out and stood outside and thought: what am I going to do? If
you stayed in, you were given some work to do, cleaning cupboards or
something else.

You had to do thirty deliveries, ten in Part 1 and twenty in Part 2. We
had a 'Brown Book' to record deliveries for Part 1 and a 'Blue Book' for
Part 2. We had to submit those books for the examination.

Grace Howie, pupil midwife, Rottenrow, Glasgow, 1941

One of the very well-known training hospitals was Rottenrow in Glasgow. This was a prestigious hospital and pupils were unpaid.

I arrived at Rottenrow in Glasgow, in a real ... peasoup fog at the beginning of January 1941. That was my year for midwifery, 1941. It was the year before lend-lease* so we were very scarce in the food line. The other thing was that sometime during that year Winston Churchill got Mrs Churchill to organise medical aid to Russia. This meant we all had to part with some of our medical stores. So we had to be very 'canny', as they would say in Scotland, with cotton wool, just little wisps. We were all well trained in economy. That was one aspect of that year, blackout was the other aspect.

About ten of us started. We weren't paid anything by the way, we had no salary. Your board and your keep, and they supplied a uniform ... one asked one's parents, went home and said, 'I'd like to do my midwifery at Rottenrow but I'll not get any money.' I was the only one so I thought they could give me pocket money. It was a voluntary hospital, they didn't have any money to pay us. They paid the trained staff.

There were always plenty of girls whose fathers would fork out the money. I went home one Sunday with one [girl], she stayed just out of Glasgow, and came home Sunday morning. I remember her mother could produce a tin of fruit or something, you know, and fed us.

Eunice Boorman, pupil midwife, Oldchurch Hospital and York House, 1944

Supervision was taken very seriously in some centres.

You always had a midwife accompanying you for the actual delivery, but often you went out on your own and you just sent back for the midwife when it was almost due. You weren't allowed to actually deliver without

---

* The United States government's scheme to lease equipment and supplies to the Allies on a long-term loan basis. This debt was repaid in 2006.

the midwife being there unless it was a very quick birth. Sometimes the baby would be born before you even got there.

We had to supply our own bikes. I had mine before the war and probably the [nurses'] home had one or two of their own.

Doris Carter, pupil midwife, Kirkcaldy and Dundee, 1941–2

In other centres a more casual attitude appalled some of the conscientious pupils.

I did Part 1 [of my midwifery training] in Kirkcaldy in Fife, 1941. That had been the home of Andrew Carnegie* and it was a lovely place, lovely grounds, and I learnt an enormous amount there. But I think I learnt more at Dundee, where I went to do my Part 2. A very, very hectic place, we never thought [anything] of being called out twice in one night and we pupil midwives, although we'd only done six months' midwifery, were sent out completely on our own; it was thought that we were getting experience and confidence in ourselves. But in actual fact, I think we were all terrified.

I remember going to one lady, in a rather remote part of Scotland, and there was just one neighbour, a cheery little soul, kept on calling me 'hen'. And to my horror, the baby was almost being born as soon as I got there and I saw it was a breech and I had never in my life delivered a breech before. There was no means of sending for any help, so I just had to get on with it. Fortunately all went well, but when it was all finished and I slumped back in a chair, the neighbour said to me, 'You sit down, hen, and look at this', and she pressed a *People's Friend* magazine on me. And I've taken the *People's Friend* ever since.

I also remember another case I went to way up somewhere, seemed to me in the Highlands, and there was absolutely nobody there whatsoever, not even a neighbour. The woman's husband was a shepherd and he's out on the hills somewhere and the woman, unfortunately, had a tremendous

---

* The Scottish-born industrialist and philanthropist.

post-partum haemorrhage and I really thought that she was not going to survive. I pressed heavily on the aorta, not knowing what else to do, and miraculously it stopped, and the woman survived. It was a terrible, terrible experience.

We had ... I think it was three midwifery sisters who controlled the district, but they hardly ever went out with us, certainly not initially. If we wanted help we had to send for them, send a neighbour or get somebody to ring up for them although there weren't many telephones in those days. One sister, a big fat lady, she just hated coming if she had to go upstairs, so as soon as you said you wanted help she would ask, is it 'high door' or 'low door'? Low door being on the ground floor, but a high door was the top of a tenement. If you said high door, you knew she wouldn't come because she didn't like going up the stairs, she'd send somebody else who probably didn't know much more about it than you did. So most of the pupils got into the habit of saying 'low door' even though it wasn't; face the music when she got there.

Kathleen Raven, ward sister, St Bartholomew's Hospital, 1939–42

Kathleen Raven was awarded a scholarship by her training hospital, St Bartholomew's, to study midwifery in the City of London.

... That was an eye-opener too because, oh dear! The ward sisters there ... The Barts sisters were ladies, but it wasn't quite the same in the City of London. But there again, I learnt a tremendous lot in a different direction there.

On the district, I was up and down the Caledonian Road; we delivered the babies on newspapers. There were perhaps five or six families living in one house but the kitchen and the cooker was on the landing. There was a lot of terrible poverty. But they seemed reasonably happy. And then I finished that and went back to Barts as night superintendent.

Janet Crawley, pupil midwife, Rottenrow, Glasgow, 1941–2

Medical students were also required to observe and conduct deliveries. Most medical students were men, and they were often very inexperienced in practical work.

If it was less than two miles, you had a medical student with you. But at their exam times you did not get a student as they were studying. I used to trot along on my own and I used to say that if anybody shouted 'boo' round a corner, I would have been off. Cowcaddens, the Gorbals, I knew them all, very well. But you were not so frightened really then. Nowadays you could not do it.

Oh the patients were wonderful. They really were so kind to you. You always got a cup of tea afterwards and a chocolate biscuit, which they saved for the midwife. Yes, even in war-time they had a chocolate biscuit for you. Mind you, I have drunk tea out of a jam jar, and you never sat down on a chair without a newspaper unless it was a wooden one.

There was always a certain amount of fear. The [medical] students did not really know what they were doing; you were more or less in charge. I remember saying to one, 'Would you like to give the enema?' And he jumped at it. He said, 'Oh yes please.' He had never given an enema before and he was quite delighted.

I had one time to call out a doctor, because I maintained it was a breech; and the doctor went, 'No, no, not at all, it is not a breech, it is a simple vertex presentation.' And it was a breech, but I managed to deliver it.

The work of a midwife
in war-time

The evacuation of civilians early in the war that separated midwives and their clients resulted in problems in some of the 'reception areas'. The numbers of pregnant women awaiting delivery were enough to pose a problem for the local maternity services.

Anna Brocklesbury-Davis, midwifery sister, Radcliffe Infirmary, Oxford, c.1940

The Radcliffe Infirmary maternity department was the centre for a lot of outlying country houses, which had been taken over as maternity units for evacuee mothers from London, most of them for normal deliveries. Well now, if anything went wrong, they were sent in by ambulance, rattling in, to the Radcliffe maternity department, as an abnormality. And I worked a lot in the main labour wards, taking in these abnormal [cases] ... I worked in the Caesar theatre with Professor Moir and Mr Stalworthy, dealing with quite difficult abnormalities.

One time we were very busy. We had several mothers come in rather strong labour, we'd got two in the admission room and two labour wards going, and I was running between one labour ward and the other and I sent a ... I think a pupil midwife, into the admission room, to see what was going on in there. [There was] one mother who had been in the shower and had nothing on and the other mother, who was on a bed in the admission room, lying there, suddenly delivered. She gave a great scream to the mother who was in the shower, and the pupil midwife came in, she said, to see a naked mother who was in strong labour herself, taking this mother's baby beautifully over the mother's tummy, as if she was a born midwife. [The midwife] called one of us to come in jolly quick. We were trying to deliver other babies in the two labour wards. It was one of the funniest stories I have ever heard, I think. She didn't stop to put anything on, she just went straight across to help this woman. So people do help each other out in emergencies, don't they?

[There was one] time when there were thirteen deliveries. There had been, I think, seven deliveries in the day and we came on at night thinking we'd be clearing up after all these deliveries, and we got six more of our own.

But it was a Sunday morning at the end of all that. Another midwife and I, she was a keen Methodist, I was Church of England, but ... she said she'd got Harvest Festival going on in her church, so I said let's go. So the two of us nudged each other when we were singing these hymns about 'all good gifts around us are sent from heaven above'. We'd had these thirteen babies all the night and day, but we didn't half sing. That was partly due, you see, to the evacuation; there wouldn't have been all that number if it hadn't been for the London bombing evacuating expectant mothers. We had a very busy time in Oxford during that time.

Patricia Lloyd, pupil midwife, Paddington London County Council Hospital, c.1943

Many nurses recalled the generosity and camaraderie of their patients with huge affection. Despite the anxiety of war, midwives in particular were still able to revel in the joy of doing their jobs well.

We used to go out in the middle of the night and there was a blackout, there was a fog, there were bombs around ... down the Harrow Road, off Edgware Road, some of the really rough areas, but people were so nice to each other. Neighbours would come in with their only egg, rationed, for the mother who had just given birth and they didn't have much to give, a lot of these patients, but they were so nice.

And I can remember, two o'clock in the morning coming back on my bicycle. I was on a bike in those days, for goodness' sake, we didn't have cars. And I think it was ... one of the happiest days of my life, having had a successful birth.

Eunice Boorman, pupil midwife, Oldchurch Hospital and York House, 1944

District midwives had a base that they returned to and where they refilled their bag containing a standard kit of instruments and medications. Analgesia was usually pethidine but might include 'gas and air' (nitrous oxide) if they had the equipment and could find a strong man to transport it. After the delivery, the midwife or pupil midwife remained for some time and certainly until the end of the third stage (the delivery of the afterbirth). She then visited and nursed her client for fourteen days before discharging mother and child to the health visitor's care. The shortage of hospital beds and the many demands on staff resulted in women being accepted for home delivery regardless of the facilities in their homes.

We had a midwifery bag that contained kidney dishes, bowls and things, also drugs, pethidine and things like that. We were issued with ergometrine. We had one for each bag, we had to sign the drug [off] when we got back and get a fresh one if we used it. We had sterilised scissors and instruments that we could sterilise. Cord ligatures and dressings; and mothers, before they had the baby, used to collect a big pack from the clinic which consisted of sanitary towels, cotton wool, and dressings that you might need for the baby's cord, and surgical spirit, and silver nitrate stick to treat the baby's cord with. That was a delivery bag which we had to sterilise and clean out after each delivery.

And then we had a normal bag that we took round as we did the nursing. We used to go in for fourteen days and the first four nights after the delivery we went in the evening to swab them down and make their beds and look after them as well as in the morning we went in and bathed the babies and made their beds, in between the deliveries that we had.

Most of our work was home births and we also had gas and air machines. They were quite big machines so someone had to bring them out for us

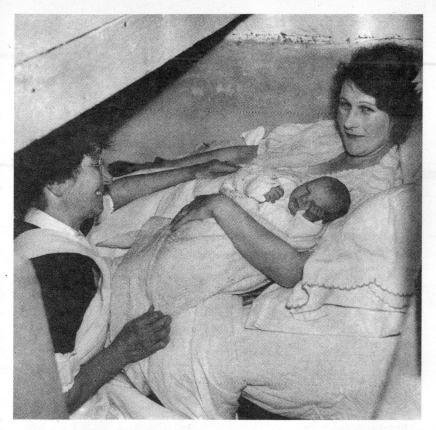

Nurse Ryman looks after Mrs Ceaplen and her baby, born in a bomb shelter during an air raid on 1 October 1940.

because you couldn't take that on the bike with the delivery bag. Often the husbands would collect it, though not many of the husbands had cars in those days and not many of the husbands were home because of the war.

Grace Howie, pupil midwife, Rottenrow, Glasgow, 1941

Many of the pupil midwives were from comfortable homes and many of the patients that they visited were poverty-stricken. Glasgow was particularly notorious for some of its poor-quality tenement housing.

District was quite something; that year was not funny. We went out to do our district cases in twos with a medical student because of the blackout. I was with a lady student. The first house, I can see it in my mind's eye to this day, it was very sad, it was no place for a woman to have a baby. She already had some family and the family history indicated severe infections which took one of the children to one of the hospitals which we called the 'Lock' hospital [the venereal disease hospital], not really polite to mention. It was very sad, you couldn't forget that. We got the baby delivered and we got back.

Then the next week, we were in a house in the same street and we went to see a young mother with her new baby, it was just a baby visit, and I can well remember a clean white towel at the side of the kitchen sink for nurse to dry her hands; everything was immaculate. I used to wonder how she managed to bring up her child and keep her husband in that home to her standard with this other sort of standard downstairs. It made you think about the social side.

Janet Crawley, pupil midwife, Rottenrow, Glasgow, 1941–2

The tales we could tell, we used to have what we called 'big game hunting' when we went back in from district. This was when you went for your bath, and you stripped off to see who had the biggest catch. You could send your uniform to the laundry every time you wanted it cleaned. It was usually underneath that you had all the bother. I had long hair in the Royal, but I had to get it cut when I went to Glasgow. I thought, I'm not risking that. It really was, well we made a joke of it, but it could have been pretty awful if you had let it get you down.

I remember one street I went into, in the Gorbals, and when you went upstairs you had your handkerchief over your nose, because of the smell of the toilet in the corner, halfway up the stair, until you got to the flat. I went in and it was beautiful, the husband was a carpenter and the wife was a French polisher, and it was beautiful inside.

Joan Savage, staff midwife, Simpson Memorial Maternity Pavilion, c.1944

There was limited knowledge of birth control and limited access to contraceptives and contraceptive techniques. Few nurses chose to mention this and the burden it posed for impoverished mothers.

I think the one thing that was a problem was the abortions, the back-street abortions. They were admitted to the Simpson's Ward 54, at the top in an isolation block that had its own theatre, and it was tragic sometimes. I mean the patient would not say anything but you'd find a bougie, a solid rubber tube that you used to insert to bring about an abortion, because it wasn't legalised then. There were people against legalisation, but if they had only seen some of those patients, I think they would think differently. It was sad, this young girl, she just could not afford to have another child because she had already got a big family.

They did not all die, but they would not reveal anything. Some would do it themselves and some would go to a woman.

District nurse at work

Like midwifery, district nursing allowed a certain amount of autonomy, not least because the nurses were already qualified and experienced. But out on the district, these highly skilled nurses co-existed with the handy women, relics of an earlier era.

Lisbeth Hockey, Jewish refugee, Queen's nurse, c.1945

After some dreadful experiences during her midwifery training, Lisbeth Hockey found her professional home in district nursing.

[It was] different [from hospital nursing] in that you were on your own and you didn't have anybody else to ask for another opinion. Different in that you had to cope with the most primitive conditions. I mean you would have a bed that was in the corner somewhere and you couldn't make it properly and you couldn't lift the patient very adequately on your own, so you know it was harder. You had to train relatives. I did a lot of teaching of relatives to cope because we did one … or might be two visits a day; we weren't allowed to do any more than that.

You learned how to adapt, and there were lots of routines you had to follow, for example, you always had newspaper. District nurses became ridiculed for the newspaper. You came into a house and you put your bag on a piece of newspaper, you had another piece of newspaper and you folded your coat on to it, because many houses were infested with vermin. It was really to keep your things clean, but in order to be diplomatic to the patient, when they said, 'Why do you want newspaper?' you would say because you don't want to, you know, bring any dirt in, on to your beautiful furniture or whatever.

So you carried newspaper with you in case a family didn't have any. And then you boiled your instruments in a saucepan and you sterilised your dressings in the oven, and you did it all yourself; for district nursing you didn't have anything that was pre-sterilised in your case.

Mrs Burley-Wilson, née Wood, 'handy woman', Tunbridge Wells, 1945

After leaving her last hospital job, Mrs Burley-Wilson began work as a 'handy woman' in her local area.

When I left, I was called 'the nurse'. I laid out all the village, I think, there wasn't a house that didn't have me laying them out.

I had a ticket from Boots [the chemist], a token which allowed me to get things a bit cheaper. I had kits for cuts and grazes and things. Women even came to me thinking they'd got carcinoma, and would I tell them if they'd got it.

Well, people just came, 'Mrs so and so's just died …' or 'My wife's just died …' or 'We've got friends staying with us and he's just died.'

I had the most horrific last offices* to do, that's being polite, in several cases. One old man with a double hernia with a great big belt round him which I couldn't get off, I had to get someone else to help me get the belt off his stomach, you know, ever so strong, belted in. He died in the garden.

I never really finished nursing. I never finished, I carried on. I had a reputation for miles.

Lisbeth Hockey, Jewish refugee, Queen's nurse, c.1946

Although the district nurse was well regarded, there was still a mysteriously superior status awarded to a hospital nurse.

The people who had district nursing care worshipped the district nurse. At the same time they felt she was less educated than the hospital nurse.

---

* Washing and laying out a dead body.

I remember patients saying to me, 'When are you going to qualify as a nurse?', that sort of thing.

People don't perceive hands-on nursing as being skilled nursing. The minute you gave them an injection – sulphonamides came in during my time as a district nurse – and as you began to be more 'technical', I think your reputation rose. I think we were valued more than perhaps district nurses are now but you were certainly not perceived to be as educated [as hospital nurses] – I mean that's why I did most of my studies at the Queen's Institute – it really worried me that patients had to go to hospital outpatients to have, for example, stitches removed, often by people far less qualified than the district nurse. And they had the inconvenience and the expense ...

Paying for care

✚

One of the things all nurses hated doing was asking for and collecting money.

Mary Anderson, registered nurse and midwife, Queen's nurse, c.1945

There were certain things that you were supposed to charge for. For instance, if you were doing last offices, you were supposed to get so much money off them. I can't remember ever doing it.

If somebody was really getting into trouble – say a widow with a few children, and she's getting into financial difficulties, and if she doesn't watch it she'll be out of her council house and this kind of thing – I [would go] to the banker, who was in charge of our nursing association, the local association. And they made some arrangement that she could pay gradually. I actually wrote down and kept a note of how much, and handed it on and this kind of thing, you know.

Dora Williams, Queen's nurse, Buckinghamshire, c.1938

As a senior nurse, Dora Williams was clear about her attitude to charging for her time.

If the patients couldn't afford it we would [sometimes] do it for nothing. It [district nursing] started as home nursing for the poor and I think there had always been an understanding that you would never charge a patient who couldn't afford it. It was a bit of a problem to decide.

Eunice Boorman, community nurse and midwife, c.1943

Insurance was a reality for only a small number of patients.

A lot of them belonged to the Hospital Savings Association (HSA) and things like that. They also had to pay so much per visit for ordinary district nursing. When I went to Hackney and did my Queen's training, we had to collect the money. In fact we were very grateful when the NHS came in and we didn't have to any longer ... because you see sometimes you couldn't get the money from people.

Lisbeth Hockey, Jewish refugee, Queen's nurse, c.1944

Finance was always a bit of an issue, and some nurses reported using their own money for payment.

Some patients had an insurance system which was called a provident scheme and they had the little yellow card on the mantelpiece so you could see it and our hearts were very, very pleased to see the little yellow card because it meant that you didn't have to ask them for half a crown. Just imagine an old lady given an enema and she could hardly afford to buy her meals and she had to give you half a crown. You had to account for the number of visits. You had to do your accounting, number of visits, money or insurance scheme they had to equate, and I remember more than once putting our own money in because you knew if you didn't you were accused of not having done the visit.

People had to pay or be members of the insurance system, they just didn't get a visit if they didn't have the money. [But] it happened relatively often, I mean those of us who were really committed and people couldn't afford to pay we just put our own half-crowns in.

Dora Williams, Queen's nurse, Buckinghamshire, c.1938; later superintendent, Plymouth

Queen Victoria's Jubilee Institute made an important contribution to community care. This was supported not only by the patients who immediately benefited but also by wealthy patrons.

The local authority used the Queen's as agents for their work. Queen's didn't pay us. The Queen's inspected us; it was a voluntary body. I mean, we had to raise all their money, you know. I used to go out and have to give talks and do all sorts of things. We had to raise the money to run the service.

Yes, [in Buckinghamshire] we had a scale, from nothing to perhaps 7/6d [seven shillings and sixpence] a visit or something like that; a means test. But what we had in Plymouth when I first came was what we called 'the Scheme'; the patient paid a penny a week for the district nurses, penny a week for the ambulance and a penny a week for ... I think it was something to do with hospitals, and they had a card with stamps and they stuck the stamps on and they showed you their cards and they were in benefit.

We had to see the cards. That was all, to see if they were up to date. But luckily when I came to Plymouth I didn't have to do that, I would have hated it.

Health visitors

Health visitors were the third element of care for the community during war-time. Health visitors wore a nurse-like uniform, but they were employed by the Medical Officer of Health and were particularly concerned with the welfare of healthy mothers and children. They worked in local authority clinics and their clients' homes, never in hospital. Inevitably the social disruption of war upon families came within their remit. They became involved in harrowing stories.

Anna Brocklesbury-Davis, student health visitor, Battersea and Wandsworth, London, c.1944

I'd been at Oxford for quite a few years, doing midwifery, and felt that I should go on and go right into public health, as a health visitor. I went and trained, with the war on, in Battersea, right in the middle of London.

The first visit on my own that I ever did, I went to see a new baby. Thank goodness we had a very good senior health visitor who was in charge [back at base]. The mother had got nappies on the line, and one thing and another, and she said [to me], 'I haven't got the baby here at the moment, the baby is round at my mother's.' I said, 'What is the address?' and got the address.

I went back to my senior health visitor and said, 'I didn't see the baby, it was at Mother's or something, this address.' So senior health visitor got a visitor to go [round], only to find that there was no such address, the mother had made it up. And, well, to cut a long story short, that mother hadn't had a baby at all. She had pretended to have a baby because she didn't think her husband loved her enough and she was told that if she produced a baby, he might keep on with her. It was very sad. There had to be a court case in the end, she had borrowed somebody else's baby to take up to the registry. There was this baby, she put down its name and everything, so [that is why] we got a card to say that there was a baby in that house.

Elaine Wilkie, student health visitor, RCN, London, 1940–1

For many, fees had to be met out of meagre earnings.

I got my name down for health visiting at the Royal College of Nursing, by which time the Blitz had started in London. So I came back to London and the college was continuing with its education courses.

The end of my [health visitor] training was in 1941. At that time the training of health visitors was by a body then known as the Royal Sanitary Institute which provided training for sanitary inspectors and a range of other people in public health. It was a very packed six-month course and considering the nature of the training, which was very stereotyped and very limited, I thought the college did very well because they did open it out and I found that training really quite exciting.

We paid for it ourselves with family support.

Anna Brocklesbury-Davis, student health visitor, Battersea and Wandsworth, London, 1944

I always felt that if the mothers of the future were trained and given the right information and educated, that the babies would be fine and get better, and be stronger. Vitamins for children and babies were only being discovered about during the war. It took the war really to make us think what was the best thing for the babies. They must have the best, so the vitamins were part of their routine. Of course breast-feeding was more the usual thing of the day; it is obviously the very best thing, it is made for that baby.

Well, we did teaching; we were trained, in Wandsworth, even through all this war-time bombing and everything. All the lectures in Battersea Polytechnic were well organised and we were given a proper training so as to be able to give classes to the mothers.

Frances Jones, health visitor, Farnborough, Hampshire, 1942–4

All these nurses had more than one qualification, and even public health nurses had to turn their hand to other nursing roles.

When I worked in Farnborough [as a health visitor], the Medical Officer of Health of Farnborough and myself were in charge of the operating theatre at the casualty centre where air-raid victims were treated. It was a terrific experience when this bomb fell because you felt the whole ground was opening up, but they missed the Royal Aircraft establishment. It fell in a road, in a residential area not very far from where I had digs actually.

Everyday reality on the home front: rationing

Rationing of essential supplies was introduced early and continued into the post-war period; sweets finally came off the ration in Coronation year, 1953. Nursing was hard physical work and student nurses had always had good appetites.

Anna Brocklesbury-Davis, student nurse, London, c.1935–9

The diet in my training days at St Thomas' Hospital was very plain food, but good food. In the Nightingale School, when we came back for our elevenses, I remember eating vast quantities of bread and dripping to fill myself up because I was always so hungry. We were given as much bread and dripping as we wanted. There wasn't very much vitamin C in the diet, I can remember that. Hardly any at all, hardly any fresh, uncooked vegetables or fruit. Everything was thoroughly cooked.

The nurses' dining room, St Thomas' Hospital. The nurses continued to wear their starched and goffered caps throughout the war despite the problems of laundering them.

Janet Crawley, student nurse, Royal Infirmary of Edinburgh, 1937–40

The introduction of rationing in hospitals produced all sorts of problems for those who were trying to create a fair system.

Rationing came in then, which was a dreadful thing really, because you could not buy oranges in the shop or any other fruit. You had to rely on somebody bringing them in to the patients, and probably a patient would sneak you an orange, which was wonderful.

Gertrude Cooper, née Ramsden, ship's nurse, later sister tutor, Park Prewett sector hospital, c.1939–42

When Gertrude Cooper left the employ of P&O, the ration book she was issued turned out to be rather unusual.

We signed off the ship and were given identity cards which apparently had some indication of our category, because the subsequent year, when ration cards were issued to all the nurses, when I was at Park Prewett, mine was a document offering me rations for three weeks. On taking it to the 'Food Office', I was accused of handling, or having received, a ration card which was issued through the Port of London to incoming seamen. I was registered as a merchant seaman! As I explained that I was now on the staff of the local hospital, I was given a fifty-two-week ration card. You know the 'Food Office' weren't very polite to me!

Agnes Barnett, housekeeping course, Territorial Army Nursing Service, c.1939–40

Rationing posed many different problems.

When I finished [district nurse training], war was on, so I joined the Territorials. I tried to do a housekeeping course in Gwent and it was a disaster. War had begun and we were just starting rationing, in fact I think the housekeeper said to us they were worried about training properly. You muddled your way through, spent all day weighing out the rations, making ends meet. It was 4 oz of sugar, 4 oz of butter ... I think it was 8 oz of sugar but you kept 4 oz back for the cooking, and you kept half the butter back for the cooking.

Monica Baly, sister, Princess Mary's Royal Air Force Nursing Service, North Africa, 1943

When posted overseas, nurses became expert at foraging or scrounging supplies.

... And there was the docks operating company, in the docks at Benghazi, with whom I became very friendly, which was a great place to be friendly, because when they got consignments in of oranges and so forth we got an orange, which was very nice. Rations were awful, I do remember that was the hardest part of the war in fact ... I went down to eight stone; we were on very low rations there.

Sue Aylmer, student paediatric nurse, Royal Alexandra Hospital, Brighton, c.1942–5

Food and hunger became a universal topic of conversation.

I think you ate more carbohydrates and stuff. Fillers-up. I mean at lunch-time, mid-morning, we used to go to change our aprons. We had coffee or tea or something and great wedges of bread and peanut butter or bread and dripping. But on the whole I don't remember ever being hungry or not liking what I was given.

Annie Altschul, Jewish refugee, student nurse, Epsom Hospital, c.1941–4

We lived in, but of course that made it difficult because if you went away to visit somebody you had to carry your rations around with you; we had rations handed out every week.

In Epsom one got to know patients pretty well, I kept having the same patients in, so if the grocer was a patient, she afterwards supplied something. I remember a greengrocer patient who let us know when apples were about. We were never hungry and the whole point about the war was that one was extremely well fed, the rations were aimed to be 1,500 calories and well-balanced and the non-rationed thing added; you had enough protein, fat and carbohydrates if you ate the rations but either bread or potatoes were always off ration. You couldn't be hungry. I used to oil the hinges [with the butter] … it was always rancid but it made quite good grease for oiling hinges with.

Ivy Scott, matron, Royal Halifax Infirmary, 1939–45

There were all sorts of inequities in the system. The quantities of food for each person varied; serving soldiers and miners were allocated more calories than nurses. Matron Scott was unimpressed by the rations of her nurses compared to those issued to soldiers on guard duty in her hospital.

Of course Halifax was a garrison town. They had what they called the 'glass house' just outside Halifax and we got several of their patients in. Well if they came in they'd have to have their guard with them and I don't say it caused difficulty but it opened our eyes a little bit, because one day I happened to be doing the round and the guards were changing and you would have thought they were in front of Buckingham Palace the way they changed guard outside that ward! And they were bringing in the rations. So I said to the sergeant, 'I would like to see what they get.' And he took this carton into the ward kitchen and I was amazed at what came out of this carton; things that we hadn't seen for months. And

I said, 'Is this for the week?' He said, 'No, this is for today.'

I said, 'But my dear man, your guards are sitting there doing nothing, my nurses are running up and down the ward all day long and getting a quarter of this.' Rashers of bacon and tins of sardines and chocolate and all the rest of it; I was amazed, so he said, 'Put it into the pool and let them have what we have.'

'Poppy' Bocock, sister tutor to St Thomas' student nurses, Botley's Park sector hospital, 1939–c.43

Once distributed to their sectors, the sister tutors and nurse administrators set about sorting out some of the inequities in the system.

When we got down there [to Botley's Park] we found that the mental colony patients [had been] on a deficient diet. We were told that we wouldn't have a meal after four o'clock each day. We would have breakfast, we would have dinner, and we would have a tea at four o'clock. So I went straight to Dr Paddle and said that this wasn't good enough, the nurses couldn't work a whole evening and have no meal – an evening meal must be put on. And they decided that they had to.

So we got an evening meal put on, but I don't mind telling you we all lost about oh, four or five pounds the first two or three weeks because we didn't have enough food. We had quite a good breakfast usually, a rather poorish lunch, and very poor supper. If we were lucky we got cheese and bread, and some coffee.

But then after that, because we began to get soldiers, everything improved. And I will say that all the patients, even in the mental deficiency wards that were left, were given the same food. So the fact that we had soldiers meant that in fact our rations were certainly very adequate. Not awfully well cooked you know, but adequate.

Everyday reality on the
home front: travel

It was not only food that was rationed; shoes, bicycle tyres and petrol were all hard to get. Travel was a particular problem throughout the war. Everything was unpredictable, raids disrupted timetables, trains were not heated and were barely lit, light bulbs were painted to preserve the blackout. Nurses became expert at hitching and scrounging lifts in civilian and military transport, and many found their uniform a sort of passport to security.

Sue Aylmer, student paediatric nurse, Royal Alexandra Hospital, Brighton, 1942–5

All nurses needed decent shoes, and they were one of the most difficult things to find.

I can remember my shoes were disgusting eventually. They were stuck together with Elastoplast. I mean, you didn't have many coupons, did you? And shoes were quite expensive and you had to wear black lace-up shoes. I had a family who gave me things, so I was probably better off than most. One of my sisters was a dressmaker and she made me things, or remade things. So I think I was very fortunate. I did go home. We still lived in north London and it wasn't very nice travelling on the trains in those days, because they were all blacked out.

Dora Williams, superintendent Queen's nurse, Plymouth, 1939

All community or district staff had to find some mode of transport, and bicycles fitted the bill for many.

When I came to Plymouth my nurses were all on bikes. I went out as a superintendent on a bike with them. I was absolutely determined that before I left, every nurse should have a car or the use of a car and every nurse should have a telephone. The city council said it was quite unnecessary for them to have telephones or cars. I fought it and I told my staff here, 'Over my tombstone, just put a little car and a little telephone.' Because I got every nurse a telephone and a car in the end but it was hard work.

Janet Crawley, student nurse, Royal Infirmary of Edinburgh, 1937–40

Nurses were issued with bus passes to enable them to travel to work and return quickly in the event of a raid.

We had a special privilege during the war. You had a special disc, which you had on your uniform that you were supposed to take out with you, so if the siren went when you were out you could go to the head of the queue and get on the bus, much to the annoyance of some of the people in the queue. I can remember being down once at Haymarket and the two of us had to get to the head of this long queue to get on the bus. There were all sorts of remarks being passed; I can remember it so well. Then of course we produced this ticket that we had. They did not know what it meant, but the conductor on the bus knew.

Afra Leckie, Queen's nurse, Brighton and Portslade, c.1942

Bicycles could be fun.

It was wonderful work; and you know that lovely feeling of going on the bike, especially on a Sunday when there wasn't any traffic really, of whizzing down that New England hill ... We used to walk up the hills, and whiz down them, on a bike. I used to know Brighton so well. My area was at the top of that hill, Stanford Road, I think it was called. That was really a great life. I enjoyed that enormously.

Dora Williams, superintendent Queen's nurse, Plymouth, 1939

Dora Williams had an eye for the future, and in order to prepare for her career after the war she decided to study for the Midwife Tutor's Certificate, even though it meant travelling to and from Bristol in a cold and blacked-out train.

I realised that my committee didn't want me to leave and I said to them, 'Look, I will stay as long as you let me go and do my midwifery tutor's certificate at Bristol University.' They let me go, it was my day off in the week. I went every week, one evening, and stayed the day and came back the next night. I think it took a year and it was pretty hard work. The theory was very hard but, of course, I could practise on my own students, which was very good.

I had to travel to Bristol in the dark. We weren't allowed any lights in the train, it was such a long ride and you couldn't see anything out or in. It was horrid but it didn't do me any harm.

Joan Crémieu-Javal, River Emergency Service, c.1940

For some nurses, train journeys nurtured romance.

I was working round London ... a period at the North Middlesex filling in time, and I went off and married ... a war-time marriage.

We met on the train, from Colchester going up to Liverpool Street, and he was going back from leave. We met in the blackout. [I] got into the carriage, I said is there room in here? Yes, yes. I said, right, I'll come in. He said, right, do come in, and he introduced himself, naval chap, same age I was, twenty-three. He said, well I can't see you, I'm going to scrape the paint off the light bulb. He got up, scraped the paint off the light bulb so that he could have a look at me, my face. By the time we got to Liverpool

Street he said, well … I'll escort you home wherever … I was going to north London, I think. We went on seeing each other, he was [from] Essex you see, and I was an Essex girl, and I think within a few, what two months, three months? he said he thought we ought to get married. By then, the River Emergency Service was about to be reformed and so I ended up, we went off to marry in a registry office. War-time was [this] fevered thing, you know everybody going slightly mad. I can remember at the time thinking, this is absolutely ridiculous, but I'll go with it.

Janet Crawley, student nurse, Royal Infirmary of Edinburgh, 1937–40

Even walking in the blackout was a challenge.

If you went out, it was in the blackout. I used to go out to one of my mother's friends; they were in Lauriston Park. I used to go down there regularly, I knew every step. I had my torch, but I mean if I didn't have my torch on, I knew everywhere I had to step down off the pavement and step back up on to the pavement, all the way down to Lauriston Park.

District nurses in Watford set out on their duties after a morning briefing.

The good times

◆

Even though they were poor, tired and surrounded by trauma, nurses still had fun. There were many vivid memories of good experiences. Some of them centred on encounters with the Allied soldiers stationed in Britain. There was a lot of goodwill towards these men, most of them from the Empire and the Commonwealth; though occasionally cultural differences could cause tension.

Sue Aylmer, student nursery nurse, Barnardo's, Sussex, 1940

The kindness and generosity of some Canadian soldiers brightened Christmas for Sue Aylmer and her charges.

One time the Canadians were stationed in the village, this was I suppose 1940, and I was in the shop one day trying to get sweets for the children. There was a Canadian man in there and, 'Oh I'll give you plenty of sweets,' he said, and I said, 'Oh yeah.' Wondering what he wanted in exchange. Anyway he was very sincere, he said, 'Where do you come from?' and I told him and said if you have sweets to give away, you get your commanding officer to contact the matron.

Well they did, and at Christmas, oh it was lovely, makes me cry even now. These Canadian soldiers came up, on parade as it were, with bagpipes playing, and they marched up the long drive, got to the front of the house, and they were all dismissed by the colonel. They had been allotted, you know, this lot went to the older children and this lot went to the younger children, and this lot went to the nursery. The rule in the nursery was that no visitor touched a baby, because of germs. Well these soldiers came in, and before you could say knife, they whipped up these children, and they were cuddling them and singing to them, oh it was really ... well, there you are. And they had brought all sorts of toys and sweets and things. We had a lovely time.

After that they used to come up one evening a week, and we used to have a little social time together. But unfortunately, they were the ones, or some of the ones, that went to Dieppe [the Dieppe raid, August 1942]. And we never saw them again.

Patricia Lloyd, staff nurse, St Bartholomew's sector hospital, St Albans, c.1941

Many nurses, not to mention their families, were grateful for the support of the Commonwealth soldiers, and tried to make the visitors welcome.

He [my brother] was stationed in Canada. It made a big difference to the way my mother looked at the Canadian soldiers over [here]. I would come back from a night's leave, if I was lucky to get it, from Barts, and arrive with a couple of Canadian soldiers who had got nowhere to sleep for the night, and my mother would make up beds in the lounge for them. People were very nice to each other in those days, and helpful; and my mother said, 'Well if somebody is looking after my son over in Canada, the least I can do is look after them over here.'

Sue Aylmer, student paediatric nurse, Royal Alexandra Hospital, Brighton, c.1942

For many nurses, their social life improved immensely thanks to the cosmopolitan influence of soldiers from all over the world.

My brother-in-law was in the army and he was stationed up on the Downs, he was ack-ack [anti-aircraft], so occasionally he came down to Brighton and took me out. People were very kind, they used to invite us out to supper. And of course there were a lot of soldiers around, a lot of South Africans [and Canadians]. The South Africans brought crystallised fruits. We hadn't seen anything like that in the war and thought they were lovely, but after a while they were on every table that you looked at, you had them morning, noon and night. Pity, but you got tired of them. They [the South Africans] were nice; we had some Australians as well.

Joan Gray, née Goddard, relief sister, Bodmin Hospital, c.1943

The mixing of different cultures did not always go smoothly. Joan Gray's was a lone unhappy voice.

The day after we arrived in Bodmin, 1,000 American soldiers were posted there, and they were awful. It's a shame really and I do perhaps regret [saying] it because they came to help us win the war …

The road from the hospital at the top of a little hill [came down into town] and this was all that there was of Bodmin, so we [would take] a walk down the hill and there would be four American soldiers on this corner, four on that corner, five or six on that corner and they would be whistling and making suggestions and horrible approaches to us, such as we had never had before. I didn't like it.

We had a dance at the hospital every fortnight, and these Americans would come, and if there were any nice-looking ones, they just stayed in the background, but there was always somebody came and got hold of you and wouldn't let you go. The only way I knew to get rid of him was … I would say, I'm going to the ladies' room. And I would get back to my bedroom and stay away. That was how I escaped. It was a shame really, it was always just these few that persisted and it was … horrid. But there were always attractive people in the background, behaving themselves, as I would say.

[Years later] my husband and I went to the Bayeux museum and as we were coming out, a chap said to my husband, 'Were you involved in D-Day?' and Jeff said, 'No I wasn't, but my wife was, she was a nurse and she doesn't think they've given much credit to the QAs.' This American said, 'They get a lot of credit from me.' He embraced me and said, 'I was looked after by the QAs, I was looked after so wonderfully, and I was always so grateful for it.' And it was really quite moving. You know, something I hadn't ever expected and he hadn't ever expected, he was with his wife and it was just so lovely.

Eirlys Rees, pupil midwife, Sorrento Maternity Hospital, Moseley, c.1945

It wasn't all dances and sweets from gallant foreign soldiers. Nurses were expert at making their own fun.

In later life, Eirlys Rees flourished as matron of the Royal Free Hospital.

When we were taking our midwifery training at the Sorrento, we used to have to go on the bus in to Birmingham City Hospital, Loveday Maternity Hospital, for our lectures. As soon as the lecture was finished we used to dash round to this Kardomah coffee place which was opposite Birmingham station and have coffee and relax. By the time we came to the end of the month we hardly had any pennies, but one of the three of us was a gold medallist and she had her gold medal.* So we found a pawnbroker in Birmingham and at least once a month when we were short of pennies, we used to go in there with this gold medal and he used to bail us out for the rest of the month. That gold medal from the Elizabeth Garrett Anderson Hospital School of Nursing used to go into the pawnbrokers in Birmingham at least once a month for the whole eighteen months. I shall never forget him, he used to see us coming through the door and he always got the money out without a word.

---

* Some hospitals awarded a gold medal to the most successful student nurse each year. The medals were highly valued by the nurses.

Kathleen Raven, ward sister, St Bartholomew's Hospital, 1939–42

London theatreland continued through some of the worst times in the war. Nurses were often able to pick up free tickets.

And then you see we were young and we all had great fun together and we came off duty and we got a lot of theatre tickets sent from the London theatres and we used to dash off and change quickly and get there for half past eight. I'd go to get an evening dress, yes we had to be in evening dress, that was the condition, and we did it and we loved it. It was a marvellous life really.

Eirlys Rees, student nurse, Elizabeth Garrett Anderson Hospital, c.1939

Based in central London and keen on the theatre, Eirlys Rees went as often as she could.

So the notice would go up outside Matron's office at two o'clock in the afternoon saying there were x number of theatre tickets for that evening's performance at whatever theatre, and it would have the notice 'evening dress'. I can remember I wanted particularly to see this show. So I thought come hell or high water I have to go, so I [went], in my evening dress. I remember coming back from the theatre and I was crossing the square opposite Euston Square station, near the fire station, and the sirens went, so I had to hitch up my skirt and start running. A policeman stopped me just as I got into Euston Road and he guessed where I had come from. He said, 'Nurse, you must go into the shelter.' I knew the shelter was under Euston station; I said, 'No, I can't, I must go.' So he said, all right, and he took my arm and I hitched up my skirt and he ran to the hospital with me and dumped me outside the accident and emergency door. I shall never forget that; I never saw him again.

'Poppy' Bocock, sister tutor to St Thomas' student nurses, Botley's Park sector hospital, c.1939–45

The sister tutors took on the task of morale-boosting.

I personally washed, starched and goffered about sixty Nightingale caps a week.* I charged the nurses a penny, which covered the starch, or what was supposed to be starch in those days, and with it I bought records. We had a record-player up in the – what had been the hall of Botley's Park, but which was now our residence. And I bought records for record evenings, because there was nowhere for the nurses to go. So we got country dancing going and we got record-playing. And years later an old student who by then had been a ward sister and retired came and told me that her love of music developed from the time that we had that record-playing in Botley's Park in the middle of the war.

Nurses who worked in the community were, as Lisbeth Hockey said, frequently 'worshipped' by their patients. There was widespread recognition that in wartime, even more than in normal circumstances, these women were a source of solace, support and comfort. For all nurses, in between the privations caused by rationing and shortages, there were moments of fun and joy to be snatched, but there could be no possibility of relaxing for long. By the middle years of the war, nurses had come through a baptism of fire and learned how to get on with whatever needed doing. But as the war rumbled on, there were more and more returning servicemen in need of care. In the hospitals, as in the community, nurses stood up to the challenge of caring for a seemingly never-ending stream of patients.

---

* Many hospitals issued elaborate, decorative caps to nurses. The Nightingale nurse wore a net confection which had to be starched and goffered into shape.

Almost all nurses thought battle dress was the most suitable attire
for nurses near the front line.

SIX

NURSING WITH
THE MILITARY

We had a few Germans and I decided, that very first day,
that they were not enemy, they were patients and they would
be treated exactly the same.

Joan Gray, née Goddard, sister, QAIMNS(R),
Normandy, 1944

For many nurses, the most obviously worthwhile war-time role was working alongside the military. Some, like Theodora Turner and Joan Crémieu-Javal, had joined one of the reserves and were called up at the outbreak of war. Others, like Elvira Thomas and her five colleagues from Cardiff Royal Infirmary, did not join but were called up anyway.

There were three main nursing services attached to their respective military services. The largest, Queen Alexandra's Imperial Military Nursing Service (QAIMNS or 'the QAs'), worked with the army. All QAs were qualified nurses, some were regulars, or career military nurses, but numbers expanded throughout the war. The Voluntary Aid Detachment (VADs) were members of the Red Cross or St John Ambulance who had completed some home nursing courses, and signed up. VADs like Eileen Willis worked as nursing assistants alongside the QAs. The Royal Army Medical Corps (RAMC) provided medical services, and although nursing in military hospitals was overseen by female QAs, much of the 'hands-on' nursing was undertaken by male RAMC orderlies who also did much of the nursing in front-line battle areas.

The other two armed services each had a nursing service organised in a similar way. Queen Alexandra's Royal Naval Nursing Service (QARNNS) and their VADs, together with male Sick Berth Attendants (SBAs) supported the Royal Navy. Their numbers were fewer and women did not go to sea on active service, but they were posted to hospital ships which were used both to transport the injured and as mobile hospitals.

Finally for the newest service, the Royal Air Force, the Princess Mary's Royal Air Force Nursing Service (PMRAFNS) and VADs were again all women. Like the other services, the RAF also had orderlies who manned hospitals and sick bays wherever RAF personnel were posted.

The regulars were conscious of their future position in their chosen career. Despite the expanded numbers in the nursing services, all the most senior posts were occupied by regulars.

Many service personnel were also admitted to civilian hospitals and looked after by civilian nurses for at least part of their care, especially at crisis points such as the aftermath of Operation Dynamo, and later the D-Day landings.

By the end of the war there were doctors, orderlies, stretcher-bearers, sick berth attendants and nurses in every theatre of the war.

Called up

✚

Agnes Barnett, nurse, Territorial Army Nursing Service, 1940

Agnes Barnett began her training in 1930, and by the time she was called up she had qualified in general nursing, midwifery and Queen's nursing.

The war had broken out, I was in the Territorials, and I got called up in February 1940.

[We went to] Oxford first, 26th General Hospital, we were there six months. I learnt to pack and unpack very quickly. Everywhere we [were supposed to go] the Germans got there before us, so you packed and unpacked. We were about to go to Finland when the Finns capitulated; we were packed ready to go to Norway when the Norwegians capitulated; we were packed to go to France when they capitulated.

Elvira Thomas, sister, QAIMNS(R), North Africa, c.1940

In North Africa one group of QAs was rescued by American Quaker ambulances.

I was posted to the Middle East, I went to Jerusalem first of all, where we were transferred; and we went to Tobruk. That hospital was captured, at the fall of Tobruk. We got the patients out by sea, and I think some of them were torpedoed. I don't know how many patients were lost, but I know one of the orderlies was lost, some of the surgeons were captured, but the nursing staff went out by ambulances, and we came back down to Alexandria. The American Friends, Quakers, had ambulances; it was they that brought us [out].

We were heading for Rommel's headquarters at one time when we were crossing the desert; we were stopped by this lookout and redirected, because there was nothing to help you to know where you were going. The poor drivers were driving blind.

Betty Boyce, QAIMNS(R), c.1944

Betty Boyce was one of a group of QAs allocated to work in a civilian hospital. She was very impressed by the contrast between the work that the QAs did and the work of nurses in the Civil Nursing Reserve, the reserve that the RCN had been called on to organise before war broke out.

So we set off with our suitcases to the Wellhouse Municipal Hospital. This ward had 40 beds, they were all men; that was about the only thing that was common to them; we had medical, surgical, army and civilian, a few orthopaedic, and a few ear, nose and throat just dotted around; and a Civil Nursing Reserve staff nurse.

I really quite enjoyed it but I don't think I've ever worked so hard for three weeks in my life, it really was killing and I thought, these hospital service reserve nurses they're doing this year in year out, while we're swanning about in the army; really I'd done very little work in six months and it didn't seem awfully fair. I had great respect for the Civil Nursing Reserve after that.

There were about three of us to run this ward. I used to come on extra early to get the laundry sorted before my poor old staff nurse who wore buttoned boots and had glasses. I think most of them had retired and come back in. My old lady must have been about sixty and she said to me, you'll take charge of the ward, and I said, 'Oh no, temporary postings never take charge,' as I had learnt in the army, and she said, 'You are a sister, I am a staff nurse, and you will take charge.' So I thought, well don't let's waste time arguing because moments were precious.

Yes they were paid, yes, she lived miles away, came in on her bicycle every morning and they had the air raids to contend with. We were supposed to go down to the cellars but I was far too tired. I thought, I shall just have to take my chance because I'm staying in my bed, I'm not going down to any cellars. The buzz bombs had just started, it wasn't the ordinary bombing we were afraid of, it was those other things that cut out and dropped – doodlebugs – they were very nasty but we were north of London, so they did fall but not too close to us.

Grace Howie, ward sister, Ayr Hospital, 1942–6

Not everyone wanted to join up.

It never occurred to us to do anything like join [up]. The older ones, some of them had their eyes set on the services. I didn't ever feel I was up to the standard of the services physically, I didn't think I was sturdy enough.

Military nurses

✚

Rose Telfer, née Hall, sister, QAIMNS(R), c. 1940–5

After completing general training at the Royal Infirmary of Edinburgh and midwifery in Glasgow, Rose Telfer joined the Queen Alexandra's Imperial Military Nursing Service. Not everyone was looking for a 'romantic' overseas posting.

My first posting was to York, Fulford barracks outside York, quite a biggish hospital. Then the night superintendent came round one night and said to me, 'There's a posting in for you, Miss Hall.' I said, 'Where do you think it will be?' She said, 'I think the Middle East.' I said, 'Well I don't want to go, Sister.' She was the assistant matron actually who was doing 'night super[intendent]'; she said, 'Why don't you?' I said, 'I just don't want to …' She said, 'You'll have to come.' She was going herself actually. 'There are a good crowd of us going, you must come.' I said, 'No, I don't want to go overseas.'

Matron was on leave and I met her in the corridor two mornings later and she said, 'I see there's a posting for you, Miss Hall. Why don't you want to go?' And before I could answer her she just went right on, she said, 'Is it ageing parents?' I said, 'Yes.' Well at that time my mother and father would be just seventy I think and, you know, not complaining unduly, but I just said yes. 'Well,' she said, 'I've got a friend in the War Office; I'll phone her tonight and see if she can do anything about this posting.' So it was cancelled. I was posted up to Stirling.

It was a little hospital up near the castle, Argyll's Lodging, an old, old building, and it was just a small sick bay with reception station. There were quite a lot of troops stationed around Stirling and you know they reported in to us. Well it was terribly nice there; there was only myself and another sister from Ireland. We had a very happy time there.

My father turned ill and I asked for compassionate leave to go home and nurse him, he was a big man, and Mother by this time was a bit debilitated with rheumatism. So I asked and the commanding officer was a terribly nice man, he had been chief medical officer with the old Persian oil company all his life, retired and offered his services in the war, and he was terribly good about me getting this leave and he was very friendly with the district director of medical services.

Then when I was there, in 1945, this posting came in for overseas and of course you didn't know where you were going but anyway it was to France. I couldn't refuse of course after all this compassionate leave I'd had.

We mobilised, I was posted to Number 8 British General Hospital, it had a very good reputation, Number 8, they had been out in the desert, in the Middle East. But they were home and this was them remobilising. So I was posted there ... we mobilised at Watford and well we just didn't know quite where we were going. I was glad to get away from the London area at the time, glad to go over to France.

We were under canvas and it was awful, I'm no pioneer; we were under canvas in our camp beds and what not. We stayed there, just waiting to find out where we had ultimately to go. Anyway we were ultimately moved up to Brussels and we drew up at this big hotel and we thought we were just stopping for a cup of tea or something. This was our headquarters, this big hotel!

Joan Gray, née Goddard, sister, QAIMNS(R), Normandy, 1944

After discontinuing midwifery training, Joan Gray and her friends joined the services.

[There was an] advert, asking for nurses, in the QAIMNS. If I'd had the choice, I would have gone to the RAF, but you had to be twenty-four and I was only twenty-three and so I decided to join the QAs. You got an application form, you were told where to go for an interview, to a hospital ... it was in Cornwall, and Matron interviewed us and decided whether she would have us or not. I think we were all accepted.

So we started ... it was some kind of training for moving over to France and these patients, these damaged and injured patients. We were nursing all these RAF people who had been injured, head injuries and that kind of thing. [We transferred] to these various hospitals, they had taken over these Oxford University colleges as hospitals and we had these patients with head and back injuries and things like that in these wards and we stayed ... where the students would have stayed.

I started off in Oxford. And then I was posted up to Scotland, to Turnberry and they had a hospital in the Turnberry Hotel, and we were sleeping in this hotel on the top floor and we had biscuits* to sleep on, on the floor. Every morning you found that they had slipped apart and one part of your anatomy was on the floor.

You looked out over this beautiful scenery, Ailsa Craig and things like that, it was just beautiful. We had a day off and you could go off to Glasgow, or you could go off and look at the place where Robbie Burns had been brought up ... there were lots of things to go and do.

The service uniforms appealed to many and were worn with pride. However, in many war-time situations the veils and tippets, stockings and skirts of the QAs and the white tropical kit were not appropriate dress. Battle dress without a nurse's cap was worn by many in forward positions.

Monica Baly, staff nurse, Middlesex Hospital, London; sister, PMRAFNS, c.1942

By the time Monica Baly joined the Princess Mary's Royal Air Force Nursing Service, her views about the Axis powers had modified.

At that stage I had decided, I had seen the light, like Paul on the Damascus road, about the whole point of the war. I don't quite know what triggered me off, I think it was something on the concentration camps. Not much

---

* Large square padded cushions, perhaps 36" x 36".

of that was getting through to us, of course; very little of that was getting through. But I met some Poles, and my feeling about Germany was changing. I decided, walking down Oxford Street one day, that I was going to offer my services to the armed forces, so I applied first of all to the navy, but the navy lists were closed, so I applied to the Princess Mary's Royal Air

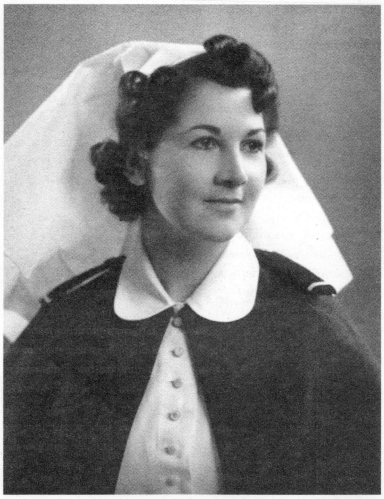

Monica Baly in Foggia, Italy, in 1944. Like many PMRAFNS nurses, Monica was proud of her uniform.

Force Nursing Service, which was an easy bet for the Middlesex because Dorothy Madge [the matron, Miss Smith] was on the interviewing panel, so I was in.

Sheena Kilminster, née Craig, sister, PMRAFNS, c.1940

Sheena Kilminster began her training in 1935 but was delayed by a period of sickness with a streptococcal throat infection and rheumatic fever. She finally qualified during the war, and as she did not want to become a midwife, she decided to join the PMRAFNS.

My brother was then in the RAF, and so I said at the recruiting office, 'Please may I have papers for the RAF nursing service?' And they said, you haven't a hope. 'They are being very, very selective, they need very, very few nurses and they're taking very few indeed, you haven't a hope, the army is taking everybody.' And in my toffee-nosed fashion I said, 'That is precisely why I have no wish to join the army, please may I have papers for the RAF?' So I got the papers, and filled them in and sent them off. And in due course I was summoned to the Air Ministry in London, it was then in Aldwych, and there were twenty of us interviewed that day and four of us were accepted.

I was given £50 to have a uniform made for me; there were tailors who did nothing else, and I must say the RAF uniform was a very becoming one, more so I think than the navy. The indoor uniform was a white dress with short sleeves, under which you could slip a long-cuffed sleeve, so that it appeared like a long-sleeved dress in cold weather but in summer you could have it as a short-sleeved dress and of course for overseas as well. You had your epaulettes with your rank, and we were flying officer rank, you were called sister, and on top of that, in this country you wore a little cape similar to the very well-known red army cape – you know they have scarlet and grey. Well the RAF had RAF blue barathea, the same as officers' uniform, and it had a pretty little rosette at the centre back, and on the front you had what we called our 'medical dogs' – the RAF medical insignia of the wings and the serpent on the stick, and your epaulettes with the badge of your rank on, and white shoes and white stockings. That was the indoor uniform.

The outdoor uniform was a white shirt, a black tie, a well-cut barathea skirt and a jacket with a built-in belt that fastened, brass buckle that needed cleaning, epaulettes with a button that needed cleaning – and as sisters we had to do our own cleaning, we didn't have batmen to do it for us – and what we called our 'Dicks'. It was really rather like a Dick Turpin hat. The naval officers had the blue and theirs were three-cornered; ours were black felt and were four-cornered, so you had a corner at the back as well as at the front, and of course the usual RAF badge. It was really a very distinguished uniform. Later on we were issued with berets; now they were very becoming and you were not allowed to wear your berets in London. So when I was stationed at Halton if I was going up to London I had to wear my Dick, but around the camp one wore one's beret and outdoor uniform, and of course you had a greatcoat.

Gertrude Cooper, née Ramsden, QARNNS, 1942–6

Gertrude Cooper taught student nurses from St Mary's Hospital, London, in one of their sector hospitals, Park Prewett, Basingstoke. By 1942 the worst of the Blitz was over, and Mrs Cooper took the opportunity to join the Queen Alexandra's Royal Naval Nursing Service for the remainder of the war.

By the spring of 1942, I realised that as nurses in training were being recalled to their training schools, since London was again functioning, their place was being filled by VADs. I felt there was no longer a need for me, as one of four tutors, to remain at that hospital. They were gradually withdrawing [student nurses] because they were conducting nurse training where the patients were flowing. So that may be purely my way of appeasing myself, because it [nurse tutor] was a reserved occupation, and they no longer allowed nurses to apply [to the services] if they were doing tutors' work. Tutors were in very short supply. But, after all, I was not trained as a tutor.

Military hospitals overseas

Monica Baly, sister, PMRAFNS, Middle East, c.1942

When Monica Baly was finally posted overseas, to Cairo and Benghazi, she found that she and her team 'should have been here six months ago' ...

That was my first trip. I'd never been to the Middle East, I'd never been further than Europe. And Cairo of course was a great revelation. And from Cairo the six of us flew down to Benghazi [Libya], to an Italian hospital in Benghazi, which had just been evacuated by the army. The army had moved on, moved up the desert.

When we got to Benghazi, I must say, everybody said to us, 'Well you should have been here a year ago, you should have been up here with Wavell, you should have been up here with Montgomery.' Wherever I went in the war I should always have been there six months earlier, because you know, that's when all the fighting was!

Betty Boyce, QAIMNS(R), c.1944

After three years as a sister at the Royal Victoria Hospital, Belfast, and one year as a tutor at the Ulster Hospital, also in Belfast, Betty Boyce joined the QAs.

I joined the army in Bangor, 25th British General Hospital, they'd been to France and been evacuated. We had a hospital in Bangor somewhere up near the railway station; I think it was probably a primary school. And from there we went to the London orphans' school at Watford where we 'packed a hospital'. Now, you see the equipment that you have in a hospital now, well anything we wanted we had to pack and take with us. There was going to be somebody to look after the tents but everything else, medicine glasses, syringes, the lot ... there was a list.

Monica Baly, sister, PMRAFNS, Italy, c.1943

Making do and keeping track of equipment was a vital skill in the battlefields.

We boarded a lighter and we went over to Italy, first to Taranto, then up the coast to Bari, and then to Foggia where we were taking over an old bombed-out Italian hospital. And this was to be Number 4 RAF General Hospital.

It was a very traumatic experience, because it was totally bombed and we had to make do. I always said I spent my war either closing hospitals or starting them up. Finding packing cases to make lockers and to improvise things, I mean we had very little equipment, and all the things that we were supposed to have were not there. Again, rations were very short. The great thing was to go out into what was known as the 'Italian economy', foraging for eggs.

Joan Gray, née Goddard, sister, QAIMNS(R), Normandy, 1944

Nursing and living under canvas was new to most of the QAs.

[Inside the British General Hospital] they had got patients on stretchers, very close together, all these injured patients and so on in rows. They had folding beds; they had got the marquees up and we were able to get the beds undone and try and treat these patients and see what we could do for them. We had to stand astride these beds because you couldn't work standing on one side.

We had a few Germans and I decided, that very first day, that they were not enemy, they were not German, they were patients and they would be treated exactly the same. That meant that if you were doing the dressings, you started with the clean dressings and went to the dirty ones, they were treated in order of [medical] precedence.*

---

* In order to minimise cross-infection, clean uninfected wounds were dressed first. Infected wounds were left to the end of the dressing round.

We had only been there a day I think when Matron arranged for us to have slit trenches in our tents. We had two nurses in a tent and it left a narrow little bit down the middle and you had this slit trench built so that the camp bed was lowered to the bottom. She wanted us to have our tin helmets over our heads while we slept.

So we did all that we were supposed to do, all of us obeyed orders; and then of course, this business of the Grey and Scarlet [traditional uniforms] made it very difficult. We somehow got the washing done, but we still had to do quite a bit of ironing. We had a little oil stove and a pan of some sort to put on it and we had our iron, an old hand iron, and we managed all that.

Agnes Barnett, sister, Territorial Army Nursing Service, Middle East, 1941–5

Miss Barnett's unit eventually returned to Cairo and she worked in a psychiatric unit for the remaining three years of the war.

We were waiting outside the sisters' mess to be escorted somewhere else, and two [QA sisters] walked by in beautiful white overalls, starched caps, sort of sparkling, and one says to the other, 'What a dirty-looking lot of sisters!'

I got my own back. I was on one of the wards and we were making beds, this girl was inspecting me making beds, and she said, 'We are really busy, we've got 900 patients.' I said, 'How many beds do you have?' '1200-bedded hospital with 900 patients.' 'Oh,' I said, 'then you will be as busy as we were in Greece, 600-bed hospital and 1200 patients.' No more talk about how busy they were. I think it was 900 patients we had in fact, but I wasn't going to drop a few hundred for the sake of making a point.

Joan Gray at work in a tented hospital and wearing traditional QA uniform. The matron of her unit did not like nurses to wear battle dress.

Esta Lefton, née Guttman, Jewish refugee, Auxiliary Territorial Service (ATS) with the Allied armies, Egypt, 1941–2; Italy, 1943

Esta Lefton had been partially trained as a nurse in Jerusalem.

The hospital was built in tents and I should say it may have been about sixty patients in each tent. The tent was dug in and was a few steps [down] just to go in. The patients were usually coming from the front line. The camp was called Tel El Kabir, and the troops there were in El Alamein, in Tobruk and of course several times it was backwards and forwards with the Allied forces. It was a very busy hospital.

We had lots of German raids over us; during the night we had to jump out of our tents and sort of hide away outside. We actually packed up the hospital twice because the Germans and Italians advanced and they were quite near at one time. Twice, we had to pack up the hospital to be ready in case the hospital had to be evacuated. But lucky for our wonderful troops, the Allied forces, they beat them back and then we unpacked.

Theodora Turner, sister, QAIMNS(R), 1939–45

Theodora Turner requested a transfer from neurosurgery in Oxford.

I was sent to a general hospital which mobilised in the north of England and was then sent out to Iraq, because at that time they thought the Germans were going to come down through the Caucasus.

By the time we arrived in Basra [Iraq], the Germans had changed their minds. So the battalion were sent over the desert to join the men, in Egypt, and we spent the winter just nursing in whatever hospital we were sent to.

I went with a friend to a hospital which was what they called an Indian combined, British–Indian combined. So we had some British nurses – the girl I went with was a New Zealander actually – some Indian nurses and we had patients from any of the armies.

Male orderlies

The male orderlies recruited and trained by all three services made a great contribution to the war. They were based in the most forward positions and tasked with stabilising and evacuating the wounded.

20 June 1944, RAMC orderlies, accompanied by a QA, transfer a patient from the operating theatre, 79th General Hospital at Bayeux.

Arthur Brompton, RAMC orderly, 1939–45

I went in the Royal Army Medical Corps, well I was put in there you know, and I was in the medics for six years. I went to Scotland for the initial training then in 1941, beginning of '41, we went abroad with the first armoured divisions to Egypt, Alamein; I was out there for three and a half years.

Then I went into Italy and when I was in Italy I got blown up. I got my eardrums burst with the blast, it didn't do any damage anywhere else so I was lucky in that respect. But for six weeks I was deaf. I got off light, a lot of my colleagues were killed in the blasts.

If we had any wounded soldiers, any wounded be it German or Italian or British injured, then we'd get out to them first. We were there first and we'd just quickly put on a splint, 'M' for morphine on the forehead, send them a bit further back to where there's a bit of peace, to a larger medical unit and so it went on.

But we survived. We used to think to ourselves, as lads we used to say, we will never be able to go back to England and be civilised again. I was telling someone yesterday, I can remember the time when drinking water was scarce in the desert, but you got what you called 'camel dung water', boiled it up to make a tea because you had to have a tea and sweetened it with marmalade. It was a horrible drink.

Specialist medical units

The advantages to the wounded of access to specialist teams of doctors, nurses and orderlies in forward positions were recognised and accepted by the end of the war. Theodora Turner worked with a neurosurgical team in Africa and Europe.

Theodora Turner, sister, QAIMNS(R), 1939–45

We used to take over schools and things like that. We set up our hospital first outside Tripoli, lovely place called Subratha, which had been Phoenician, a village.

While I was there some of the people I had known in the head injuries hospital in Oxford were wanting extra sisters. It's the kind of work that you either like or else you're no good, because it's rather like looking after grown-up children. Head injuries with ... brain damage. Very severe and it was very hard work, really was. We also treated spinal injuries so there was head and spine, chiefly head. They asked for me to go back, because I liked the work and I'd done it before. The unit I joined had three ward sisters and one theatre sister and a masseuse, and then we had our own officers, a surgeon and a medical man, and our own orderlies.

Rose Telfer, née Hall, sister, QAIMNS(R), c.1940–5

When Rose Telfer's unit arrived in Brussels in 1945, they discovered that their hospital included many specialist units.

The hospital had been a private clinic for cancer patients, a great big six-storey building. We were terribly busy because we had all the special units; we had ear, nose and throat, chest ... plastic surgery, just every speciality we had, whereas a hospital outside of Brussels, they weren't half so busy as us. We really had a very hectic time.

Decorations

Many nurses were reluctant to speak of their decorations, despite their evident pride.

Theodora Turner, sister, QAIMNS(R), Italy, 1944

Yes, well it was in 1944 in Bari, that'll do. And it was a very unpleasant time and so many gongs, as they called them, were given out and I got one then. I was delighted.

Monica Baly, sister, PMRAFNS, Italy, 1944

Monica Baly struggled to provide a reasonable environment and decent care to Yugoslav partisans in a hospital in northern Italy.

And for that I got mentioned in dispatches. I can't think why, I can never think why, but I was.

Working with allies

In every theatre of war, nursing staff had to work alongside colleagues of different nationalities and with different cultural and political perspectives. As Agnes Barnett discovered, in some areas, such as the eastern Mediterranean and the Balkans, loyalties switched as the fortunes of war changed.

Agnes Barnett, sister, Territorial Army Nursing Service, called up February 1940

Agnes Barnett's unit was posted to Palestine in the Middle East and then moved on into Greece.

We went to Sarafand, which was the Aldershot of Palestine, if you like; we were there three months I think, sitting twiddling our thumbs because they hadn't decided where to send us, and then the Italians invaded Greece, so we went to Greece in November '40 and we were there until April 1941.

The British forces were not very great in number, so we weren't very busy. There were fifty sisters in a 600-bedded hospital and if we had 200 patients at any one time, it was all.

The colonel offered to accept Greek patients, we started taking in the Greek soldiers because their hospitals were overrun and we were twiddling our thumbs.

One convoy came down from Albania round Christmas time, 200 casualties came into Athens and not one man had four limbs, not one man had gunshot wounds, they were all frostbite because the Greeks were not ready for war, they were not expecting to go to war and their uniforms were not ready. You'd go into a shop and the shop assistants were sewing uniforms, putting buttons on and making buttonholes; but they were a marvellous race. They pushed the Italians out of Greece into Albania.

By the end of hostilities there were two million troops in the Indian army committed to the Allied cause. In 1946, medical and nursing staff returned home with the troops.

Our big casualties were the RAF, the pilots and the gunners and they either came back whole or they didn't come back. If a plane came down there wasn't much chance of a recovery.

[I remember] a patient that was shot down in Albania and his leg was fractured. There were three aeroplanes in the formation, and the other two saw what had happened. One of them landed on a strip of flat ground in a mountain village in Greece, told the Greeks what had happened, and they went through the Italian lines with a couple of donkeys [into Albania], brought this lad back to the village, got the local doctor … he had fractured his femur. [The doctor fixed up a Thomas' splint], two long steel sidepieces that extend six inches below the foot, and put straps across the two sides to support the leg. And they put one of these on this patient, strapped his femur down, and sent him down to Athens to us. A friend of mine, Johnny Campbell, went down to the station to pick him up in the ambulance and there was the lad waving his leg around in the air, Thomas' splint or no Thomas' splint. 'I've only got a fractured femur,' says he.

Then I had my appendix out, I was off a month and I just got back on duty* in time for the Germans to enter Greece.

The Germans started coming down through Yugoslavia and we really were hectic. I had a light ward because I had just come back from sick leave and the patients that I had in the morning were not the patients that I packed in their beds at night, and they weren't there in the morning when I came on duty, they would be another lot by then. They were coming in and getting them out as fast as they could. The ones I had were what they called walking wounded, their wounds would be dressed and they were shipped out.

Agnes Barnett finished her war working alongside Russian medical colleagues repatriating soldiers who had been prisoners of war, an experience she found highly disturbing. The Stalinist view was that Russian soldiers should die fighting; to be captured or 'rescued' was a disgrace.

The war was practically over, it was the April of '45, and I went to Brussels first, and was in Brussels about a month and then got posted to Norway. We were taking over from the Germans in Norway, and we were taking Russian prisoners of war back to Russia. We did two trips to Archangel [the Russian port city] and we weren't allowed to do anything with the patients; once we docked in Russia a Russian group came on, medical officers, nurses and orderlies, and they went round and said who could walk and who couldn't and their idea was if you could talk, you could walk. Stretcher cases were arranged ready to be carried off the ship. I had got an injection ready to give to a patient to see him safe on his journey and one of the lads said, 'Sister, come and see this man, he

---

* Illness was dealt with on the spot and many were then returned to the battle front.

is bleeding badly.' He was ... froth was coming out of his mouth; TB lungs. There was a Russian medical officer came over, took a look at him, stepped over his stretcher and walked away. Can you imagine our men doing it? They would have been out on their ears, but I think that was the attitude. Then also some of the amputees were going down the gangways, and you know how steep they can be going down on to deck, one of the men going down was an amputee, he had lost his crutch and fell. [At first] no one went to pick him up. And they stopped one of our orderlies who wanted to go down, he was on top of the gangway and they put their arms across and stopped him going down. But he went and picked the Russian soldier up.

Betty Boyce, QAIMNS(R), 1945

Betty Boyce arrived in Europe not long after VE Day. The atmosphere was chaotic and torn between celebration, exhaustion and horror at the news emerging from the concentration camps.

We went from Bangor in Northern Ireland up to North Rhine-Westphalia. We were in a nunnery this time and I worked on day duty. One day Matron said, 'I think you could go on night duty, Sister.' So I said, 'Well I haven't been very long in the army.' I knew very little about army nursing because I hadn't really done much. So she said, 'You can go on tonight with the night superintendent, she'll show you what to do.' We had a quiet night; the most important thing seemed to be to get the midnight report written at the right time and something ready for the colonel's desk in the morning.

Next night when I went on by myself Matron said, 'Forty Free French arriving. I don't think they speak any English, they're on their way up to Belsen.' And she told me where I would find beds for all this lot and said, the food has been issued and kitchen staff will cook the meal for you whatever time you tell them.

I said, right, so I checked where the beds were. Then a nurse was to have her appendix out and there was no sister on night duty in the theatre and the rule was that if it was a female being operated on there must be a female there. So the day sister wasn't very pleased when I went to tell her that she must be there, because there was going to be a dance that night to celebrate VE.

The next thing was the Free French arrived, very excitable, and I showed them all round to their rooms and then they'd heard there was a dance so they said they'd go. I said, 'Well the meal will be ready at eleven.' I went down to the cookhouse and said, 'What about the meal?' They said, 'No food.' I said, 'Nonsense, you knew the rations …' 'There's been forty patients in since eight thirty, all the food's used.' So we had to go to the man in charge of stores, he wasn't pleased at being disturbed, got him up, arranged more food. And then I went to see that the table was laid, switched on the light, no light. It was summer time and our last meal was at eight o'clock in the evening, broad daylight, nobody had ever tried the lights in this room. So I had to go round and try to borrow hurricane lamps, and people who only have one hurricane lamp are very unwilling to lose it. Of course they had to.

So I eventually got them [the French] rounded up, got them back, got their meal, and then had to show them all to bed, they'd all forgotten where they were.

And I went to the ward and went to my office and thought, well, one o'clock, better start the twelve o'clock report, hadn't been long at it before there was the awful sound of tins clanging and I thought that means a fire, that's really all I need. I opened the door and an orderly was panting by with two buckets and I thought, I'll follow him because he must be going to the seat of the fire … it was the sterilising tent had gone on fire.

I met a sister and I said, 'What are you doing?' She said, 'I'm evacuating my patients.' I said, 'You are not.' Hers were head injuries, delirious and everything else, so I thought, they're a lot safer where they are. I said, 'There's a good wall between you and it and I think the fire's out anyway.'

Then I thought I'd better go and see the matron, so I went up, and she said, 'Sister, it's been a very noisy night.'

In many ways those who served with the military had a very different war from their colleagues who nursed in Britain, but the core experiences were the same. Military and civilian nurses alike struggled to care for their patients against a backdrop of confusion and with the burden of trauma always threatening to overwhelm them. A great deal of suffering was of course relieved, but despite the pride in all this hard work, nurses were only too aware that many were still wounded, in mind and body.

Recovery was hard. A nurse and wounded soldier board the *Arundel Castle* to return home.

SEVEN

WOUNDED BODY, WOUNDED MIND

We had a lovely sister in charge of that burns ward ... and she worked
and worked incessantly and one evening she flaked out flat on the floor,
she just passed out and the others said, 'You've got to go ... *go.*'

Eileen Willis, student nurse, diary entry, 1945

Nurses, doctors and of course the wounded all suffered. Modern warfare created modern injuries. Men who survived the tank battles of the North African desert or were ejected from crashing aircraft, as well as civilians trapped in incendiary raids, sustained terrible burns. Like soldiers in the First World War, injured troops who lay out on the beaches of Dunkirk and Normandy suffered from gas gangrene. And many combatants and non-combatants were left with mental trauma.

The medical world responded by developing new strategies and treatments. The powerful antibacterial drugs, of which penicillin was the best known, saved countless lives. Many nurses were excited by the challenges and the potential to alleviate suffering that war-time nursing offered them. Sheena Kilminster worked at one of the RAF's specialist burns units and found her work inspiring.

The emotional toll of war

Nursing work has always involved emotional tensions and traumas. Nurses now found themselves working desperately hard under pressure to care for adults and children, military and civilian, Allied and enemy. They struggled to continue working as their familiar world crumbled around them.

Eileen Willis, mobile VAD, 1939

As an enthusiastic eighteen-year-old VAD, Eileen Willis was helped by a more experienced colleague when her emotions threatened to get the better of her.

The first death that I saw was this very handsome young artillery boy, a volunteer as the early soldiers were; it was only later on there were conscriptions. He was on a gun site and he had got a bad cold and hadn't gone off sick, and it had turned into pneumonia. We didn't have penicillin during that first stage of the war, and he just went down and down and he died.

Sister said, 'Come along, Nurse Willis, we'll have to lay him out.' And we washed him and laid him out and you know, I'd loved that boy, the tears were just running down my face. She told me what to do and then we put his hat and his badge and everything on him and they wheeled him out. You had screens round so that people didn't see them going but everyone knew he had died. She said, 'Go and wash your face. If you are going to be a nurse you will have to control your emotions.' She said, 'You have got to be strong enough, it's no good breaking down.'

David Proctor, RAMC orderly, 1943–7

Although he was an inexperienced orderly, David Proctor summoned up his emotional resources when it was asked of him.

In Jerusalem, that was the only time I was a coffin-bearer. One of the QAs had died, she had TB, and she's buried there in the army cemetery. That was a bit terrifying.

Margaret Thomson, student nurse, Royal Hospital for Sick Children, Edinburgh, 1944

Greater experience did not always help resolve the tensions that nurses had to come to terms with.

The most dramatic moment that I had, which seems curious looking back on it, was when I was the staff nurse on a medical ward. I was coming to the end of my training, I hadn't actually sat my final exams, and I was taking the matron round the ward and telling her about each patient. Just prior to Matron coming a child of eleven or twelve had died and that was the first death that I had seen in anybody other than a baby. And I just broke down and the matron had to take me away. I remember her being very kind indeed, and reassuring, but I always remember that incident having quite an effect on me.

Janet Crawley, student nurse, Royal Infirmary of Edinburgh, 1937–40

Private pressures added to the demands of nursing.

It was really a sad time because all the fellows you had been at school with, they were all away. Eventually you saw deaths in the paper, some of them had been killed or drowned at sea.

Burns and plastic surgery

This was the first war in which such large numbers of men who suffered hideously mutilating injuries survived. The work done by Harold Gillies and his colleagues in the First World War was now moved on by Gillies himself, his nephew and student Archibald McIndoe and others, and plastic surgery emerged as a new medical speciality.

Arthur Brompton, RAMC orderly, 1939–45

On the front line, where orderlies gathered their injured colleagues, they had to deal with almost unbearable situations.

We had to get into tanks and pull the soldiers out but often you couldn't because they were just burnt to cinders. It was awful and of course it was hot, there were flies so you had sand-fly fever, that kind of thing.

Kathleen Raven, assistant matron, Hill End, St Bartholomew's sector hospital, 1943

After remaining at Barts throughout the Blitz as one of six ward sisters, Kathleen Raven was appointed assistant matron and directed to run the plastic surgery unit in the Barts sector.

I was appointed assistant matron and I went down to Hill End, Barts sector hospital. First of all I ran the plastic unit; I had seventy-two beds there. I'd children and soldiers and civilians, it was very interesting, McIndoe's second in command came down to run that unit, marvellous people.

We had all the burns and people blown to bits nearly and burns on their eyelids, it was dreadful. We put on pedicle grafts, new noses and new ears; it was awful.

It was quite an experience for two years and then as I was assistant matron, I left Hill End.

Eileen Willis, student nurse, diary entry, 1945

Originally a mobile VAD, Eileen Willis was now a student nurse assigned to the plastic surgery unit at Rookswood House. The surgeon working in this unit was Sir Harold Gillies, pioneer of plastic surgery in World War I.

[Reading from her diary] … now I am [at] Rooksdown [House] in 1B ward. We have twenty-six Normandy men all very badly burned, most have face and arms affected; some legs and buttocks as well. They are able to do nothing for themselves but have to be fed, cigarettes lighted, letters opened and read, even if you [bring] a bottle [urinal] for them you [have] to do that for them; they [can] do nothing.

[Interview] You see when somebody catches fire, the first thing they do is try and beat it out with their hands, which is obviously … and some of them, they were just bones sticking out, all the flesh had gone, it was dreadful. The one with the buttocks, he had been on a tanker and it had been hit and the thing of acid had burst and he had been lying on his back in acid. Unspeakable. It was a nightmare on this ward.

[Again reading from diary] It is a terribly hard ward to be on, we are understaffed, overworked, under-equipped, and the ward is filthy but we don't have time even to clean that. But the experience is excellent, of course it is wonderful to be able to do so much for these poor fellows, they are immersed daily in a saline bath.

[Interview] They would be wheeled out to the bathroom, and there was a bath drawn of lukewarm saline and they were lowered into that. They all got infected, and the smell of the pus, the wards reeked of it. You went off duty and you still smelt it in your nose and your throat, it seemed almost solid particles that stayed with you. And the old dressings and the pus all floats off and of course they loved being in that water, it was the only time they were out of pain, in the soothing liquid.

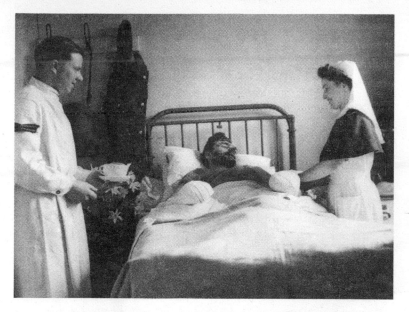

A member of the PMRAFNS and an RAF orderly in a burns unit in England, April 1943.

And then they were lifted up and that was the really agonising part because all the raw areas were exposed, but we all worked and we put on *tulle gras* which was squares of light mesh material in a sterile tin, a mixture of Vaseline, balsam of Peru, and a mild anaesthetic agent. These square strips were put over all the raw area and you had to cut so that you didn't waste. Then you put them on, and you sprayed them with sulphonamide. Then [the patients] just lay like that, we did put bandages on, but of course the awful part was the flies used to come in and re-infect them. When the healing was sufficient ... after a bit, it over-granulates and the granulation tissue will go up above the skin level, of course you don't want that, you don't want it to be sticking up. So when it was up to a certain level they would do swabs, they'd take swabs and provided there was no infection they would go for skin grafts, but of course time and time again when they would be ready for grafting they'd be infected and they couldn't be done. Of course that was a terrible disappointment to them and to us.

Their hands had these strips and Vaseline and they just lay there like that. They had junket all the time, a lot of them, their faces were badly burned, they could hardly open their mouths, could only get junket and fluids down, it was awful. It was worse when they weren't covered; you see the *tulle gras* had a slight anaesthetic quality, it did help. They had morphine and things like that but of course they were lying down, a lot of them, so you didn't want them to get pneumonia, which [they] can if they are too dopey, not able to breathe.

You had to read their letters to them. You had to do everything, clean their teeth, everything, it was awful, and their eyes, they were supposed to have their eyes irrigated with saline and a drop of penicillin, I think it was, that was put in. Ideally they should have been done every two hours. Well if they got it done three times a day we thought we'd done well.

It was simply awful, you never went off duty if you could help it but you just got so tired you had to, you were ordered off.

I always remember, we had a lovely sister in charge of that burns ward and she used to spend nearly all her time in the bath house, it was very hot, it had to be warm if these men were lying naked, and she worked and worked incessantly and one evening she flaked out flat on the floor, she just passed out and the others said, 'You've got to go ... *go*.' And when she went off duty she was crying. Apparently she'd heard that day that her fiancé, who was in the RAF, had been taken prisoner by the Japs and she'd worked on all through the day with that awful worry on her mind. But she was on duty next day.

You couldn't not do it; when you went home all the time you just thought, 'Why have I left? I haven't done this, I haven't done that.'

That is one of the hardest times I think I have ever had in nursing. Awful, reading their letters to them, that was ghastly. I didn't mind feeding them, giving them bottles, but reading their letters to them was dreadful.

A youngster about twenty, his mother and father came to visit him, and he was terribly burned, and I tried to tell her that he was very bad but they would do marvellous things but it would take time. But she said, 'Let me see him.' Well of course when she went in and saw him, her face just went chalk white and she burst into tears. I'm afraid I just burst into tears too, I came away, but that was the only time I've broken down on a ward.

Monica Baly, sister, PMRAFNS, Taranto, Italy, 1943

As an RAF nurse Monica Baly was assigned to take charge in a burns unit.

I started on a surgical ward and then I was promoted to run a burns unit.

Now I had done some burns training at Cosford; and I knew McIndoe although I had never worked at [Queen Victoria Hospital] East Grinstead,* but I mean I knew enough about burns treatment in fact to be given this blessed ward. And it was the time of saline baths of course, and we had baths, but we had no water. We had to carry the water up the stairs, I well remember that. I remember organising this place, and organising saline baths with water that we carried up the stairs. I was doing this when the principal medical officer came to inspect us. It was hard going, it was really hard going because the temperature was very high, and sweating up and down stairs with buckets of water!

And this was fascinating actually, because what we were getting as patients were partisans from Yugoslavia, and by Jove they were tough. I think now of the Yugoslavian war [of the 1990s], and you know, you're never going to beat guerrilla warfare because they really were so tough. The difficulty in dealing with them of course was communicating. I spoke some German, they spoke very little Italian and very little German, so it was difficult.

Some of them were very badly burnt. I can see that ward now ... very badly burnt. Airmen too, mostly not flying accidents but accidents in the camp, blowing up Primus stoves and that sort of thing.

---

* Archibald McIndoe's specialist plastic surgery unit.

Sheena Kilminster, née Craig, sister, PMRAFNS, burns and plastics, Halton, c.1943

After joining the air force, Sheena Kilminster found that she spent her entire career at RAF Halton.

It was said that if that happened either you were very good or very bad; I never knew which category I fell into!

Halton was 600 beds, it was the biggest RAF hospital in the country, and of these beds sixty, 10 per cent, were allocated exclusively to plastic surgery, and this was quite apart from the very large burns unit that we had and all the other specialities in the hospital.

Most of the patients were air crew, as you can imagine, and the wing commander in charge was an absolutely wonderful man for whom I have, and had, the greatest admiration. Wing Commander D. N. Matthews, he was known as Dennis. He was not only a first-class plastic surgeon but a wonderful communicator. He would sit down at a patient's bedside and tell the man in terms that the man could easily understand exactly what he planned to do, and if that was successful what he would go on to do – because many of them had a whole series of operations. And these men would have gone to hell and back for him, they absolutely thought the world of him, and rightly so; and so did I.

The faces, the hands, the arms, the legs that he repaired were really wonderful, and I particularly admired his facial work. For that he used, nearly always, the finest of fine platinum wire to do stitching. Now that needs skill to put in but oh boy it takes trouble to get out. If they are what are known as interrupted stitches – that is one stitch and you cut off, and you do the next stitch and you cut off – that is reasonable to remove, with care, but if it was what is known as continuous suturing – that is like sewing a seam – that was hell to remove. Very often he took out his own stitches, and when you had watched him do it, and he thought you were sufficiently competent, he would say, 'Now, Sister Craig, you take out these stitches today.' And there he was breathing down the back of my neck, and I can assure you it took not only a steady nerve but a remarkably steady hand to take out those stitches, and when he saw that you were competent then he let you get on with it.

I think probably the most fascinating case that I dealt with was rebuilding a nose, the man's nose most of it had been shot away, and he ended up with a very much better nose than I have. It was called a 'pedicle graft'. They raise a graft from the abdomen, a pedicle graft preserving its own blood supply, and attach it to an arm then to a site close to the lost tissue. There it was shaped to resemble the missing part and stitched into position. This was just simply what's known as empirical surgery, there were no books to tell you how to do it, you just had to invent the method for yourself; and that is what Matthews did.

Now how do you feed a man like that? You know, the pedicle is covering half his mouth. Well, we devised means of feeding him because plainly he was a young man with a good appetite, and he needed to keep his strength up. But it was some of the most fascinating work I've ever seen. I was all of a year there.

They came and went and sometimes came back for more. And all too often, the man would be rehabilitated completely, he would go back to his squadron and the next thing you heard was that he'd been killed. It happened time and time again, and it was so, so sad.

Well, really it was so fascinating that one didn't feel it stressful because you could see results and this was a great thing. One certainly felt awful when one heard of the death of somebody that one had known and nursed, but that apart, there was so much forward looking and success that it was stimulating rather than stressful.

Penicillin

Research into antibacterial medications began before war broke out. Among the first sulphur drugs to appear was M&B 693, named for the manufacturers, May and Baker. The earliest sulphonamides had become available before the war in 1936. But the breakthrough that everyone remembers was the arrival of penicillin.

All these drugs, when first used, were experimental and initially were given to patients whose prospects were hopeless – the new medications were their last chance. Once successfully tested on these patients, early supplies were restricted to use by the armed services. By the end of the war penicillin and streptomycin were both available for civilian use.

All nurses had memories of the introduction of these 'miraculous' drugs for the care of infected wounds. Christine Chapman recalled that in its earliest form, crystalline penicillin administered by injection was painful enough to make brave men cry.

Doris Carter, staff nurse, Royal Hampshire County Hospital, 1939–41

As a student nurse, Doris Carter recalled the introduction of the new 'miracle' drugs.

Yes, Prontosil was the very first wonder drug, as they were known, that I remember giving and I think it must have been about 1935. I remember which ward I was in at the time, it was horrible stuff and it was red, it made the patient's buttocks all red, messed up the syringes. But it seemed to be a very great innovation at the time. I later remember M&B 693, I think it was, and then bit by bit the other wonder drugs came.

It was given for pneumonias, some things like that as far as I can recall. We used to have some very, very ill pneumonias in those days. Well if they got pneumonia there wasn't really much hope for them because there were absolutely no drugs at all, no antibiotic of any sort, so it was pure good nursing that got them through. Some of them were desperately, desperately ill.

Winifred Hector, ward sister, St Bartholomew's Hospital, London, c.1940

The restricted use of these new medications was hard to accept when their power was so visible.

Penicillin was becoming available but we weren't allowed to use it. It was being used for research. So patients who might have lived weren't getting it. It was going to people who were perhaps likely going to die but as though [they] were some interesting organism that they could test it against.

Isobel Balmain, ward sister, Royal Infirmary of Edinburgh, 1936–45

Some diseases and their complications disappeared almost entirely after penicillin use became widespread. Infections of the bone and mastoid that made lives a misery are now rarely seen.

... Mine was the ward that got the first penicillin in Edinburgh. It was made over in the Wilkie department in the university and in the early days we could only give it to army and war people. I remember the first little patient that got penicillin, and it saved his life. It was a wee boy called Billy McKinnon who came in to us moribund. He had osteomyelitis of the tibia, he had pericarditis as well, general septicaemia, and we gave him penicillin continuously into his muscle. I had to get up on to a chair and milk this tube down occasionally because it would stop running, and I was up there on the third day when Billy suddenly opened his eyes and said, 'Is that a thermometer?' and I nearly fell off my chair in excitement.

I said, 'No, Billy, it isn't though it looks like it. What do you know about thermometers?'

'Aw there is to ken.'

So of course I rushed into the doctors' room and told them all and Billy by this time was unconscious again but he came out of it every now and again. He was like an old man ... [though] he was about sixteen to seventeen and I'd had a feeling what was wrong, so one day I sat down beside him and I says, Billy, when you're better will you come to the flicks with me? And he looked at me, I can still remember his expression. 'I'm not going to dee, Sister?' I said, 'Dee? Of course you're not, Billy', tongue in ma cheek, he was still a very ill little boy, but from that day he got well and everybody that came into that ward would still say, 'Got a date with the ward sister?'

So in the end we got a taxi and went off to the flicks, that picture house in Lothian Road.

Lotte Heymann, Jewish refugee, student nurse, Addenbrooke's Hospital, Cambridge, 1945–8

These powerful new medications were administered almost reverently.

I recall the introduction of penicillin when I was at Addenbrooke's. We had nothing like that when I was at the children's hospital, hence all the mastoids and also ... osteomyelitis, children with the leg burns and things, and all they could get was M&B and it wasn't very good. So the introduction of penicillin came while I was there, I think in '46, in my second year there, and that was, of course, a great advance.

This particular patient had been written up for penicillin and the hospital had it by that time. The senior night sister had to be found, she had the key to the particular cupboard where it was kept, and then ... double-checked and triple-checked and then finally this injection was given and everything went back under lock and key till the next dose, but it worked.

Gertrude Cooper, née Ramsden, sister, QARNNS, 1942

While in New Delhi with the QARNNS, Gertrude Cooper was called on to nurse Brigadier Marriott, who had developed septicaemia following a simple hernia operation. He was one of the first in India to be treated with penicillin.

After sick leave, I came back to be told by a local doctor in the blood transfusion unit that Brigadier Marriott had deteriorated and was now on the dangerously ill list, because he had got general septicaemia. I was taken to see him, and it was arranged I should cycle to and fro and care for him. On Thursday the RAF dispatch rider came to the nursing home and handed me ... he said, 'Package from Cairo.' It was the penicillin, which we immediately started to administer. He made a dramatic recovery and I was released from those duties within two weeks. But it is a memorable association, because from that date, penicillin was introduced into the India Command, and the sick patients wrote home to their parents, telling them they had the wonder drug and they were getting better.

The penicillin was solid, it floats sufficiently to draw it up into a syringe already loaded with saline, and when this mixture was mixed, it was given into the buttock of the sick patient. Even three and four years later, it was still administered in that crude preparation. It was not given by mouth; it was given by intramuscular injection.

Christine Chapman, student nurse, Birmingham, 1946–50

Administration was so painful that it reduced otherwise stoical patients to tears.

... Penicillin was terrible crude stuff that had to be given every three hours day and night. They used to cry when they saw you coming with the syringes because it was so painful. People who had it for a long period, we used to put kaolin poultices on the injection sites to try and ease the pain, it was horrendous really, but it was a life-saver.

Winifred Hector, ward sister, St Bartholomew's Hospital, London, 1941–2

These new drugs that wiped out the infectious diseases that had crippled so many changed the nature of nursing work.

There were really few medical cures and when they then began to be able to cure patients, then the nurse's role began to be questioned, you see, because up to then we'd been master of our own field, giving comfort, you know. 'Nothing more I can do, Nurse.' 'All right, sir, I will look after him until he dies.'

But now we are suddenly told the treatment for this condition is penicillin. Nursing has gone out of the window. You could stand him up in the corner of the room as long as he was having penicillin; it really did alter our feelings.

Esta Lefton, née Guttman, Jewish refugee nurse, ATS, posted with Allied troops, Italy, c.1943

Reflecting on her preference for caring for wounded surgical patients, Esta remarked on the absence of the 'magic' antibacterial therapy soon to emerge.

We didn't get any penicillin until I was in Rome and then we had to go to the black market to get it because the Americans used to sell it to the black market; oh yes, there was lots going on.

Alwyn Friar, RAF orderly, 1938–46

The appearance of the new medications at the battle front allowed injured troops to be rapidly returned to the front ready for action.

Yes we had a lot of antibiotics in the air force. In Italy, we had 75 per cent of the world's supply because they were fighting the Battle of [Monte] Cassino at the time and every man that came out sick he had to get back quick.

Blood transfusion

By the time war broke out, safe techniques of blood transfusion and methods of handling and storing blood and plasma were known. Whole blood was collected and could be stored in glass bottles. Giving sets were made of red rubber tubing with glass connectors; these had to be sterilised between use by boiling or using an autoclave. However, the availability of blood for transfusion depended on local organisation. On the home front, in many places, this meant a panel of donors who could be called on in an emergency. During the war civilian blood banks became available more widely. In the services, troops could donate for their colleagues and local policies had to be worked out to provide whole blood for patients. However, dehydrated plasma was increasingly available to forward military units.

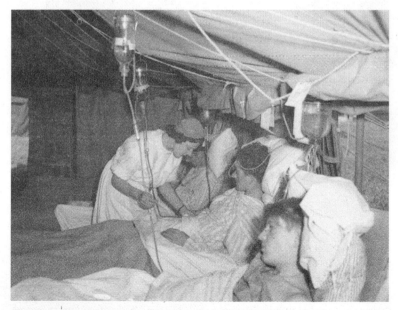

15 August 1944, a nurse tends to wounded soldiers in a field hospital in Normandy.

David Proctor, RAMC orderly, 1944–7

The selection of personnel for special tasks such as blood transfusion was a bit of a mystery, but David Proctor did at least volunteer for the work.

In 1944, when I was eighteen, I was called up and we went to Ireland; you do six weeks' training while they sort you out. I don't know whether it was luck or whatever but I was then drafted into the RAMC from Ireland and I went to the RAMC depot, where you have a basic training of square-bashing [military drill], little bit of first aid, mostly square-bashing as far as I remember. From the base depot you're then asked what you'd like to do and I think there was an operating room attendant, blood transfusion orderly, or 'the wards', and I chose blood transfusion orderly, I don't know why but that appealed to me.

We were then drafted to Bristol where we were in civvy billets, but we did our training for blood transfusion at Clifton College and Southmead Hospital and we were upstairs in the college and downstairs were the Americans and ne'er the twain shall meet. When we came down, at the bottom of the big lovely wooden staircase there was the Americans' dining room where they had serve-yourself, with lovely chicken and things, and never once did they invite us to join them.

February, I joined up, it would be 1944, before D-Day. We were trained how to assemble giving sets and taking sets, how to cross-match blood and how to take blood; we took blood from each other, we were told you will never have to do it but you might as well see how it's done. Then from Bristol I was drafted to Moretonhampstead in Devon, Manor House Hospital. We were waiting for posting, and while we were there 6 June, D-Day, passed and we thought, 'This is when we're going to go', but we didn't, I don't know how we missed that, but I was then off to Egypt.

We got to Cairo in December 1944 and [were] again in the RAMC base depot waiting for a proper posting. [We spent] six weeks there, which was very interesting because we visited Tutankhamen's tomb and the pyramids and all the sleazy streets in Cairo and I was young and innocent and looking round thinking, 'Well, what's this?' But from there I was then posted to Number 4 General Hospital, which was a tented hospital in a place called Kassassin, which was in the desert somewhere, and I was the only one posted there. So I arrived all lonely with my kitbag and was given a tent, we were all in tents, and introduced to the chap who ran the blood transfusion unit, he was the same as me, he was a lance corporal. The next day I went up and joined him and he sort of ran through all the routine. We had, on the outskirts of the hospital, a German prisoner of war camp and an Italian prisoner of war camp. So they were our chief blood donors. We went over, we had to take sample blood for Kahn tests, for syphilis.

First time when I was asked, you know, 'A patient on such and such a ward needs blood', I phoned the houseman, or he was a young lieutenant doctor then, and he said, 'Well what about it?' I said, 'Well what time shall I meet you?' 'Meet me? You can do it better than me, you do it.' So that was our introduction, we not only took the blood, we cross-matched the blood and gave the blood and also did saline drips and things like that. I got on well with that, I enjoyed that.

Mental health

Mental health or psychiatric nursing tended to be looked down on but it was an important area since the mental health of civilians, service personnel and nurses was under great pressure throughout the war. In some places, such as Mill Hill hospital, pioneering therapeutic work by psychiatrists, psychologists and specialist nurses was practised. Elsewhere sympathetic nurses found themselves sent to care for traumatised troops without any special preparation for the role. Interviewed many years after the war, some of these nurses were still repeating 'we just coped', 'it was really ghastly', 'one could hardly cope in a way really', 'it was terrible'.

Monica Baly, ward sister, PMRAFNS, c.1942

Early in her career in the air force, Monica Baly was surprised to find herself assigned to run a psychiatric ward.

The thing about the air force was that you went by your seniority in the air force, not your seniority in nursing. And so I found myself due to take a ward of my own, in spite of the fact of having people coming in later who were really senior to me in nursing. So when I was due to have a ward of my own, I was given a psychiatric ward, and all my friends commiserated with me, this was terrible, and the squadron leader didn't like women and didn't like general trained nurses and so forth, and this would be awful.

However, we battled it out. He didn't want me because he was a Scot; he had no time for people who came from the south of England. I was a woman, according to him I was middle-class bourgeois, and I wasn't mental-trained. So I more or less said to him, well train me! And he gave me Henderson and Gillespie,* which I've got to this day, and decided that he'd got to put up with me so he would train me.

---

* A standard medical textbook widely circulated in the UK after World War I.

I found it absolutely fascinating, and I am so grateful, because it filled a big gap in my training. I'm very grateful to Squadron Leader Ashford. Before I went out to the Middle East he asked me to be his wife, but I thought, no. No, he was a misogynist, I don't think he really liked women. But I enjoyed my time there and I learnt so much, and as I say it was a big gap in my training and has stood me in very good stead when I came to the Royal College of Nursing and came to go round mental hospitals. I can talk their language.

Because I must say, Squadron Leader Ashford trained me well. And of course what happened was, when I was due to move, he wouldn't allow me to move! And there was a great battle between him and the matron whether I should be moved or not!

Betty Boyce, sister, QAIMNS(R), Europe, 1945

Betty Boyce was in Europe after D-Day and at one time was caring for British prisoners as well as enemy prisoners of war. She had a rather frightening encounter with one soldier.

One night I'd taken one of my ordinary patients' temperatures, because I was the only one there, and I was just leaving the ward when he got up and advanced towards me, and fortunately it was his throat he was busy holding. And I thought, well no, I won't excite myself because after all he won't die on me, but then he looked as if he was attacking me so I thought, no, best not, so I took the Italian guard and said, 'Guard this one.'

By breakfast time, they had about four British soldiers watching him and I thought, yes, [but] they're prepared to leave him all night with one QA, one QA and one hurricane lamp. Then he went off under escort to the nearest psychiatric place.

He was a British soldier … I couldn't blame them, they had breakdowns after being shot at and things like that. I think they thought this was a mild one, he probably was mild, but [sometimes] they acted up to be sure that they were transferred back to Britain and not just stuck in a sick bay somewhere.

Joan Gray, née Goddard, sister, QAIMNS(R), France, 1944

When Joan Gray crossed to Normandy soon after D-Day, she and her colleagues became aware of 'unusual' wounds.

At the time that I was there the injuries got very strange and it was thought, or it was suggested, that they were self-inflicted. And then we got more of those and in the end we were having these army investigations, 'Was it a self-inflicted wound?' We were asked did we think it was a wound that was self-inflicted or not and I always said I didn't think it was. I always said that, I didn't know whether it was or not. It was horrid. And then I was posted, out of the blue, to a psychiatric hospital, just the other side of Bayeux, and I was horrified. 'But they can't send me to a psychiatric hospital!'

But of course they could and off I went the next day. And I hadn't been there a day before … I loved it. And I loved it so much through my period of time with the psychiatric hospitals that I arranged to go and do two years' nursing at the Maudsley Hospital in London. I was going to go and do psychiatric nursing. And the only thing that stopped it was that I met a man [who was] on the way home from Ceylon and I wasn't free to go really!

There was something about it, I think … I had had all these patients with awful wounds and blood and very bad injuries and I think it was quite a relief not to have the bodily injuries. I certainly didn't like the self-inflicted wounds, or what were supposed to be self-inflicted. I think it was mainly that I got away from the really nasty injuries and got on to this other, and I just loved the work.

We were instructed to try and get them to speak about their injuries and there used to be such a lot of weeping, [they were] really quite distraught and I was able to sort of cope with it, I think I'm really quite able to listen to what people have to say.

Nearly all of them had done such serious things. There was one fellow had done about four landings in enemy territory, parachute landings, and you can't stand much of that. There was another fellow, such a lovely young man, and he had been sitting in the front of a tank with his best friend beside him and they were struck by enemy fire and the best friend's head was shot off on to his lap. Now you can just imagine the sort of distraught feelings of that. It's the sort of thing; you can't do it without a lot of feeling. And I think that is what I liked about it.

Some of them did go back to active duty but a lot were sent home. Others were kept in for a while; they did have to keep them in till they had settled a bit better and perhaps got over the worst of it and could face the next part of the journey and go back home.

Patients and VADs on the terrace at Longdon Hall, a convalescent home equipped by the Joint War Organisation of the Red Cross and St John.

Esta Lefton, née Guttman, Jewish refugee, ATS, attached to Allied forces, Egypt, c.1941

Esta Guttman was a member of a Polish Jewish family which moved to Palestine in 1936. She volunteered for the Auxiliary Territorial Service (ATS) in Palestine in 1940–1 before completing her nursing training. She then undertook ATS training for some six months in Sarafand, Palestine. After that she was posted to Egypt, where she worked in a military hospital caring for the wounded from the North African campaigns.

I worked on the wards, so we not only had to deal with the injured soldiers, we had to deal also with their mental state. I think we were very good in trying to convey to them our concern and our care for them. If they couldn't write we wrote letters for them and we read to them at any time we were free, and I used to do it quite often, used to go back after duty and sit on the bed of the soldiers and talk to them. In the war you're traumatised and particularly if you are on the front line it takes quite a while, if you're a young soldier, experienced or inexperienced; mentally it takes quite a lot. We had to be very strong – I say 'we' because we were really all together – and to talk, and to talk about other things, talk about life, talk about children, talk about trees although we were in the desert. And really it was a lot to make them laugh, to make them get away from hearing bombs, hearing shells, and hearing this noise in the air.

But at the same time you had to be very realistic, smiling, and really giving them courage, giving them hope; because when you come from a front line and when you see your comrades, your friends, being killed and you are alive, it's not easy. They had to get all this out of their system, so by you talking to them and by you sort of taking them into your confidence and giving them confidence, they recovered much quicker.

Later Esta was moved to a hospital in Suez, and here she was assigned to morale-boosting activities.

You are told by the army to go and you go. So we went to Suez, it was a very large compound and a hospital, and there I stayed until 1943. We were guarded; we had a guard at the entrance of the compound. Suez was an eye-opener for all sorts of things. We had different troops from all over the world, East Africans, West Africans, they came in all different shapes and sizes.

I was in charge of welfare. I used to bring books and they used to read and then we used to have a meeting and whoever got the gist right or the questions right used to get a book as a present.

This type of nursing is not like in civilian hospitals. You had to sort of nurse the whole person, in other words, reading to them, holding their hands, I know you have to hold their hands in normal hospital, but ... You need all the time to make them really aware how much they're wanted and how much you really care. We used to give the troops, as I said, dances, organise having a meal together, it all was part of ... just trying to carry on life as it is, because you can't think all the time about the war, you have to think and do other things as well.

From the same base (Suez), Esta found herself assigned to escort mental-health patients to the military mental hospital in Jerusalem.

When I was at Suez we had lots, unfortunately, of mental cases of staff; and they had to be transferred from Suez, or wherever it happened to be, to Jerusalem, because Jerusalem had a mental hospital for troops with the army. The [patients] used to say, 'We want Esta to come, Nurse Guttman.' So I would travel with them and [the authorities] used to arrange an escort because you never knew what was going to happen and if you had two or three and one wanted to go to the toilet you couldn't leave the other ones on their own.

So I used to go to Jerusalem. And [we] used to go by train right through the Sinai Desert to Jerusalem, and [the authorities] always used to say, you know, you can stay for a few days and visit your family but it was too hurtful because it really unsettles you, what you see.

Agnes Barnett, sister, Territorial Army Nursing Service, nursing psychiatric patients, Middle East, 1943

Agnes Barnett had completed general, midwifery and district nurse training and volunteered. Following service in France and Greece, her unit was posted to the eastern Mediterranean.

I was posted to a psychiatric unit and I stayed there until I came home [after three years]. It was on the Bitter Lake, in Ismailia, you know. I've forgotten the name of the camp, but Ismailia was our nearest town and we were near a big prisoner of war camp, well it was a big base. There was a repair depot; ordnance corps had a great camp there, because everything went there.

They were battle casualties, but they were all psychiatric, some of them should never have been in the army, [for] some it was the stress of war. I think we did very well really. Out of 2,000 in the nearly three years we were there, we only had one commit suicide, although there were a lot [who were] suicidal and showing signs.

Afra Leckie, night sister, Maidenhead Hospital, c.1944

Not long after Afra Leckie began the health visitors' course at the Royal Sanitary Institute in Buckingham Palace Road, she had personal experience of the trauma of bombing. Her digs lay in the path of the flying bombs.

One night a flying bomb fell on the house opposite. It was one of the first doodlebugs to come over I think into south Croydon; and the roof of where I was staying came in. We were sleeping in the cellar anyway by that time. The house was so badly damaged that we were never able to go back. We all went to a hall, and spent the night there.

I remember saying to my friend Muriel at the time, 'Oh I'll go and get your cigarettes.' When I went to go and get them I couldn't run. You know that was an extraordinary feeling [because] I wasn't [normally] frightened or anything, I was never nervous.

I remember having to go, on the Monday afterwards, to give a talk – I think it was about immunisation, and when I got up to speak, I couldn't speak, the words wouldn't come out. I gradually took a deep breath and then managed to do it. I was giving a talk to the students, a practice talk, because you were given lectures on how to give talks, in those days.

Annie Altschul, student mental health nurse, Mill Hill Emergency Hospital, 1944

When Annie Altschul arrived at Mill Hill Emergency Hospital, she knew she had found the branch of nursing that fascinated her. Her account of war-time psychiatric nursing is exceptionally detailed.

Anyway, I got to the end of training and by that time one had to go into a branch of nursing where there was a shortage. I knew I didn't want to stay in general nursing, and the ward sister that I was working with at the time said her sister was working at Mill Hill, perhaps I would like that. So I went there for interview. It was an emergency military psychiatric hospital, in Mill Hill school, it's a boarding school which evacuated to Cumberland I think and became an emergency military hospital.

I got there in '44. I had no idea that I would enjoy it as much as I did. I certainly knew that I would stay the moment that I arrived. [I liked] everything, the patients, the fact that one was expected to think and there was opportunity to think, the patients were fascinating and you were encouraged to talk to them.

In retrospect I think Mill Hill was a much better mental hospital than any of them are now or have ever been since. I keep on hearing people telling us what marvellous progress psychiatry has made. I can't find it, nothing is as good as Mill Hill was. I know that may be rose-coloured spectacles about the past but I don't think it is.

There were all kinds of reasons why it was possible: there was a back-up of other military establishments to which you could send people who couldn't be alone on the wards. It was a school, everything was wide open.

One had military police who could have gone and looked for absentees so that we didn't have to bother about whether people were missing, and that meant that you could do all the things that one later thought were such marvellous ideas – wards and a completely free environment – without the slightest difficulty. Everything that anybody thinks they have invented since!

For one thing, there was a superb occupational therapy, only they didn't call it that; what they said is that every military person had to do a job unless he or she was too ill to do a job, so there was an 'employment centre' who allocated jobs and they took advice from the nursing or medical staff about what kind of job would be advisable or wouldn't be advisable and they made sure people were there. If they weren't there, they went and found out why.

They accepted advice if you said the patient was too ill to do any work but in fact every patient had a job and every patient learnt something. There was a marvellous horticultural department, that's now called something therapy, it used to be called gardening. But there was a thriving market garden going on in Mill Hill which of course during war-time rationing was marvellous anyway. There was a jewellery department where people learnt to make jewellery and some made excellent work. They did all the work around the hospital, all the cleaning, all the gardening, all the repair jobs, all the woodwork. There was a gymnasium so certainly every person, every patient, had exercise at some point. There were people around who could do dancing, whatever anybody could manage to teach, they taught.

There were enough staff about who knew about football and of course plenty of facilities for playing team games and doing everything else, and the swimming pool in the school and open doors and individual psychotherapy and group psychotherapy. Of course, drugs were not as plentiful as at the moment but I think we were a good deal better at managing very disturbed patients.

For a long time I was in the female ward and some of those patients were as disturbed as I've ever seen since, some of the Wrens and women's army. But it was marvellous, the fact that it was quite new to me that the doctor would ask the nurse what she had observed or what she thought, what her opinion about something was. I enjoyed the feeling of being expected to contribute something, but certainly it was the patients rather than that that caused me to feel I had a future in psychiatric nursing. The fact that the working conditions were pleasant and that the staff were nice added to the pleasure but that's not why I stayed in psychiatric nursing, it was the patients that made me stay.

Not too many male nurses during the war but they rapidly came at the end of the war; came back from the army medical corps, and many of those who had been in psychiatric nursing came back. I think my first ward sister's job, in fact my first staff nurse's job, I was entirely guided by some very senior men who really knew what they were doing.

The training had no structure of any sort. There were two tutors at that point, one who was supposed to be doing something with the students who were doing a three-year training, new recruits. Theoretically we were divided into the three-year and the certificate group, and those of us who were general-trained had as our tutor Olive Griffith. She was an assistant matron who was supposed to teach us but she didn't give any lectures or anything like that, she had an endless library and we met her in small groups or singly, when we discussed what we had just read and she produced the next thing and said maybe you would be interested in that. But she also did rounds and asked you the sort of questions that you didn't know the answer to … [as well as] a lot about patients and about the work.

[We learnt from] the ward sisters, the doctors, ourselves, we discussed [things], one talked all the time. I don't think there were any particular didactics about it. I think it was something that emerged but there was also an ethos about which … we had nurses' notes which were written up about every patient, and a nurse was made responsible for keeping a patient's notes. Now it could be [from] a student, it could be [from] a trained nurse but it was your business to collect information about the patient for the time you weren't there, it had to be written up weekly and you had to know what exactly had happened to the patient and what should happen and what was going to happen. If the patient didn't go to occupational therapy when you weren't there, that was reported to you by the nurse [on duty] that day. These notes were fully taken into account by the medical staff, who discussed them when they met you again; you were continually discussing patients, there was no break in this. One kept very good records of what was going on and you knew which patients you were responsible for and the patients knew who was keeping records about [them].

There were very different-sized wards because they were school 'houses'. I think the female ward I was on longest probably had about thirty [beds]. Maxwell Jones was there; his ward was one of the smaller ones. He dealt with anxiety states, shell shock or whatever it was called at the time, and developed an interest in therapeutic community work.

The returned prisoners of war from Japan literally came back thinking that nobody else knew anything about the war and that the whole world owed them a living because of the terrible experiences … they really were quite insufferable as people when they came back. They were never going to work, that was beneath them. He [Maxwell Jones] managed to get these people motivated in the sort of therapeutic community atmosphere.

All the psychiatrists who ever made a name for themselves were there. If you look at the psychiatric literature of the time it was Sargent, Slater, Goodman … psychiatrists who didn't have the sort of god-like belief about themselves that developed later. There was something about their attitude both to patients and to nursing staff which made it possible to work with them, in fact more than possible. Maybe they couldn't have worked solo or maybe they got the kind of nursing staff who made it clear to them that they had something to contribute. To me it was new when I first went there but once you were surrounded by people who thought and who had ideas [you grew accustomed]; there was certainly more teamwork there than I have ever seen after that.

We went back to the Maudsley and it took on its pre-war pattern immediately, immediately, as if the whole war had never existed.

If the new injuries could be horrifying, the new treatments, developed out of necessity, were sometimes so amazing that they appeared miraculous. In the best situations nurses, whether civilians or part of the medical services, were inspired and excited by the teamwork they shared in. Many nurses still recalled their own trauma and their patients' with great distress even years later, but nonetheless they rose to the challenge of moving on.

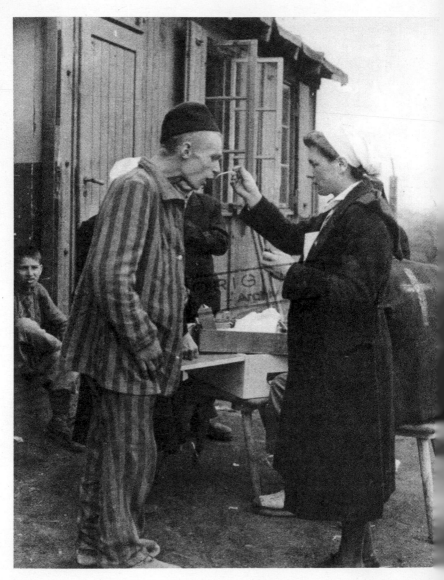

A Red Cross nurse assists concentration camp survivors, April 1945.

EIGHT

NEARING THE END

The longer I was in the army, the more startled I was
that we ever won the war.

Betty Boyce, sister, QAIMNS(R)

The six long years of war ground on. The theatres of war changed. Allied armies from North Africa invaded Sicily and fought up the length of Italy. The Russians continued a fierce campaign in the east and pressured the Allies to launch a second front in Europe.

New weapons such as the flying bombs put in an appearance and there was no let-up for civilians.

The Allies prepared with the greatest possible secrecy for 6 June 1944, D-Day, and the beginning of a desperately fought Allied combined operation, the invasion of the mainland of Europe. Planning for this invasion included both rehearsals of military strategies and preparations for the medical support of the armies to be deployed across Europe.

It was anticipated that in the early days of this campaign the wounded would be evacuated back to Britain. In readiness for this, hospital beds were emptied and some patients in the south of England were transferred with their nurses as far away as Scotland.

D-Day

✚

Joan Gray, née Goddard, QAIMNS(R), 1944

After completing only Part I of their midwifery training, Joan Gray and her friends were now enrolled in the QAs and preparing for the invasion.

It all was quite rapid. And then came the time when we were mobilising, so we had to go to Luton and we were stationed in private houses. I remember that this person I was staying with wanted to charge me extra for my daily bath. However, we weren't long there. Then we were sent down to Southampton, where we had the night in an army camp and circular tents and they gave us the most lovely food. Oh it was lovely, tinned peaches, and we said, 'They are feeding us up for the kill', and then off we went to France with British General Hospital 84 on 16 June 1944.

Elwyn Jones, sick berth attendant (SBA), Royal Navy, 1943–5

Elwyn Jones joined the Royal Navy in 1943 at the age of nineteen. He undertook training as a sick berth attendant and found himself in a fleet making its way to the Normandy beaches around D-Day.

We sailed that night, it was dark, and we were called down because [we were] part of the ship's company. So the skipper of the landing ship tanks (LSTs) spoke to us. It was like a cross-Channel ferry, and he took us down into the tank space and told us that we were now on our way to the shores of France. Well that was something. Before we sailed we had taken on board mainly Royal Army Service Corps people with trucks, and there was a contingent of Canadian airmen. We were crammed in, but … cramming and overcrowding was part of the war days. But it was a marvellous system where these trucks came in, down a ramp, on to a lift, and the lift took them up on board and then we were able to fill all the space.

The space down below was called the tank space but we never took any tanks. We used the rails to anchor the stretchers because, what happens with these LSTs, you go in with the tide and then you discharge everyone and then you wait for the tide to come back in before you go back. We were protected, you know, by the big battleships firing over our heads.

You never questioned anything and therefore you never asked; you'd be surprised what people told you [but] you did it.

So now we were part of the naval SBA detachment that was controlled by the chief petty officer fellow from Swansea who was our operating theatre technician SBA. It was well organised with the army ... we had no call to use the operating theatre, which was a mobile thing, because the Royal Army Medical Corps (RAMC) had dealt so exceptionally efficiently with the so-called patching-up. The morphine had been done initially by the RAMC. I could never praise enough the work that was done by them. They operated, but all the people who had amputations were taken to a hospital ship. So, you know, a lot of ours, in the LST, could walk.

They had a label and they had a document with detailed information. In those days I didn't realise the significance of SI ... 'self-inflicted'. A lot of them were accidental, you know, shooting off their toes ... I was innocently unaware of what it meant and of course we treated everyone the same because they were casualties.

Going back, because the ship was lighter having discharged the heavy lorries and transport, I used to get very seasick. Our destination was the Southsea area. There was a bay where you came in, unloaded, discharged the casualties and then you went to another base to load up. So as soon as you unloaded you went, loaded up, and off again. I found that the journeys weren't too long, not as long as it takes to go from Dover to Calais, but I would say it was about the same rate. We did this back and forth until as they advanced into France you could see then that the casualties were getting fewer, they were able to do their own and fly them back, I suppose, fly the casualties back.

[We slept] on the way back. I suppose we got tired but being young we were able to keep awake and active. It was when we were in port and after unloading [that] we sort of snatched hours before we loaded up again.

Eileen Willis, student nurse, Westminster sector hospital, Basingstoke, June 1944

Now a very competent student nurse, Eileen Willis was part of a civilian team poised to care for the wounded brought back from the D-Day beaches.

[Reading from her diary] 1944 on 5 June, I was sent with other nurses to Basingstoke, which was part of our training and also part of looking after the army and other casualties. Everywhere was empty. We were cleaning and getting the wards ready, there were three large and one small, sixty-eight beds in all.

The first convoy [was] due to arrive on the 8th, great expectation and excitement but in the event only one patient came, a sailor with arm wounds. He was transferred after a couple of hours so the ward was empty again and we waited again.

Six days later the first convoy, about thirty men, admitted to the ward, filthy, dirty, walking cases, nearly all Canadians, very cheerful but worn out, shrapnel wounds, some bullet wounds of arms. They were bathed, wounds re-dressed, fed, and then they sleep in bed non-stop, they say it was hellish over there, murderous crossfire, some of them stayed in the water over two hours, they said some of the Germans are only boys of fifteen and sixteen.

On the 10th, all these patients evacuated, ward empty again.

Convoy reported to be coming in tonight. Then at six a.m., then at ten a.m.; eventually it arrived at midday.

[Interview] We used to take it in turns to be on call, so after a heavy day on duty you had supper and, if you were wise, you turned in to bed immediately because if a convoy came in the night and you were on call they came and they woke you up, shouted, 'Convoy coming in half an hour' so you got up and hurriedly dressed and you walked up through the

Members of QAIMNS arrive at a Normandy bridgehead, June 1944.

dark to the admission ward, which was about ten, fifteen minutes away from where we lived. I used to go along and see the searchlights going, it was all a bit scary but you got used to it.

[Reading again from diary] The 11th: convoy consists of six Americans, very quiet, nice chaps, they are appreciative of our efforts but horrified at our primitive set-up. A Frenchwoman of twenty-four had been brought over but is on another ward, apparently she and a few others were sniping our men on the beaches and had accounted for seven Americans before being captured. A lot of the men said when they were going through French towns they got ball shots in the back from the French, the enemy. They had been overrun and a lot of them had collaborated with the Germans anyway. That's war for you.

On the 12th another convoy comes in at last. This crowd is nearly all Canadians and good fellows too, they have nothing but praise for the Americans, saying they can do their stuff when they have to. We were supposed to be having five walking Germans tonight but they didn't come to us after all. One night in three you are liable to be called out; London passes are still taboo but I am having a day off at last.

On the 14th, small convoy coming in, British this time, all the Shire regiments, Northumberland, Durham light infantry, the Dorsetshires, the KOYLI [King's Own Yorkshire Light Infantry], etc., such nice men and very grateful for everything.

15 June. Convoy departed again, sorry to see them go, they were all overwhelming with gratitude. Two men left, one with nasty through-and-through wound of the shoulder which bled profusely after operation; the other with malaria.

A convoy arrives, ten admissions this time, all are in cracking spirits and all tell the same thing, you cannot trust the French, they wave and cheer you from the window and as soon as you are past, a bullet gets you in the back. Many French girls are married to the Germans.

Norma Batley, student nurse, St Thomas' sector hospitals, 1944

Through all this, student nurses and their tutors tried not to lose sight of the training requirements.

By the time we got to the second front, and we were sent to a sector hospital for that, and we had convoys coming back, I was in the theatre for six months at that time, I did actually miss a section of my lectures but nobody ever discovered it.

Joan Gray, née Goddard, sister, QAIMNS(R), June 1944

Joan Gray's unit did not leave Luton and cross the Channel until 15 June.

The army had all gone over, the RAF and everything, they had all done that and it was about the … 15th [of June]. And we went over in this 'landing craft infantry' it was called.

And when we got over there, in this boat ... they lowered the ramp and they said, now you can wade ashore; there was great shouting and waving from the beach and the men there saw that we were women. They hadn't seen women there before and they found a DUKW ... an amphibious vehicle, and they sent it out so we landed dry. Then lorries came for us and we got in and were driving off to ... where the hospitals were being set up. When the French saw us they were clapping us and cheering us and waving to us ... it was really very nice.

Betty Boyce, sister, QAIMNS(R), France, August 1944

After a successful career as a sister in accident and emergency and later a nurse teacher in Belfast, Betty Boyce joined the QAs and was transferred to Europe in August 1944.

We were in Wellhouse Municipal Hospital, Barnet, a bit north of London, for about three weeks, and then we moved down to what I later discovered was the New Forest, where the army ran a camp for those who were getting ready to go over to France, must have been early August by this time.

And then we went under canvas. I'd never slept under canvas; I'd never been a Girl Guide camping out, so you learnt a lot. There was a lot of dew on the ground, even in August; you took your clothes into bed with you and put your shoes up in the bottom of the bed so that they didn't get damp. We didn't have anything to do except report in at meals in the evenings in case we were summoned to go over to France.

We went over in one of the Ulster boats. D-Day had happened in June so we were the back-ups because the ones who went over in June were mobile so to speak; ones who were going over now were going to be running 500-bed hospitals, tented hospitals like that.

Well nothing happens very quickly in the army; I mean the longer I was in the army the more startled I was that we ever won the war.

We got over to Bayeux in this large field where we slept in a tent which slept twenty-five nurses, and that's what you had, your bed, that was it.

We'd all been told to get tent pole straps. And I had my tent pole strap, and my tent pole strap was built to fit a tent pole of one size but nobody had told the tent pole straps manufacturer that the poles were now different. Naturally enough it didn't work; you were all supposed to have three hooks each to hang your things on. We didn't have any hooks because you couldn't keep your tent pole strap up so all you had was literally your bed and your suitcase underneath it.

The kindly pioneers had provided latrines across the end of the field, twelve-seater, six back to back, a piece of hessian round the outside and that was it. Unfortunately the road was higher and the three-ton lorries were higher still so that soldiers could wave at you when you were seated on your loo. So our matron found some hessian and put some hessian round about four and labelled them '25 BGH only'. So we had a little privacy, it wasn't ideal, and for some of the forty/fifty-year-olds really it was not the ideal kind of life.

V-1s and V-2s

There was no let-up for the civilians. There were new unmanned weapons to face. The V-1 flying bomb, or doodlebug, and later the V-2 rocket were targeted on London. The particularly terrifying thing about the doodlebugs was that their engines made a noise as they came over, and when the engine cut out and the noise ceased they fell to earth and exploded. Eunice Boorman and her fellow nurses in Oldchurch Hospital were on the route followed by the flying bombs and rockets launched from the Netherlands.

Eunice Boorman, pupil midwife, Essex, 1944

Once she had completed her general training, Eunice Boorman began midwifery, all around the same area close to London.

Of course we caught the majority of the doodlebugs that came because from Holland, where they were launched, we were in a direct line to London. If they didn't bring them down here … this was the last place before they got to London.

Anna Brocklesbury-Davis, student health visitor, Battersea and Wandsworth, London, 1944

After qualifying as a general nurse, Anna Brocklesbury-Davis continued to further her career. In 1944, at the time of the flying bombs, she was undertaking her health visitor training.

I did my health visitor practical visits in Wandsworth, and I remember, I was visiting out in the region of Tooting Broadway. I thought, I'll leave time to bicycle back to Wandsworth Town Hall, to have my lunch. So I'll leave about ten minutes to bicycle down Garrett Lane.

As I was bicycling down Garrett Lane, the Tooting Granada rocket bomb fell, in the exact area where I had been visiting, and if I had been there I might have been killed. I was more or less carried up in the air on my bike and put down again with the blast. I felt I should go on. I thought that, well, they would have their team of experts to 'do the incident', as they used to call it, I'll get on with my own work.

So I went on and got back to the town hall, but I found that one of my fellow health visitor students had also been in that area, had not left herself ten minutes to get back for her full hour lunch and she was very badly hurt. She got her skull broken, but she managed to get better and went on with her training later. Brave girl.

Afra Leckie, student health visitor, Royal Sanitary Institute, London, 1944

Exasperated by her many clashes with authority over petty discipline, Afra Leckie resolved to undertake health visitor training. She was struck by the stoicism of her colleagues and was impressively stoic herself, despite the trauma of being bombed.

Then of course the doodlebugs were still coming over. One of the things that I remember most clearly was when we took the health visiting exam, one of the things we were told was in the event of enemy action you must not leave your desk. So in the event of the doodlebug coming over, you would just stop writing and wait till you hear it boom, and then you would get on with it. That is exactly what happened. Two went over while we were having the exam and most people stopped and nobody moved. Nobody turned their head, you had got used to it by this time.

I can't tell you that I was ever really frightened, not even when we were bombed. The Fagg family, my landlady's family, were wonderful. Somebody came in and cried their eyes out, and I thought she was quite stupid to come in and cry, because it's no good worrying about these material things, you had to put up with it, as this was war, and so on. They were a fantastic family. They were the parents of the friend that I had trained with at Margate.

Rita Gascoigne, student nurse, St Helier Hospital, Surrey, 1943–4

The impact of the V-1 and V-2 raids on her training hospital was such that Rita Gascoigne and her fellow students were transferred elsewhere.

1943–6 that was ... we were right in the line of the doodlebugs and ... our work was so interrupted by the doodlebugs that in the end we [decided we couldn't rely on just] the local warnings – we had a little man up on the top of the sixth floor who used to ring his bell when it was coming in our direction. We had tin helmets and we had to lie down wherever we were, with our tin helmet on, when we heard that warning coming.

We were hit. One doodlebug landed on the front of the nurses' home ... and the medical doctor's house which was just in front of the nurses' home. His house was demolished and the front of the nurses' home was demolished. I lost all my stuff in my room.

So then we all doubled up in the back of the hospital and plodded on and then we had another one land about ten days after that, on the other end of the hospital, which was the boiler room and the main functioning part of the hospital, so we had to be evacuated then.

I went to Epsom Hospital for about a month, until they had patched up some of St Helier. We had a skeleton staff and the two bottom wards open just to receive casualties; they were assessed there either for immediate surgery or to be transported up to Scotland somewhere. They went to surgery and then again straight away for evacuation to Scotland.

Nursing in mainland Europe: concentration camps

The advance across Europe brought new challenges. Immediately after D-Day the wounded were evacuated home. Later, hospitals were set up as the medics followed the troops across the continent. For the nurses in these units an unexpected and most horrifying experience was working with the victims in the concentration camps they encountered. Staff were encouraged to write to family back home to assure them that the awful tales they heard were true.

Mary Copland, QAIMNS, 1944

After completing fever and general training, Mary Copland had joined the QAs to find herself transferred to Normandy on D-Day+12. The invading forces were held up by the enemy and several army hospitals were held up for some time around Bayeux.

I went over on a hospital ship, D–Day plus 12, to Normandy. We landed on the Arromanches landing stage; I was in the 91st BGH. We went into an orchard near Bayeux, we were a tented hospital, and we had casualties coming in from Caen. Gunshot wounds mostly. As our troops advanced through France we followed along. The whole hospital travelled in trucks and lorries. We set up hospital in a convent in Rouen, we were only there about three days and then we moved on to Brussels. I always remember going through Brussels; the people came out in the streets and they threw peaches and all sorts of things; they were so delighted to see us, and we were in a hospital there for about a month I think, and then went on to Antwerp, and then on to Holland, and then eventually into Belsen.

The unit Mary Copland was with had not been especially prepared to deal with the horrors they found in Belsen.

And we went into Belsen, I suppose, about ten days after it opened, and it was absolutely horrendous. I have a letter here that I wrote to my sister at the time, we were all told to write to as many people as ... friends and relations, to tell them all about the horrors of it, and this is my letter written to my sister on 13 May 1945.

Perhaps you know where I am? If not let me enlighten you. The place I am in is none other than Belsen. We have been here almost three weeks, just ten days after this ghastly place was taken. I cannot begin to describe to you the horror and degradation of this concentration camp, but you will have read about it. Please believe everything that is printed and tell anyone doubting the newspapers or the information which is released that the accounts and stories of the place are absolutely true.

In fact it seems incredible to believe our own eyes here and to realise that all this misery and suffering really has happened at the hands of the Germans. Someday I will be able to tell you all about our work, the brick wall obstacles, the seemingly hopeless task that we are trying to do with a thousand and one pitfalls.

However, this gigantic task is being tackled by various branches of the army. The Royal Artillery guns are doing jobs they never in their wildest dreams imagined, so are the Military Police, and even the RAF are here doing everything but RAF work.

When we first came up I was in charge of five buildings with 850 patients of every nationality imaginable. Each building had its own staff of internal nurses, at least they were called that, but none of them had had any inside hospital experience, and the only qualification they had which prevented them from being patients themselves was the fact that they hadn't got typhus or dysentery, typhoid or TB, and were able to walk.

Apart from the frightful language difficulties, international prejudices are existing among the internees themselves; it is no picnic trying to cope or organise. But now we have the German army medical personnel in, they run the buildings and look after the patients, and there is a British sister over them. I am now running a building with 180 patients who are being looked after by ten German orderlies, three German sisters and two German doctors, and I might add it is not an unpleasant position to be in, that of supervising doctors, and telling them what to do, quite apart from them being Germans.

Actually these Germans profess as much horror and disgust as we do and pretend they knew nothing of what was going on. However they are really working hard and seem to be trying to do their bit to make amends. And, of course, the patients do not like Germans looking after them, but there was no other solution with 60,000 of them.

However, as long as they know the British are supervising they are happy. The buildings the patients are being nursed in are the late SS barracks and are mostly small rooms. I do quite frequent visits of all the rooms and you should see the delight in their faces as I walk in.

Perhaps one in a hundred speaks a little English so conversation is nil. Gesticulation and signs etc. are the order of the day.

Conditions in which they are being nursed would really shake you. We have no mattresses, just hessian sacks filled with straw. The patients have no clothes or sheets and just lie rolled up naked in blankets.

Oh it is terribly pathetic.

However they are now living in comparatively clean and luxurious surroundings compared to where they were, and as each day goes by a few clothes are brought along. This area of Germany around Celle, Hanover and Bremen has been completely ransacked for clothes and food for these inmates. Every day our troops are sent further into Germany to demand more clothes etc. at the point of a bayonet if necessary, so in time perhaps things will be more plentiful and the bare necessities at least will come.

There is a great demand for magazines, newspapers and anything with pictures in it. If you could send them along I would be only too pleased to distribute them. Until three days ago we had seen no newspapers ourselves.

We are under canvas, it is nice in this weather of the past few days, but when we first arrived the rain, wind and cold was terrible. We are fortunate in being able to get frequent baths. The super, super SS barracks we use for that.

Yes, the camp is a most ironic mixture of unspeakable living conditions where the internees were, and luxurious accommodation for the bestial SS Germans.

Whilst we were there, there was one big funeral for 300 that were put into one large pit and then covered over because they were dying all the time.

It was absolutely horrendous.

Rose Telfer, née Hall, sister, QAIMNS(R), 1945

Once her unit arrived in Germany, Rose Telfer found herself assigned to caring for patients liberated from Buchenwald.

...We were posted up to Germany, and our first intake there were the patients from Buchenwald concentration camp and it was ghastly, those poor souls. Our hospital was a hutted place; it was in the Bremen area.

I was put on night duty. There was a little Jewish boy, he'd only be about eighteen or nineteen, he could speak ever so many languages and I used to get him to go round with the trolley at night. It was mostly chests and diarrhoea, and of course they were mentally incapacitated too, very much so, a lot of them. This little fellow would help me with the medicines at night, was it their chests or was it their bowels? It was really ghastly and they were dying like flies, dying off like flies they were so debilitated, so many of them; it was really terrible.

Russian a lot of them, I've got a long list of all the nationalities. Matron met me in the corridor again one morning, this little matron, she said, 'You've been on that ward long enough, Sister, I must get you off.' But she took me off night duty and put me on to day duty. There was all this awful sputum and diarrhoea, one could hardly cope in a way really, it was terrible.

They'd go running away ... it was during harvest time and they'd run, the ones who were able, they just ran in their pyjamas, their jackets tucked in, ran through this corn to go to a farm and they'd ... whether they frightened the folk or what, they'd come back, and they'd have a chicken and eggs. They were so mentally deranged. And we had to lock the kitchen door at night because the food for the breakfast, the bread was all buttered and fixed the night before, you see, and if they got into the kitchen they'd just ram this down their throat, this bread, and then it would aggravate the diarrhoea. They were actually too ill to move ... waiting till it was time for the move, you know, wherever they were going.

Well we just coped ... just got on with it, and it was really dreadful. I feel all your generation should know about it and see it.

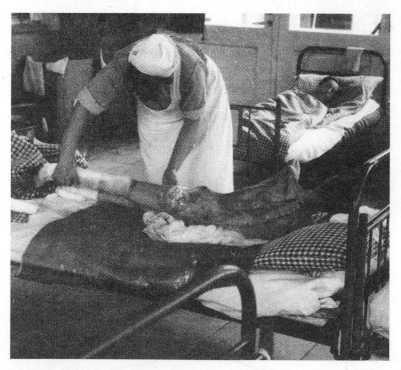

June 1945, a nurse at Roundhouse Hospital, previously the HQ of the German Army in Bergen-Belsen, tends a former inmate of the concentration camp.

VE Day: 8 May 1945

✚

After more than six years of war, Victory in Europe Day was declared. All the interviewees had vivid memories of the end of the war.

Margaret Broadley, nurse teacher, the London Hospital, 1945

The first step towards the end of the war was what was known as VE Day, the day when victory in Europe was proclaimed. I told my nurses that they could do anything they liked for the rest of that day and I myself went where I had previously been on the day of George V's jubilee and stood on the gates of Buckingham Palace, and I also stood on the gates of Buckingham Palace later that year on VJ night. I felt that my presence was essential to get peace established!

Betty Boyce, sister, QAIMNS(R), Netherlands, 1945

The most conscientious nurses were frustrated by the delays that arose around VE Day.

I remember coming back from leave … I left England on the afternoon of VE Day, so that by the time we finally got to Brussels and a train up to somewhere like Nijmegen to hopefully get transported to our units, every time the train stopped there were hurrahing crowds outside cheering. We didn't really know that the war had ended until they told us because I think although it was said in the afternoon it wasn't until about midnight that night that it was actually declared.

When we were offloaded at Nijmegen they said, 'And how are you getting back to your unit?' and I suppose now we would have said your guess is as good as mine, because we had no idea how we were getting back to the unit. But [another] unit said, 'Well we're not very far from there, come with us.' So we started about a six-hour journey in the back of a three-ton lorry with just benches to sit on, eventually got to their unit and they said to come in and have a meal, so we had a meal with them. It was well after midnight when we got back to our unit. But Matron couldn't complain because of course nobody had made any effort to collect us.

Mary Copland, sister, QAIMNS(R), Belsen camp, 1945

One of the worst places to celebrate VE Day had to be one of the liberated concentration camps.

At first we were absolutely miserable and hated being there and everyone was very upset by the horror of it all, and needless to say very disappointed that Belsen was the spot we were to celebrate VE Day.

I can remember the little service that we held, that was held with the chaplain in a field on that day.

Sue Aylmer, staff nurse, Royal Alexandra Children's Hospital, Brighton, 1945

Sue Aylmer remembered the intoxicating freedom to do simple things like going to the beach.

You couldn't go on the beach in those days. They had barbed wire … normally you weren't allowed out after ten o'clock, you had to have a pass. But VE night you could go where you liked, come back when you liked. Brighton was absolutely alive.

Margaret Thomson, student nurse, Royal Hospital for Sick Children, Edinburgh, 1945

The restrictions of discipline still impacted on some celebrations.

… I do remember the day war stopped and in Sick Children's we were told that we could go out but we must be back at ten o'clock. Well a lot of the girls did not come back and they climbed in windows and all sorts of things and there was the most terrible row the next morning and these girls were all severely reprimanded.

Joan Savage, staff midwife, King's College Hospital, London, 1945

Oh yes, I was up … outside Buckingham Palace. I thought that I was going to be squashed to death going through the gates when it was finished. It was just great. Great companionship and comradeship. I got back home on a lorry, you know there was no transport, you had to get what you could to get back and the doctors and even the consultants were put on, anyone wanting a lift to London, you put your name down and you'd get a lift.

Eunice Boorman, pupil midwife, Dagenham, 1945

Then when peace was declared, we had bonfires in the streets; burnt all the tarmac. For weeks you couldn't cycle because they had burnt the tarmac on the roads.

Gertrude Cooper, née Ramsden, QARNNS, Kandy, Sri Lanka, 1945

In every corner of the world where there were Allied servicemen and -women, there were celebrations. Out in Sri Lanka, Gertrude Cooper was nursing at Lord Mountbatten's headquarters.

Two days later, early May, VE Day occurred, when Europe was *en fête* because of the surrender of the Germans. We had celebrations in Kandy [Sri Lanka], I think there were celebrations all over the world, and that evening Mountbatten had his favourite recreation, a film show, in his bedroom. The film unit from the American section moved in, and we saw *Mrs Miniver*, and we had fruit drinks. That was our VE Day, and we continued with very great activity going on, although the patient (Mountbatten) was submitting to prescribed treatment.

Sheena Kilminster, née Craig, sister PMRAFNS, Halton, 1945

Assigned to work in the plastic surgery unit at Halton for the whole of her service, Sheena Kilminster was well positioned to enjoy VE Day.

VE Day, it so happened that Nell Campbell, my roommate, and I had both been on night duty and we both had nights off … no, no she didn't, sorry, she had to go back on night duty, but I had nights off. We did three weeks straight up from eight till eight, which was a long stint. Then you had a sleeping day plus three full nights off, and then back on day duty on the afternoon of the fifth day.

Instead of going to sleep of course on VE Day we went up to London, and we somehow or other got ourselves into Whitehall when Churchill was speaking. You couldn't put a sheet of paper between the throng in Whitehall, and I found myself hard against the lamppost with my arms pinioned to my sides, and my handbag – we had shoulder bags in those days – slung over my shoulder, and we listened to Churchill's speech there. And then she and I had arranged to meet her cousin who was Board of Trade and who was a member of the Royal Ocean Racing Club no less, in St James's, and we managed to make our way to St James's and we saw Ian there, and Nell had to go back to be on night duty for eight o'clock, so she had to catch a train from Baker Street down to Wendover.

Ian was going on his cabin cruiser, thirty-foot cabin cruiser, to have a pub crawl down the Thames, starting off at the Royal Yacht Club. There were buses running, and we caught a bus and went down and went on board his cabin cruiser and we had drinks at the Yacht Club.

We more or less did a pub crawl down the Thames, and Hampton Court Palace was lit up, floodlit, and it was fabulous to see the lights after four years of darkness. It was something quite, quite phenomenal, I'll never forget it.

Anyhow, we ended up at the, I think it was called the White Swan at Thames Ditton, and that really was enough and I was just sleeping on my feet as you can imagine, anyway we had lost the rest of the company somewhere en route, and Ian being a complete gentleman – my husband I think is never very sure how I behaved that night, but I can assure you my behaviour was impeccable – I just simply passed out like a light and Ian tucked me up with a rug on one bunk and he slept on the other. We slept all night and he surfaced in the morning and he went ashore and got some food and then got me back. Because I had arranged to spend the weekend with relatives in Hertfordshire, out near Hertford, and I had to go back to Halton to get my clothing, of course, so it was all a fairly tight schedule. I had to ring up these relatives and explain my absence but I eventually spent the rest of the nights off with them. But it was a quite, quite unforgettable experience.

Esta Lefton, née Guttman, Jewish refugee, ATS, with Allied forces in Italy, 1945

Esta Lefton was assigned to duties attached to the Allied armies as they moved up the Italian peninsula. She never forgot the church bells that marked the celebrations in Rome.

There, in Rome, that's [where] I think we knew the war was going to end. I was dreadfully interested to find out as much as I could about what the soldiers actually felt when the war was coming to an end, hence my visiting Cinecitta. That was the Italian film studios and was given over to refugees. We were going, after our duties, to have a look. Some rooms were just made out of straw and there were lots of refugees in a terrible state; mainly they were mothers and children, and they quarrelled. Nobody, neither nurse nor anybody, prepared us for what [it was really going to be like] when the end came.

We had also different clubs there, for troops, for ATS. In Rome we had a wonderful YWCA as well where we met and we talked about nursing and we talked about our experiences.

The day the war ended the only thing we could hear were the bells ringing over Rome and there are a few bells I can tell you! Myself and the other nurses that were off duty, we were in this big sitting room which overlooked the Rome university, and the other side it overlooked the ambulance depot. The women ambulance drivers, they had the most wonderful building, it was just opposite the hospital. And we just stopped still, I mean none of us could move, and nobody said a word to each other. And then we just walked out. We had to go on duty.

The aftermath of war

The damage, the destruction and the unexpected consequences now had to be dealt with.

Patricia Lloyd, student nurse, 1940–4; later staff nurse, St Bartholomew's sector hospital, St Albans, 1945

Patricia Lloyd trained at Barts during the war. For much of the time she was based in one of their sector hospitals caring for children evacuated from London. Some of these children lost touch with their families completely.

Patricia Lloyd, tallest of the three nurses, with the 'failure to thrive' children in the Barts sector hospital in St Albans. Many of the young patients were war orphans.

I had to find places for all these children; one special little boy, I've got his photograph, who had been evacuated during the war without a name or an address. They had been bombed out. So he couldn't be adopted or have any permanent place. Every time we discharged him, he would come back again because he had this dysentery. He was perfectly all right while he was in with us, but the moment he went out ...

And this little boy, oh dear, I tried to get my mother to adopt him, but oh dear. I had to find someone. He went into a local hospital in St Albans where the children were head to toe, you know? A real 'home', wet beds, the lot. And I couldn't bear to think of this little boy being left there. But anyway, I got to know the consultant who was head of the hospital and his wife came over and got fond of him. He was an enchanting little boy. And [they] decided that they would like to adopt him, but they knew what the picture was – no chance of doing it legally.

So I actually had to hand him over to this pair. They were a very nice couple and they ... I didn't really have the heart to go back and see him ever again. That was a heartbreaking business trying to find places for all these children when we were closing down.

The remnants of Empire

✠

War might be over in Europe, but this was a world war, and the most powerful combatants in other parts of the globe included the USA and Japan. Japanese forces had shown both how ruthless they could be and that they could successfully challenge the European colonial powers. This theatre of war closed down brutally quickly with the dropping of two nuclear bombs by the Allies on the Japanese cities of Hiroshima and Nagasaki on 6 and 9 August 1945.

The situation in the former colonies in Asia was now extremely worrying. Allied troops were known to be prisoners of war of the Japanese, but their numbers and exact locations were unknown. European colonial administrators, planters, traders and their families were also known to be held in prison camps. How could they be 'liberated' into a country that did not want their return? An enormous amount of work needed to be done by administrations exhausted by war.

Gertrude Cooper, née Ramsden, QARNNS, Far East, 1945

Gertrude Cooper remained in Sri Lanka where all were waiting to see what was next required of them. When it began to emerge that there were hundreds of prisoner of war camps all over south-east Asia, she and a friend volunteered their help.

They had an awful lot of post-war chaos to deal with, which had never, never been anticipated. You see they were prepared to fight a war, but not to deal with all those other things. They were very badly organised.

August, when the atomic bomb was dropped ... I was still in Kandy, in Sri Lanka, helping in that military hospital, because everybody was mobile, because they were all at the ready, but nobody knew what the next task was.

Lady Mountbatten turned up, and the Prime Minister who was then Mr Attlee, gave her the authority to move around the whole of that fighting area and locate prisoner of war camps, and repatriate them. And she did it with the chief medical officer, and a Japanese staff officer, who travelled in the aeroplanes with them. They were eventually able to locate 250 prisoner of war camps. That was a very great shock to everybody, because we had no knowledge, we'd had no liaison or knowledge about this.

Lady Louis said, we fear that there's going to be civil war in Java and we can't release the women and children from the prison camps, would Lucy and I fly there. And we said yes, we'd go. We set off in the dark of the morning, flew from Singapore to Batavia, which is now Jakarta, and were received by an army officer, who'd had a rather garbled message about this group of four VADs and two sisters who were coming to help in the prison camps.

Well, disarming the Japanese wasn't easy, because as they laid their arms down, the Indonesians moved in and acquired them, so that the beginning of civil war was happening and there was trouble in the streets and fighting at night.

There was an empty bungalow, and it was suggested that we move in; it became the Red Cross mess because of the VADs, and we shared their 'compo' rations. That was a great asset because we had variety, although very stodgy bulky food, but we had a daily delivery of compo rations.

There was no currency accepted in the island other than what they called 'banana money'; they were bank notes turned out of the machine, all with the same number on, but it was currency and we found that if we went into the market, the fresh fruit in Java was beautiful.

The Indonesians were charming to us, and we had by this time acquired khaki drill skirts, bush shirts and Royal Marine berets, on which we put our flash, and we looked like official servicewomen; because it was made very clear to us, by all the troops present, that we must look very British and not learn a word of Malay, because we might be mistaken for Dutch, that is the former colonial power.

We were collected each morning at six thirty by a driver from the mess, crossed the town in a jeep and were delivered to the camp. We stayed at the camp till two o'clock. It was very hot and [there was] very inadequate care.

We saw people in various degrees of starvation. The drains didn't work, and there were 9,000 people in about a hundred houses, unimaginable. The squalor and the dirt ... those Dutch women and children were heroic. The women had organised that camp splendidly. The young women came round to see us; we were welcome; we were novelties, and they wanted to tell us what they'd done. We admired the women and children for surviving.

We were there until November and then some Red Cross workers and an officer were killed out bathing. That was their folly, because we were told not to go to remote places, there was a curfew, and we were always in long before, because our day was long, having started at six thirty.

Following this episode, Gertrude Cooper and her team were transferred to Surabaya, also in Indonesia. Here they worked in two civilian hospitals until March 1946, when a British military hospital moved in and the two nurses discovered that their age group had long ago been demobilised.

The next time Lady Louis came in, I said had she room in the plane, because the army sisters said my age group had been demobilised. So she said yes, hop in, and she gave me a lift to Singapore.

I knew a man who was a movement officer. He offered accommodation on a troop ship that would bring me home, and I left in April. I got to Southampton five weeks after I set off. In Southampton we went in the queue, and the disembarkation officer said, 'Oh no, what are you?' I said, there's [me], another sister, and thirteen VADs. Well what are we going to do with you? he said. Would it suit you if we got transport to collect your luggage and you went to Haslar Royal Naval Hospital?

When I got there, they said to me, what do you want to do? I said whatever the procedure is. Well, they said, you get disembarkation leave ...

Getting home

✚

The disruption and confusion in all the theatres of war was reflected at home, where health professionals were struggling to help the returning servicemen and their families. Following the bombing, the national housing stock was depleted. In many areas with traditional industries, plant had been destroyed; everywhere the economic problems were acute. Young men and women who had perhaps married in haste and who barely knew each other had to begin their lives.

Anna Brocklesbury-Davis, student health visitor, London, 1945

During the war, I was basically a trainee health visitor. By the time the war was over, I was just trained and working in Bethnal Green. I was visiting [people's] homes, and there [were a lot of] returning soldiers. The wife at home, and the soldier was coming back from the war. There were all the problems, what he thought of this bride that he had left behind; sometimes there was hardly anywhere to live, living in mother-in-law's house and all sorts of things like that, and him having to try and find a job. There was great need and difficulty, just after the war.

When I went for my interview for that job, the medical officer who interviewed me said, 'All I can say to you is, don't come here unless you really feel that you've got a calling for this kind of area and this kind of poverty and this kind of work, because it is very difficult.'

He just challenged me, rock bottom, not to come, and that made me want to come all the more. So I did go.

It was this spirit of bloody-minded determination that carried people through those first days and weeks of total confusion. There was widespread anxiety and exhaustion mixed in with jubilation and relief. Everyone had worked tremendously hard, few more so than the nurses. Now they were looking forward to the future with some apprehension but above all with hope.

A British policeman and a German soldier share guard duty outside
St Helier Town Hall.

NINE

OCCUPIED BY
THE ENEMY

We nearly got caught once. We were cycling back from visiting friends and we knew it was nearly curfew. The three of us, my brother and Lorna and I, passed this German on guard and he said, 'Halt!' He was looking at his watch. We didn't stop, we just carried on and we heard a gun and of course as soon as we heard that we went faster, but he was firing over us.

Brenda Hervé, née Quevâtre, assistant nurse, Emergency Hospital, Guernsey, 1940

The Channel Islands, in the Gulf of St Malo and closer to France than England, were the only part of Britain occupied by German forces during the war. For five years between June 1940 and liberation on 9 May 1945, the population lived alongside an occupying force which at times equalled the civilian population in numbers.

The Channel Islands have retained national links with Britain but their French antecedents are obvious; place names, family names and the local patois are more French than English. Each bailiwick, headed by a bailiff, retained local autonomy in many aspects of government and administration; the Channel Islands did not return MPs to Westminster, rather each had an elected representative body, the 'states'.

In 1939, at the time of the declaration of war, the population of the main islands was around 72,000.

The 'phoney war' saw the islanders experiencing an uneasy security. Life seemed to go on much as usual, vegetables were harvested, tomatoes and potatoes were still exported to Britain. However, all this changed in May and June 1940 when the Allied armies were forced out of mainland Europe and the Dunkirk evacuation took place.

In June 1940, the British government reviewed their priorities and decided to withdraw troops from the Channel Islands, leaving them with the status of an 'open town'; that is, unarmed and undefended. Surprisingly, this change of status was not made clear to the Germans, an oversight that was to have tragic consequences. Free passage was made available to civilian evacuees, and many left. However, some remained, either inadvertently, like Ann Baudains, or deliberately, like Dr Darling.

Evacuation

Ann Baudains, née Thomas, staff nurse, Overdale Isolation Hospital, Jersey, c.1940

It was almost an accident that brought Ann Baudains to Jersey. She was in search of an interesting job in a pleasant place.

I was asked to come to Jersey for six weeks in 1940 by my agency in London, so I took a three-month return ticket. It was only a matter of weeks after arriving in Jersey that the Germans came. Dr McKinstry had asked me to stay until the last moment, but I left it a bit too late and couldn't get away even though I had got my return ticket, even booked a berth to go back!

It was a bit of a shock really to be trapped like that because I didn't know anyone on the island and I had only brought my uniform and a few changes of clothes.

Dr Averell Darling, resident medical officer, General Hospital, Jersey, 1939–45

Recently qualified, and recently arrived from England, Dr Darling was obliged to work in a general hospital. It was his empathy for the Jersey people that led him to stay.

I came to the island in 1939, in September, and I was one of two resident doctors at the General Hospital. We were there for one year because the government had said all newly qualified doctors had to spend a year in a general hospital before they could join the forces.

In June 1940 it became very obvious that things were about to happen and we knew that the islands would soon be occupied by the Germans.

There was panic in many quarters. We all registered [to evacuate] but I had a conviction that I should stay. We had some quite seriously injured people in the hospital at the time, and I went to see Mr Halliwell [consultant surgeon] and asked him would it be better if I went or would it be better if I stayed? I would be quite happy to stay. Oh, he said, if you are willing to stay – stay … We settled down to what was going to be a long haul.

Brenda Hervé, née Quevâtre, assistant nurse, Emergency Hospital, Guernsey, 1940–5

As her family decided they wanted to stay together, Brenda Hervé did not consider leaving.

A lot of the Guernsey people evacuated, a lot of the schools … oh it must have been more than half of the people of Guernsey who evacuated. They went to England. My father wanted us all to go [though he was planning to stay]. My mother said, 'If you're not coming, we're not going.' So we stayed.

The Germans arrive

The Germans reconnoitred the islands from the air, and as they were unaware of the withdrawal of all Allied military personnel, they concluded that the lorries they saw lined up at St Peter Port, Guernsey, and St Helier in Jersey contained munitions. In fact the lorries in Guernsey were filled with tomatoes and those in Jersey with potatoes. As a result the innocuous lorries and their civilian drivers were bombed and machine-gunned. Eleven lost their lives in Jersey and twenty-three in Guernsey.

Beatrice Le Huquet, school teacher, Jersey, 1940

News spread quickly in the small community; before long everyone knew what had happened.

The day we were occupied was very sad because the island had been declared an 'open town'. Towards the end of that Friday [28 June 1940], things happened very quickly; the Luftwaffe planes hovered around and flew over and bombed the harbour about six thirty to seven p.m., leaving many casualties. The ambulances were alerted and the men taken to the hospital for immediate operations. Sadly, we lost several men; they died.

The surgeons and nursing staff were working all night in the operating theatre. Leaflets were dropped by the Germans informing us to be ready to receive them at 07.00 on 1 July.

Organising medical care

Around 18 general practitioners remained in Jersey. Other medical staff included the Medical Officer of Health (MOH), Dr McKinstry; and in the hospital the consultant surgeon, Mr Halliwell; the consultant physician, Dr Hanna; and a resident medical officer, Dr Darling, who worked closely with a medical student stranded in Jersey at the time of the evacuation.

Dr McKinstry, the MOH, looked after the laboratory in the hospital and oversaw Overdale Isolation Hospital, where infectious disease patients were cared for. He maintained a blood transfusion service throughout the war. Donors were encouraged by the offer of extra rations for a month after they had given a unit of blood.

In preparation for war, the States of Jersey had prudently laid in what they estimated was two years' supply of medical stores and dressings. Some medications and duplicates of all surgical instruments had also been stored.

In both Jersey and Guernsey it was soon clear that the occupying forces intended to use the existing hospital accommodation, and civilian needs would just have to fit around that.

In Jersey, as well as the Overdale Isolation Hospital there was the General Hospital in St Helier, which housed German and civilian patients, each cared for by their respective nurses and medical men.

In Guernsey, an Emergency Hospital was set up to house civilian patients. This was managed by Matron Rabey, an experienced nurse who came out of retirement.

Mary Le Sueur, née Jouny, nursing sister, General Hospital and Les Vaux convalescent hospital, Jersey, 1940

In the General Hospital, Mary Le Sueur could only watch as the local patients were ejected from their wards.

The Germans took over a whole men's ward of forty beds; eventually they took the female ward of thirty beds, and the operating theatre. All this meant that we had a massive rearrangement programme moving patients to different departments and even taking over large properties and getting them equipped. We were very short of staff. Luckily several Jersey girls joined us to train as nurses and were there during the five years of occupation.

To add to our difficulties, the Germans demanded that some of the staff worked on their wards. The Irish nurses who were 'neutral' volunteered. Some time later some German nurses were brought over, which made things much easier for us.

Once the Germans had their own wards and casualty department and their own staff, we had very little contact with them.

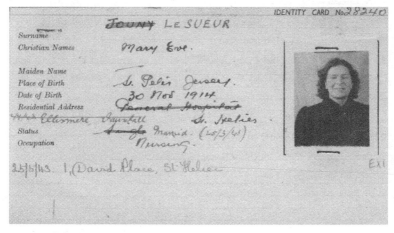

Under occupation, the population of Jersey was required to register with the German authorities. This is the identity card of Mary Le Sueur, sister in charge of the men's wards in Jersey's General Hospital from September 1939.

Nurses and nursing

Before the war there had been a training school for nurses in Jersey, recognised by the General Nursing Council for England and Wales (GNC); the national syllabus set by the GNC was implemented locally and a sister tutor, Miss Bissell, taught Jersey students. In normal times, if students met the requirements of attendance and were successful in passing the national or state examination, they would then register with the GNC and earn the right to describe themselves as SRN, state registered nurse.

After the evacuation of civilians to England in 1940, only 15 qualified nurses remained in the Jersey hospitals and there was a shortage of staff able to deliver nursing care.

The physician, Dr Hanna, was a keen supporter of the St John Ambulance. He appealed in the local press for those who had completed the St John's Home Nursing Course to consider assisting in the hospital. Young women like Brenda Hervé of Guernsey responded to this. Yet others like Cathy Minty were recruited as student nurses or probationers and arrangements were made for them to undertake training. They sat a preliminary examination, or 'prelim', so that they could progress in their training. The examination was set and marked locally and the scripts were stored so that the GNC could endorse or reject them in the future. Students, of course, were unable to sit the GNC examinations during the war.

In spite of their enforced separation from the GNC and the mainland, nurse training and the delivery of classes continued in Jersey throughout the occupation, and in 1945 at least 10 Jersey nurses were successful when they sat the GNC final examination and were able to register as SRNs in 1946.

Cathy Minty, née Mollet, student nurse, Jersey, 1941–5

Eager to undertake nurse training, Cathy Minty began her studies in 1941.

I started my training a year after we were occupied by the Germans. It was obvious then that the occupation was going to continue for some time.

Our pay packet was 17/6d a week to start with. The nurses' quarters were sparse, as many as four in a room, and with blackout curtains. Our morale was good, most of us had our bicycles to get around in our off-duty, which was usually headed for home, hopefully to find a bit of a nibble cooked by our mothers.

There had never been a training school in Guernsey, and here recruiting young women and men who had some experience from their association with St John Ambulance was even more important.

Brenda Hervé, née Quevâtre, assistant nurse, Emergency Hospital, Guernsey, 1940–5

It was in 1940 that Brenda Hervé's long-standing interest in nursing began. She was still involved in nursing at the time she was interviewed for this project.

I had been to visit my great-uncle in the hospital; he was very deaf and I was busy watching the nurses. From then on I was very interested in nursing.

I did a course of home nursing and I passed that. Then someone from the St John Ambulance came in to ask any of us if we were interested in nursing and at once I said, 'Oo, I would like to be a nurse.'

So we went to see the matron [Matron Rabey] at the hospital. We had a tandem; my mother couldn't cycle but with me in the front she just had to pedal. And I was accepted and I started nursing.

I loved it; I absolutely loved it so much. I really fell into it quite happily. And then Matron was so nice … she was a Guernsey lady.

Betty Baker, née Butlin, staff nurse, Overdale Isolation Hospital, Jersey, c.1940–5

After qualifying as a fever nurse in Portsmouth, Betty Baker spread her wings and found a staff nurse's post in Jersey. She did not expect to stay long. However, nursing work was tough during the occupation and nurses did not feel they could walk away from it.

One person usually looked after a ward … we did have a maid and then later, during the occupation, we had girls [who] came and worked and we trained them; they were great helps.

We were supposed to have been off three hours a day but we weren't always, and if there was another nurse off we'd often have to do two wards. You'd run and give one lot their tea and then you'd run over to the other ward and give them their tea and then it was the bedpans. On night duty it was terrible because if you were on alone, you went to one ward and gave out the various bits and bobs that they all needed and gave them a drink, then you went to the other ward and did the same, and so you went right round the hospital and then you started again from the first ward. Collected up the bits and bobs, made them comfortable, gave them their pills, or whatever there was to give them, cough mixtures and stuff, then on and around the ward you went again and you did that all night because you daren't sit around in case anything happened on another ward.

Brenda Hervé, née Quevâtre, assistant nurse, Emergency Hospital, Guernsey, 1940–5

The new nurses quickly fell into traditional nursing ways.

We had to wash the patients first thing in the morning, then we had to bath them, blanket-bath some that couldn't get out of bed. If patients had been in bed a long time, there [were] the backs to do, the heels to do. We used to do it with soap first of all and rub and rub until the soap had gone and then we used to use spirit, rub the spirits on, and then powder. And a lot of patients had terrible sores on their bottoms because they were malnourished, they were suffering from malnutrition and I think that was the cause but I only remember one very, very bad one.

Food and hunger

The islands were beautiful and fertile. In peacetime they had exported vegetables and flowers, mainly to Britain but some to France. However, the marketing of island produce was now overseen by the Germans and much was exported to Germany, leaving food shortages in the islands that became steadily worse. Hunger and the search for food and fuel was at the front of everyone's mind.

The islands had always been dependent on imported fuel for heating, gas and electricity; this, coupled with increasing shortages of food, confronted the civilian population, especially the housewives, with an almost impossible task. Many had gardens and were able to add some variety to their diet. Farmers were the most fortunate of all.

Brenda Hervé, née Quevâtre, assistant nurse, Emergency Hospital, Guernsey, 1940–5

Commenting on the patients' food, Brenda Hervé was sure that Guernsey milk had been crucial in keeping their strength up.

There wasn't much assortment of food for the patients. Vegetables and potatoes there was plenty of, but very, very little meat. I think it was the milk that saved a lot of the patients because we used to give them tea … but a lot of it was bramble tea, it was never real tea. Coffee was roasted acorns and all that sort of thing, it was never the real thing, you know. But the milk, yes, it was full-cream milk and I am sure that saved a lot of people because we had the farm on the premises.

Cathy Minty, née Mollet, student nurse, Jersey, 1940–5

Everything edible was consumed, even when it was not very appetising.

The food at the [General] Hospital was mainly potatoes, and the meat ration at the time, 4 oz a week, was lengthened out in the way of mince or stews. Overripe Camembert cheese would come into the island from time to time and was often mixed up with the mashed potatoes and baked in the oven, which was pretty ghastly.

Brenda Hervé, née Quevâtre, assistant nurse, Emergency Hospital, Guernsey, 1940–5

Some use was made of communal ovens, in the traditional way.

At home we had bean jars twice a week. You put five pounds of beans, which we used to grow, and any vegetables that you could lay your hands on in [a large earthenware crock with a lid]. There was no meat, not even a bone, and my brother would carry this jar in a big bucket on his bike down to the bakehouse on Monday night and go and fetch it on Tuesday for our tea and we ate the lot. We had one on a Saturday as well.

Peggy Boléat, née Still, TB patient, 1940–5

When you are confined to bed, bored and ill as Peggy Boléat was, food becomes very important. Even so, she found some things almost too awful to eat.

The hospitals had priority and one of the priorities which I hated was that they got all the offal, tongues, cheeks, tails, all other parts that I couldn't tell you what they were and they were all stewed up for us and of course there was no food colouring or anything and they all came out grey. We should have been thankful for it, but I don't think we were.

We had a dreadful concoction that was cod liver oil mixed with Carrageen moss, which was supposed to be very health-giving. It's a seaweed gathered off the rocks and washed and dried and then it's soaked and it's like a gelatine. People made jellies and blancmanges out of it and it was added to the cod liver oil to make an emulsion, but these little twigs used to float about … I thought it was a most dreadful thing but I had to have it, because it was going to do me good.

We were not on short commons but the food was always the same.

I [remember I once] had an egg for my birthday, a fried egg, and it was a great big treat; I don't think I saw another one the whole time I was in hospital. And that was lovely because it had to be sought for. They were like gold, you know? Little things were so important, [it was] the fact that somebody had thought about you and made the effort to get the egg and it was presented on a plate with 'happy birthday' written all round it in blue ink.

Peggy Boléat spent nearly three years suffering from tuberculosis. When she was discharged from hospital, she found that her family had been deported to mainland Europe.

Brenda Hervé, née Quevâtre, assistant nurse, Emergency Hospital, Guernsey, c.1942

Others found that when they were hungry, they could eat anything.

One day when we were served with our pudding at the hospital, macaroni pudding, there were things floating on top and there were all these tiny little white maggots which you get … you know … in old food. So I just pushed them aside round my plate and ate the rest. I didn't look inside the macaroni [to see] if there was any more. I just enjoyed the rest. I wasn't fussy at all. Some could not eat certain things, but I ate anything.

Joyce Norman, school leaver, Jersey, c.1940

Joyce Norman was one of 10 siblings and her mother worked hard throughout the occupation to keep them safe and fed.

My mother got very thin as well. Because she used to give the food to us, I suppose. I can always remember her saying, 'To see the children hungry, to see the children hungry.' I remember her telling a neighbour and when we were kids you know I used to think, 'Well we're hungry, but we're used to it now, you know', you didn't sort of think it mattered.

Eileen Picot, assistant nurse, Jersey, c.1940

The elderly had particular problems. Hospital food was positively luxurious for many.

My first ward, I was put on the top floor with the patients who were all geriatrics. The patients we admitted were underfed and they had no hot water and no soap. And so to arrive in hospital and the first thing was a good old bath, it was a great luxury for them. The food we had was far better than anything they could do. Many of these old people lived on their own in damp houses. Some of them came in with fleas.

Rationing and shortages

As the islands settled down for the long haul, shortages began: clothing, shoes, petrol, bicycle tyres and more were hard to find. Uniforms and working shoes were especially difficult. All communication with Britain was cut off, but some trading could still take place with France. The bailiffs invested considerable effort in building and maintaining a position in relation to the occupying power that kept some responsibility for civilian administration in island hands. Both bailiwicks created purchasing committees that sent representatives to France with instructions on what to buy.

Brenda Hervé, née Quevâtre, assistant nurse, Emergency Hospital, Guernsey, c.1943

There were a few things that you could buy that came from France. I mean there was someone from Guernsey, a Mr Fala, that used to go to France to buy whatever was needed like food or clothing … my shoes came from France.

Cathy Minty, née Mollet, student nurse, Jersey, 1940–5

The sewing room was constantly patching our uniforms and we kept on darning our black stockings, the feet being one big darn.

Health and illness

Initially doctors recorded an improvement in general health as excess weight was lost. This they attributed to a reduced alcohol intake, absence of high-calorie foods and an increase in exercise now that petrol was in short supply and cars had been confiscated. However, with malnutrition, the traditional infectious diseases returned: outbreaks of scarlet fever, whooping cough, diphtheria and typhoid all affected nursing and medical staff as well as the general public. Tuberculosis (TB) also gained a new lease of life; not only pulmonary TB, but also bone and joint TB. Sadly several children died of tuberculous meningitis. Once again staff were affected: one sister died and Dr Harold Blampied, who worked as an anaesthetist throughout the occupation, contracted TB and died shortly after the end of the war.

Insulin-dependent diabetics on the islands were in a terrible position. There was no way to obtain the drug. The doctors in Jersey admitted all diabetic patients to the hospital in order to help them manage their condition. Attempts were made to acquire insulin via the Red Cross, from France and Sweden, and it is reported that one German doctor occasionally made it available. By the time the Red Cross ship *Vega* made the acquisition of insulin easier in December 1944, almost all diabetic patients had died. Caring for these people who had no future was taxing, as Cathy Minty remembered.

Cathy Minty, née Mollet, student nurse, Jersey, 1940–5

I worked on a male ward with the diabetics, which I must say was dreadfully frustrating, because all these [men] without having insulin, they had to have all their food weighed out and in fact they were very, very hungry and in fact got a little bit sly; if they could get hold of a bit of food brought in for them they … I am afraid they did eat it. It was really difficult to keep them to their allowance.

[One] ward was given over to scabies patients, mostly children. Each child had to be bathed every day, scabs treated with sulphonamide cream, some of them had to have their hair shaved off and their fingers and feet bandaged daily. These bandages had to be washed over and over again and we became quite expert at rolling bandages.

The day after the liberation, the ward was clear [of scabies] after having one application of the lotion brought in by the troops.

The horrible cocktail of malnutrition and lack of fuel set off events that affected health. The most accessible fuel was wood; chopping up wood and furniture resulted in an epidemic of injured fingers. People were cold and many suffered from dreadful chilblains on their swollen fingers and toes. Finally relatively minor injuries to the lower limbs of people whose general health was poor led to chronic ulcers. Dr Darling called these 'occupation ulcers', a term that irritated the Germans. Children particularly suffered from these diseases of deprivation.

Venereal disease

Cathy Minty, née Mollet, student nurse, Jersey, 1940–5

War and occupation disrupted social norms and introduced some young women to new experiences.

The Germans kept to their wards and never interfered with us in any way. The only time they were linked up with us was on the isolation ward with patients suffering from VD. The ward was at the rear of the hospital outside and reached by some iron steps. These girls were locked in, their treatment was a daily bath and douches and sulphonamide tablets were prescribed. Weekly swabs were taken and they were only let out when they were clear, which sometimes took weeks. We did have some French girls from the German nightclub sent in. German doctors treated those girls. These girls were very colourful, beautifully dressed and loaded with perfume.

Betty Thurban, née Le Corre, student nurse, General Hospital, Jersey, c.1942*

A student nurse during the war, Betty Thurban was a match for anyone.

I worked on that ward [venereal diseases] with an assistant nurse who went off ill. I was on my own, aged eighteen! The German doctor used to visit once a week, he had been a consultant in Berlin. I recall him coming up. He was in his late forties, he clicked his heels at me and said he didn't think I would want to shake hands with him because we were on different sides

---

* Betty Thurban was interviewed by Michael Halliwell who kindly permitted her comments to be cited.

and he respected that. And as he went out of the door he said to Averell Darling, 'I think she's too young to be up here.'

The door [of the ward] was always kept locked and male visitors were never allowed. One day there was a knock on the door and there was a rather tatty German soldier standing there. In broken English he said that he had permission to visit a girl, and handed me a piece of paper. I didn't speak German and had no wish to speak German and so I was very obtuse and said, 'I don't know what this is' and marched him up to the German ward and got the interpreter. He looked at me and smiled and said, 'It's a leave pass.' About an hour later I had a repeat performance, so up to the German ward we went and found the interpreter. He looked at me and smiled and said, 'Another pass.' So as I was walking away I turned back and said, 'Would you like to tell them, I might be young but I'm not stupid.' Apparently they had heard that there was a very young nurse on duty so they decided to try it on.

Tuberculosis

Peggy Boléat, née Still, TB patient, 1940–5

There were no effective medications to combat tuberculosis, and the incidence of the disease increased as the general health and level of nutrition deteriorated. Patients were admitted to hospital, ordered to rest, exposed to fresh air and sunshine, and, as far as possible, offered good food. Many were cared for in the isolation hospital, Overdale.

One young woman, Peggy Still, was in hospital continuously from June 1941 to July 1943 with tuberculosis of her pelvis. It was not until January 1944 that she was mobile enough to return to work, almost three years after the long process of treatment began.

I had a test for tuberculosis. I was surprised, bowled over really, when Mr Halliwell said to me, 'You have TB and you will have to lie on your back for a year.' I don't think it really sank in for quite a little while, not what it would entail. I was eighteen, I believed a year meant twelve months to the day and I never imagined anything else.

It's very uncomfortable at first lying in a cast because you ache … you hurt just where the cast ends, it ended just above the knees, so there was a little gap under the knees and then it ends just above one's waist and there is another gap. Where the plaster begins and ends is very uncomfortable. But little pillows were given and that helped. Just the fact that you can't raise your head is very trying and everything seems all wrong.

The nurses were very efficient and looked very good in their uniforms. I think the nurses were special, they didn't just leave their patients to run down to the harbour [and evacuate]. Quite a few were English, Irish, Welsh nurses who stayed through the occupation, and we were very well cared for up there because the 'making do' must have been terrific.

Nurse Butlin [Betty Baker] was brisk and efficient. She didn't actually run everywhere, but she gave the impression that she did. Nurses never had time to talk to patients so we had to enjoy their company *en passant*. Nurse Butlin could make outrageous remarks; she could also make someone laugh at the same time as she was delivering a home truth. Nurse Thomas [Ann Baudains] was Welsh and moved more slowly than Nurse Butlin, but with equal purpose. Sometimes she sang 'David of the White Rock' for us. In nearly all ways she was the direct opposite of Nurse Butlin, but both were equally kind and I owe them much.

I think when you are in hospital you are in quite a different world; you're not concerned with what's happening outside. It was very lonely.

Betty Baker, née Butlin, staff nurse, Overdale Isolation Hospital, Jersey, c.1940–5

There was nothing for TBs, nothing … only fresh air and rest, though Dr McKinstry would collapse their lungs if he thought it would do them any good. He would push air into the thorax and push the lung down and then that would stay down for so many weeks, then you would have to go and do it again. That would rest the lung and you hoped it would heal itself, and it very often did.

Living through the occupation

Ann Baudains, née Thomas, staff nurse, Overdale Isolation Hospital, Jersey, c.1942

In an occupied country, individual privacy was barely regarded.

I was asleep, having been up all night, and there were very loud noises, banging of doors and heavy footsteps. I woke up and then my door burst open and this German barged in with a fixed bayonet, poked under my bed with his bayonet and then opened my wardrobe and did the same in my wardrobe, then went out and banged the door, didn't say a word, they were evidently looking for a deserter. He went through all the fever wards, Matron Secker tried to stop them but they didn't take any notice of her. They searched the whole place. Didn't find the crystal set [radio] that she had got hidden!

Once when I was on duty on the male TB ward, down what we used to call 'the dip', this very high-ranking German officer, elderly man, came with four or five other juniors I suppose, to shoot the pigeons down in the trees at the bottom there. And I was so annoyed by their arrogance that I went and told the men to pull the shutters on the ward and to make as much noise as they could and they were very, very annoyed with me because the birds all flew away.

Bunty Le Seelleur, student nurse, Jersey, 1940–5

We had lots of amusing things that happened, but it was a real time of togetherness and the staff worked very well together. You know at that time, as nurses, we just didn't think anything of how we felt. I didn't. I don't know what the others felt. But we were doing our duty, we were nurses and I suppose we just felt we were doing our duty and working and helping other people.

Curfew

Throughout the occupation there were restrictions on civilian movement. Military zones around the coast were closed to civilians and there was a night-time curfew. Stiffer curfew conditions were also used, from time to time, as a form of communal punishment. Towards the end of 1940, all radios were called in from all islands as a reprisal for the assistance given to two Guernsey escapees. The radios were handed back in December 1940 only to be removed again in 1942. Everyone was aware of the importance of radios for morale. Instructions for building a 'crystal set' were dropped by the RAF.

Brenda Hervé, née Quevâtre, assistant nurse, Emergency Hospital, Guernsey, c.1940–5

Curfew could be nine o'clock, but it was mostly ten. We were punished, if someone escaped by fishing boat or the Guernsey people cut wires or did something. The whole island was punished with an early curfew for a while and then they would change it back to ten o'clock. We had to make sure if we were out anywhere at the other end of the island that we'd leave in time.

Florence Jouan, St John Ambulance member and assistant nurse, Jersey, 1940–5

The curfew did not deter fit young people from living their lives to the full.

I remember once, a friend of mine, well we were gleaning out at St Brelade's because we were really hungry, and on the way back her [bicycle] chain broke and it wasn't long till curfew. Now she lived at Le Bourg, St Clement's, and I lived at Le Bourg, Grouville, just below Boulivot. 'Oh,' she said, 'what am I going to do?' 'Well,' I said, 'there is only one thing to do.' I had a carrier; I said, 'Put your hand on my carrier and I'll go with you as far as your house.' 'But,' she said, 'you'll never be home by curfew.' I said, 'Never mind me, I'll get you home first.' So I got her home, and by this time it was pitch dark and I managed well until I went to pass Radier Manor. Then near Radier Manor it was pitch dark and somebody suddenly shouted, 'Halt, halt' and the louder he shouted 'halt' the quicker I cycled. I don't think I ever cycled so fast in all of my life, and as soon as I got home I locked the door and sat almost fainting on a chair waiting for the Germans, but they never came.

Fun

✚

Cathy Minty, née Mollet, student nurse, Jersey, 1940–5

The camaraderie amongst the medical community was very important to this close-knit group; even years later, Cathy Minty remembered Mr Halliwell's morale-boosting efforts in particular.

Mr Halliwell was our surgeon, also very overworked and quite wonderful, caring about the nurses. He started up a social club for us and we had an occasional dance in our dining room. Rounding up enough men was a bit of a problem, but Mr Halliwell, better known as ACH, would turn up. He also organised with a friend, Mrs Gruchy from Ronceville, now Howard Davis Park, a wonderful dinner for all the nurses. One evening after duty we were all transported in ambulances to Ronceville. Mrs Gruchy had employed a chef and obtained some black market pork and some delightful meringues. It was the highlight of the occupation.

Cathy (Kathleen) Minty, née Mollet, was on duty when the liberating forces arrived with chocolate for patients and nurses.

Brenda Hervé, née Quevâtre, assistant nurse, Emergency Hospital, Guernsey, c.1940–5

We made our own fun because we were in our teens. We enjoyed ourselves. I'd leave the hospital at eight o'clock to cycle a mile or two to go to a dance, and sometimes we weren't allowed to go without an evening dress. So I had three evening dresses that I borrowed from a cousin. And I used to tuck the bottom of my dress right up here, tied it up, and it was pouring with rain and I had an old plastic mac full of tiny little holes. But I went, and I was only there really for about half an hour and then I had to come back to the hospital, you know, because of the curfew.

Christmas we would have a party with the doctors and the nurses at the hospital. We would invite other people to come but of course they wouldn't be able to go back home because of the curfew so they used to sleep in one big room somewhere; they would make, you know, the best of it. I was taught to dance. I could never dance before I was a nurse, but the male nurses taught me to dance.

Deportation

Several individuals were deported following various escapades which annoyed or inconvenienced the occupying power. Some eventually returned, but others disappeared into the network of camps on the European mainland. Some died in concentration camps.

In October 1940, the Germans requested a list of all foreigners in the Channel Islands. This drew the attention of the German authorities to Thérèse Steiner, originally from Austria, now working as a much-liked and able young assistant nurse in the Emergency Hospital in Guernsey. Thérèse's family had Jewish associations and she had left Austria around the time of the *Anschluss*. On reaching Britain, she found employment as an au pair. Her employers took her with them to the Channel Islands on an extended family visit. At the time of the evacuation, the family returned to Britain, but, as an enemy alien, Thérèse was not permitted to go with them. She settled into life in Guernsey and found work as an assistant nurse in the Emergency Hospital. Both Thérèse and Gustie Spitz, another 'alien' who worked as a ward maid in the Emergency Hospital, were deported to Germany. Both were sent to Auschwitz, where they died.

Late in 1942, all residents who had not been born in the Channel Islands were to be deported to Germany in retaliation for the arrest of German citizens by the British in Iran in 1941. The feeling of impotence and distress felt by their fellow citizens can hardly be imagined.

Florence Jouan, St John Ambulance member and assistant nurse, Jersey, 1940–5

Oh yes, we watched and oh we were all so upset. Some of us were in tears to see all these people going. And then all of a sudden we saw a couple, an elderly couple in a trap driving with their coachman, and they were looking as though they were going on holiday. Oh they really made it; you almost wanted to cheer them. The courage in their faces and they looked as if they wanted to send the Germans to a very hot place, you know. And then some while later we saw them coming back, and someone from the crowd shouted, 'Why didn't you go on the boat?' So they pointed to their white hair ... oh but, you know, the courage of those people.

Some of the St John Ambulance nursing members went over with the deportees, they deserved a medal because they were crossing the sea and they didn't know if they were going to be torpedoed, they didn't know if the planes would attack them and they just went with the deportees as far as St Malo.

Slave labourers

The massive German Atlantic Wall defences were continued around the islands' coasts. These huge structures were built by Organisation Todt using mostly Soviet prisoners of war as forced labour. Fritz Todt was the engineer responsible for the successful construction of the autobahn network in Germany and went on to found the notorious Third Reich engineering firm that bore his name.

The islanders were very aware of these unfortunate men. They were not always locked up securely at night and were often out foraging for food. Several islanders attempted to assist them as far as they could.

Bunty Le Seelleur, student nurse, Jersey, 1940–5

I was in the nursery, I was in charge of the sick children's nursery for some time. At midnight we used to go to each other's wards to have a little chat and that sort of thing, and [one night] we had got the bread and butter all ready for the morning and when we came back of course the bread and butter had gone, the Russian prisoners had come to take it.

Beatrice Le Huquet, school teacher, Jersey, 1940

I didn't actually see the slave labourers. But my sister and brother-in-law went cycling one day and they lost their way and found themselves in the midst of a camp and they were horrified and sickened to see the state of the prisoners. They had rags around their feet, which were bleeding, they were helping themselves to soup which had been brought to them in dustbins. Their clothes were in tatters.

Cathy Minty, née Mollet, student nurse, Jersey, 1940–5

Night duty was a bit scary as lights were dimmed and at times we had to guard our precious food against prowling little Russians from the sick bay at the back of the hospital [that had been] taken over by the Todt workers.

Deteriorating conditions

⊕

Once the Allied forces landed in Normandy, Channel Islanders were confident that the war was nearing an end. However, the Allies chose to bypass the immense fortifications in the islands, leaving around 25,500 enemy troops blockaded in their rear. The consequence for the islanders was increasing discomfort and even starvation. No more supplies arrived from France after the end of August 1944. Coal stocks were depleted; there was no gas in Jersey after 4 September 1944 and in effect no electricity. Nurses were working by candle- and lanternlight.

Betty Thurban, née Le Corre, student nurse, General Hospital, Jersey

I have a very vivid memory of the night the wounded were brought in from St Malo.* We heard from a nurse on the German wards that there was trouble and that they were expecting a number of patients in. I was going off duty just before eight o'clock and they had bodies on the floor everywhere and all round the rotunda on each floor. [Mr Halliwell] asked if he could help and they said no, and finally they gave him an American, and he took him to surgery, to the little operating theatre which was at the back of the hospital.

Brenda Hervé, née Quevâtre, assistant nurse, Emergency Hospital, Guernsey, c.1944

The worst thing was towards the end when there was hardly any food. My mother was twelve stone when the war broke out and she was seven stone when it finished.

---

* Wounded Axis soldiers were evacuated to the Channel Islands on 4 August 1944.

Mary Le Sueur, née Jouny, nursing sister, General Hospital and Les Vaux convalescent hospital, Jersey, c.1944

It was 1944 I think when they really became short of drugs and there was talk of someone going over [to France], that was after the British and North Americans had bombed the north of France. But fortunately for us the *Vega* [the Red Cross ship] came over with medical supplies in 1944.

Ann Baudains, née Thomas, staff nurse, Overdale Isolation Hospital, Jersey, 1945

Well of course, the last four months of the war was the worst. I was on night duty and in charge at night. We had no lights, I had a hurricane lamp that I was told only to put on in an emergency. There was no heating at all in the wards. I could only give the patients who were very ill extra blankets. My food was kept warm in a hay box. The food consisted of vegetables usually. On my rounds I used to go and feel for the patients' pulse to see if they were still alive, the very ill ones. I used to have to lay them out by just the light of the hurricane lamp. And I had eight deaths in that last four months of the war. It was a small hospital, I mean usually around about sixty or seventy patients I suppose, except during the epidemics when of course we had a lot more.

Betty Thurban, née Le Corre, student nurse, General Hospital, Jersey, c.1942

There are two things I remember especially. Because Averell Darling was in Overdale [as a patient], Mr Halliwell had to come in and live in the hospital … The electricity went off, so we had two candles a night for each ward; if you were busy that was all you had.

I have one very vivid memory. About ten o'clock you used to go to the night sister for your tray of drugs for your patients, this was Dangerous Drugs. I went down one night and we had the morphine tablets which had to have water added. I was carrying this tray, walking about like

Florence Nightingale with my lamp, and all of a sudden, at the top of a longish corridor, there was a bright light and it shone straight down. There was nobody else except the Germans who had a lamp like that, so I was furious and I said, 'For goodness' sake put that bloody light out', to which a very Arthur Halliwell voice said, 'Nurse Le Corre, please don't speak like that.' He was laughing like mad. And I said to him, 'What are you doing with that light?' And he said, 'Ah, that's my secret weapon.' He was doing his rounds.

As night nurses, we had one night a week off, and you used to try not to have Saturday night off. People used to get paid on Friday night and anyone requiring an abortion would go to the abortionist so that by Saturday night they were ready to be admitted to hospital for surgery. The theatre staff used to get everything going, possibly [Mr Halliwell] would come in. Everybody would go as slowly as possible, particularly in the clearing-up stage, because theatre had to be ready for more cases [and for as long as we were working there was heat and lighting]. They [the Germans] used to keep the lights going until four o'clock in the morning for us. [Mr Halliwell] and Averell Darling would help like mad with the night staff in keeping things going. It was terrible working without any light.

Red Cross parcels
and the *Vega*

Following negotiations via the protecting power, agreement was reached for the dispatch of a Red Cross ship from Lisbon in December 1944. The *Vega* had a Swedish master; it delivered supplies to Jersey and Guernsey late in December 1944. The conditions attached to the supply of this relief included careful policing and supervision of the unloading and distribution of the supplies, which were exclusively for the civilian population. The Germans observed these conditions scrupulously at the unloading places. It was later that individuals stole supplies.

The Red Cross parcels delivered to the Channel Islands were provided free of charge by the Red Cross in Canada and New Zealand. In Jersey, the St John Ambulance were involved in sorting the parcels and issuing them to civilians.

Ann Baudains, née Thomas, staff nurse, Overdale Isolation Hospital, Jersey, 1945

Vega was wonderful, oh that was one of the best things that happened towards the end of the war. I can remember eating a whole tin of Nestlé's milk. Just imagine eating a whole tin of Nestlé's milk! Horrible! But I thought it was wonderful at that time.

Eileen Picot, assistant nurse, Jersey, 1945

When the Red Cross parcels came, of course, it was absolutely terrific, I never had to waken up at night with hunger pains. Some of us in fact felt rather sick if we ate too much, too soon.

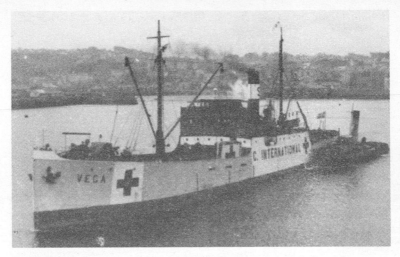

The Red Cross vessel *Vega* laden with Red Cross parcels in St Peter Port, Guernsey, December 1944.

Cathy Minty, née Mollet, student nurse, Jersey, 1945

The arrival of the Red Cross ship the *Vega* was a very great day. I remember going up on to the hospital roof to see her coming in – a wonderful moment.

I think the tins of Spam were marvellous and a tin of marmalade too because we didn't have oranges. Sugar, the cream, Klim [dried milk], was lovely to have, and of course we would eat it by the spoonful though we weren't so deprived of milk as we might have been.

Florence Jouan, St John Ambulance member and assistant nurse, Jersey, 1945

We really worked hard. Now the Canadian parcels were fine because the cardboard was thick. But the New Zealand parcels sometimes were absolutely broken up and it used to break our hearts, us who were hungry, to see the trampling on some of this foodstuff that had fallen out of these New Zealand parcels, you know.

Brenda Hervé, née Quevâtre, assistant nurse, Emergency Hospital, Guernsey, 1945

Regulations may have been respected within sight of the Red Cross officials, but once the civilians had left with their parcels, all sorts could happen.

My mother-in-law had hers, she had walked to town with an old pram to collect her Red Cross parcels, it would have been three, and she had just arrived home, and she had difficulty walking, when a German came and took them all from her.

I used to go with my brother on the tandem and he would have two parcels on the front handlebars and I would have two on the back. We cycled from St Martin down to St Vincent. But we had to hide them.

Liberation

Ann Baudains, née Thomas, staff nurse, Overdale Isolation Hospital, Jersey, 1945

Liberation is still celebrated in Jersey and Guernsey on 9 May, three days later than VE Day was celebrated on the mainland.

Oh it was exciting, because I was asleep in bed when war was finally over and one of the young junior nurses knocked on my door and pushed a note under the door. I've still got it in my room actually. To say that [Admiral] Dönitz, was it? had surrendered and the war was over! So I got up, put my Welsh flag out on the flat roof of the nurses' home and went with the other nurses down to the gun emplacement, which of course, before, we had been 'verboten' to go near. This high-ranking German officer came up to me and told me to go away, it was 'verboten' to be here, and I told him, look, the English are coming, pointed to the destroyer coming round the point, aye aye he said, and turned away. And we had a great big bell and, you know, our flags and it was wonderful, just wonderful.

Eileen Picot, assistant nurse, Jersey, 1945

A thing I shall never forget, of course, is Liberation Day. On that day I was on night duty and I was supposed to be sleeping, but of course I didn't sleep at all. I was on the pier to welcome the Royal Navy bringing the British army. We all rushed to put our arms around the Tommies … and I remember Colonel Robinson was carried shoulder high, there was no marching [for him], and he stood at the door of the hotel and he thanked us for the warm welcome that we had given him. And he said, 'I have given the German commandant my orders.' Well, the roars and the laughter went on and on and on. If you can imagine when you have had to take everything from a soldier or the authorities and if you didn't you had a gun pointed at you, you will understand our reaction.

For the whole of the liberation festivities, I went out every day and you would see one local person and a whole crowd of British soldiers and we would ask them, 'Do you know so and so? Do you know so and so?' Of course it was so stupid but we thought, you know, they would know everything.

When these DUKWs [amphibious craft] came up the beach at St Aubin we had never seen anything like it. And a destroyer waiting in the bay and the British arriving in these 'Duck' things, first of all they were on water then on dry land, we couldn't believe our eyes. And the wonderful days that followed ... I shall never forget them for the rest of my life.

Beatrice Le Huquet, school teacher, Jersey, 1945

The Le Huquet family shared in the rejoicing, but like many citizens they were physically weakened.

On the morning of Liberation Day, not one German was to be seen, they had disappeared into their tunnels. Father and brother-in-law prepared our Union Jack to hoist it as soon as I indicated that I heard Sir Winston Churchill's words, 'our beloved Channel Islands are about to be liberated'. This came over my crystal set, my sister and I raised our arms as a signal and up the flagpole went our Union Jack flag, a pleasant and welcome sight after the German flag with the hideous black swastika. Greatly relieved, we sang our national anthem, 'God Save the King'.

We managed to cycle into St Helier on Liberation Day when General, I think Snow, spoke. My cycle was in good condition because I had it hidden behind barrels in one of the sheds and occasionally I saw that the tyres were pumped up and kept in good condition. I borrowed a cycle from our next-door neighbour and there was a rubber tubing instead of a tyre. We joined the crowd but we did not stay long because my sister was unable to stand for long, you know; we were weak for lack of proper food.

Cathy Minty, née Mollet, student nurse, Jersey, 1945

Cathy Minty was one of the Jersey girls who began her training during the occupation.

Then that great day 9 May 1945 … I was on duty when the troops arrived, but within a very short time our soldiers were walking through the wards handing out soap, toothpaste, chocolate and cigarettes. We were all hugging and kissing them. They had a wonderful time as the celebrations which followed were quite fantastic.

I went down with Sister Renouard with empty Red Cross boxes collecting for the Red Cross. Everyone was most generous, getting rid of their Reichmarks, and we collected near on £1,000. We were on a high for days afterwards. With all the excitement, I remember losing my voice with all the cheering.

Mr Halliwell arranged for a photograph to be taken of all the staff of the Jersey General Hospital before they dispersed. It was much to the credit of this hospital team that medical services kept going throughout the occupation and that Jersey-trained nurses were presented for the GNC examination in the autumn of 1945.

Now that the war was over, the rebuilding and restaffing of the hospitals became the focus of attention. It was even more of an urgent issue in Guernsey than it was in Jersey, since Guernsey had seen far more of its population evacuated to the mainland. The Guernsey authorities approached the St John Ambulance with a request for help. Four qualified Canadian St John nurses came to Guernsey to assist with the rebuilding of services.

Above: The entire medical and nursing staff of the General Hospital. Jersey, June 1945.

1939-1945

PRAISE GOD
REMEMBERING
THOSE NURSES FROM
THIS HOSPITAL WHO
GAVE THEIR LIVES
FOR THEIR
COUNTRY

After the conflict, reflection and mourning led to respect and gratitude towards war-time nurses. Some local memorials were constructed and a nurses' chapel consecrated in Westminster Abbey.

TEN

BEGINNING AGAIN

One thing that I always feel a little bit guilty about, I've got a whole row of medals to show I've been in the army but I think the women who worked in the civilian hospitals at home had a tougher time than I had.

Agnes Barnett, Territorial Army Nursing Service

The war ended in 1945, but the aftermath would take years to resolve. Europe, the Middle East and the Far East were littered with camps filled with displaced persons, many of them ill and with very little hope. Some wanted to return immediately to the country they had left or been driven from. Others saw their homeland in the hands of an occupying power whose ambitions filled them with fear. Participants on all sides of the conflict, from former prisoners of war to traumatised ex-combatants, from returning evacuees to harried nurses and health visitors, faced an uncertain future.

The tumultuous six years of the war had completely reshaped the lives of thousands of nurses. There had been loss, suffering and huge amounts of hard work, but also an accumulation of experience and confidence that would prove invaluable as British society struggled to rebuild itself. Careers now had to be reviewed and reshaped and energy found to begin again. These were the people who must build the post-war world.

There was a palpable feeling of anticipation and hope, with many people now expecting to share in the fruits of victory. This was typified by the results of the general election of July 1945, in which special arrangements were made for the armed services to vote. A socialist government was returned with a mandate to nationalise key industries such as mining, steel and transport. Most excitingly of all for nurses were plans to create a health service for all citizens. The dream of the NHS, excellent care for all who needed it, free at the point of delivery, was set to become a reality.

Nurses such as Kathleen Raven, who had spent the war years working in Barts and its sector hospitals, went on to crucial roles influencing policy at the highest level. The spirit of idealism was personified in Mary Abbot, who entered nursing in the immediate aftermath of war because she saw it as the surest way to help in the nation's reconstruction.

For the tens of thousands of nurses who served their country during World War II, their war-time experiences remained vivid for the rest of their lives.

When they were asked about those times years later, their stories were filled with the struggle and courage that got them, and their patients, through some of the darkest times in the nation's history.

The refugees

Some refugee nurses were able to build a satisfying new life in the country where they had ended up. A tiny number of them found family members they never thought they would see again.

Rosa Sacharin, née Goldschal, staff nurse, Royal Hospital for Sick Children, Yorkhill, Glasgow, 1945

Rosa Sacharin's father was taken away by the Gestapo in 1935. She and her sister arrived on the Kindertransport in December 1938 after their mother took the courageous decision to let her children go alone into an unknown foreign country. When the war finished, Rosa and her sister were uncertain about their legal standing in Scotland but were working hard at their careers when in early 1946 they received amazing news.

I received two letters from Germany. One was from an American soldier and one from a British soldier and they told us that 'a woman who said she was your mother has asked us to write to you to say that she is alive. Her general state is very poor and if [you] want to send parcels to [her we will] make sure she gets them.'

That was the first we heard that she had survived. Well after that, my mother wrote to us and she said on no account will she remain in Germany. We had to do something.

We then wrote to the commandant in Berlin of the British sector and asked him to allow my mother to come over. It took a long time, a lot of bureaucracy, and my sister and I had to guarantee that we would look after her and she would not be allowed to work while here. And of course, that's what we did. My mother arrived eventually in February 1947.

I was very intrigued about her story, I wanted to know how she survived, how was it possible?

At the end of the war there were only about 1,000 Jews left in Berlin, Berlin which had a Jewish population of 160,000 before the war. The majority of these Jews were actually hidden by Germans, but my mother wasn't.

Her story starts off when the Jews were the first slave workers in Germany. My mother was working in a poison gas factory in Berlin and while there she had a haematemesis, must have been quite a severe one and she was taken to hospital; the hospital was St Hedwig in Berlin.

The Nazis were constantly looking for Jews; the hospitals were searched and the nurse in that hospital, realising that the Gestapo were coming, took my mother out of bed, put a nursing gown on her and sat her in a room and told her to clean instruments, and when the man came, the nurse opened the door and said, this is one of our helpers. He was quite satisfied and just walked out.

That nurse saved her.

The important point there is, the medical superintendent was against the Nazis and his order was 'no Jewish patient will be handed over to the Gestapo'. When my mother left the hospital, she was safe.

She then decided that she would go into hiding and wrote a letter stating that she was committing suicide, left everything that she had and went what they called 'underground'. She also then started what I called the 'black market thing'; because, of course, she had to earn her living somehow. She knew her Berlin very well and she knew where there were smallholdings where she could get a chicken, potatoes, things like that. She sold these things and got money, so that she could survive.

It wasn't just the Nazis she had to watch. There were Jewish informers; these people were promised that their families would be saved, though they weren't. One day my mother was coming down the stairs and met a woman who asked her, does (my mother's name) live here? My mother said, 'Oh, I am a stranger here, I don't know who lives here.' She knew who that woman was.

My mother was in Berlin during the last days and the hand-to-hand fighting between the Soviet forces and the remnants of the German army.

The Russians were really vicious; she kept hiding and she waited until the elite Soviet troops came in. When they arrived, she was looking for a Jewish face and she stopped a car and she said to this man, *baruch habaa*, which is Hebrew for blessed is your coming.

He looked at her, and he said, 'You are alive!' He couldn't believe it, that there were any Jews left. He had come through Poland, he had seen what had happened there, and here was this little woman, greeting him in Hebrew. And he protected her because he recognised that what the Russian troops were doing was evil. They sought revenge and the revenge was actually on the German women; they really suffered. But that's what they do, soldiers, and they were angry with what had happened.

Rosa's mother was alerted to the imminent closure of the Russian sector by her Russian contact. Getting recognition as a Jew in the British sector proved to be difficult. Her position was unusual and she had no papers.

There were a whole lot of people claiming to be Jews, so she had difficulty, but during the days that she was living in hiding, she supported some Jews who had escaped from the labour camps and were also in hiding. Because they couldn't speak German they were in constant danger. She managed to get food for them and helped to protect them, and one of these men wrote out an affidavit to say that she was Jewish … it's a tremendous story actually.

Later, when she was with us, she received a letter … After the war they had what they called 'de-Nazification' tribunals where any German who could show that they had not been a Nazi would be able to get work. This man had claimed that he saved Jews and therefore was entitled to be de-Nazified. There was a huge form to fill in and I sat [and did it] with her and most of it was innocent enough and there was no difficulty in answering. And then it came to the question 'Did he ever demand money from you?' And my mother said … 'Money! He demanded gold.'

And she sat and there was silence and it was a long, long, long, long struggle. I said to her, what will I write, and she looked at me and she said,

'Achh, let him be. Just say no.' She said, 'There has been enough killing.'

Rosa Sacharin's education was disrupted by her move from Germany. However, she was supported by the City of Glasgow Corporation and earned her School Leaving Certificate. She trained in nursing at Yorkhill children's hospital in Glasgow, and enjoyed a full and rewarding career. She qualified as a tutor, and wrote a textbook of paediatric nursing. Since retiring, she has been involved in recording an oral history of Yorkhill hospital.

Edith Bown, née Jacobovitz, Jewish refugee, student nurse, Newtownards Hospital, 1942–5

Edith Bown never forgot her promise to her parents to look after her younger brother Gert. Despite the heartbreaking loss they had experienced, they continued to look after each other, and Edith went on to support Gert in his education.

Then of course during my training I had the last letter from my mother through the Red Cross, 'I must go now, we won't see each other again, have a good life. Go to the hairdresser sometime. Love Mum' … kind of thing. And my father writing to my brother, 'get your hair cut, look decent, be smart'. And we didn't tell each other for six months, so the other wouldn't know, that this was the final thing, you see.

Her experiences as a young woman and a student nurse shaped Edith Bown's views of life.

I have only had one baby, because I was a refugee. I thought, I can tuck the baby under my arm and have a rucksack but I wouldn't be able to carry two babies, so … one it was.

   You see, I still think the most important part is food. So however hard up I ever was or we were, food is always the most … well it has to be, hasn't it? [My grandson] rang up because I send him a food voucher for Marks and Spencer every month. So that he can get what he wants …

Esta Lefton, née Guttman, Jewish refugee, nurse, ATS, posted with Allied troops, Italy, c.1945

The confusion of the immediate post-war period put obstacles in the way of Esta Lefton, who wished to complete her training in Britain.

From the army, the release was according to age group. When the war ended, I was twenty-four and a half. They always used to say in the hospital, particularly the director of medical services and the matron, 'There's a shortage of nurses, why don't you go to England?'

But my Polish passport was stolen, I couldn't go to England without a passport because I couldn't get a visa, and I couldn't go from Italy straight to England, so instead I had to go back to Jerusalem. I went back in August 1946.

In Jerusalem, Esta made contact with her family. She worked in a mental hospital for a very short time as conditions were so appalling. She witnessed some of the traumatic events in the tense situation in Palestine. However, using the contacts she had made during the war, she was able to find a job with a British army dentist. After getting her passport and visa sorted out, she came to London and worked in the London Jewish Hospital in Stepney. Here she resumed her nurse training. As she had preserved the certificates she had earned during various placements during the war, she was not required to begin her training again from scratch.

Many of the refugees who became nurses remained in Britain and followed their careers here. The contribution they made to British nursing has been significant.

After an inspirational experience as a psychiatric nurse at the Maudsley during the war, Annie Altschul completed a degree at Birkbeck College of the University of London and qualified as a nurse teacher. She was later one of the first British nurses to be awarded a doctorate, and the University of Edinburgh appointed her the first professor of mental health nursing in Britain.

Lisbeth Hockey pursued her fascination with research and her interest in community nursing. In 1971 she was appointed the first director of the national nursing research unit in the University of Edinburgh. Her contributions to community nursing were valued by other professionals internationally. The Queen's Nursing Institute awarded her a special gold medal, the Royal College of General Practitioners made her an honorary member, and she was awarded an honorary doctorate by the University of Uppsala, Sweden.

Charlotte Kratz qualified as a general nurse at St Thomas' in London. Her interests later focused on research and community nursing. In the 1950s she was involved in the development of a district nursing scheme in Dar es Salaam, Tanzania. Back in Britain and together with 'Poppy' Bocock, then senior tutor, she developed a pioneering role as a public health tutor in the Royal Free Hospital School of Nursing. She had an interest in the politics of nursing and wrote regularly in the *Nursing Times*.

Lisbeth Hockey, awarded an honorary degree from the University of Uppsala.

Moving on

The war affected individuals differently. War experience encouraged nurses to use their initiative at work, and take responsibility. Often the prospect of returning to nursing in a traditional, hierarchical hospital setting was not appealing. Norma Batley and Agnes Barnett were both attracted to public health and the work of the health visitor.

Norma Batley, health visitor, later director of the Health Visitor Training Council, c.1947

I was interested in preventative medicine. I knew a health visitor and she had some influence on me, and then I thought this makes sense to me. This makes sense so, after midwifery, I did my health visitor course; it was only six months in those days. Had a high old time there, one or two in my set who were equally exuberant in our youth, and we used to argue the toss about the great affairs of the world. I remember of course it was just after the war, '47, and we were still of course on rationing and we had great freeze-ups, there wasn't any fuel, quite a lot of hardship in those training days, but there we are. So I went on the beat as a health visitor in Surrey and really I could have done with an awful lot of help, and I see now, having been the director of the Health Visitor Training Council, that the ideas these days are so very much better.

Agnes Barnett, student health visitor, c.1945

After a challenging war in the Middle East, Agnes Barnett undertook health visitor training.

My first post was health visiting, visiting mothers and babies, family care. They said that once the '48 Act came in, you treated the whole family –

the grandmothers and the aunts – but you always did! You couldn't ignore the grandmother if she was sitting in the corner, and probably she was minding the children; you definitely had to take notice of her and see that the mums took notice of her too.

Usually I got on very well with them. You would stand chatting and in that immediate post-war period there was a lot of 'What were you doing?' and I'd say, 'I was overseas during the war.' 'What was it like?' and it broke the ice. You didn't explain that you had done this, that and the other, been here and there, you said you were glad to be home.

Monica Baly, PMRAFNS, later health visitor, c.1946

Although she had enjoyed life in the services, Monica Baly also headed for the health visitor role and a career in public health. However, when the Foreign Office was looking for a chief nursing officer to the Displaced Persons Division in the British zone of Germany, the secretary to the public health section of the RCN urged her to apply.

The government had not had a chief nursing officer in the British zone of Germany for a year. United Nations Relief and Rehabilitation Administration (UNRRA) had packed up and gone home, but they were still left with a quarter of a million displaced persons in camps in Germany. The Foreign Office were all in favour of letting the whole thing run down, but they were being monitored by the International Relief Organisation, which sat in Geneva, which had kicked up a lot of fuss and had insisted that they appoint a chief nursing officer.

So I was duly interviewed at the Foreign Office, a very friendly affair. I saw my interview notes afterwards, which simply read, 'Monica Baly is just the job.'

Now why I was 'just the job' was that I wasn't going to be a challenge. One of the people who'd applied was Evelyn Pearce,* and they wanted

---

* Evelyn Pearce was a distinguished nurse tutor at the Middlesex Hospital and author of a standard textbook.

somebody junior who would not cause any trouble.

The [displaced people] left [were] mostly what was known in the parlance of the day as the 'hard core'. UNRRA and the first wave of repatriation had gone. The nurses had been resettled because nurses are easy to resettle. There was a worldwide shortage of nurses, and they went to Canada, the States, and a lot went to Australia.

I consulted with the one nurse that was left there from UNRRA, and we decided that we needed to get a British nurse into each region, to go for a public health programme, and to try and have a public health nurse in every camp.

The only thing, it seemed to me, would be to train German nurses, and this of course was anathema to the DPs [displaced persons], and to the Foreign Office. After some unseemly set-tos with my medical officer, I went to London to plead my case, and apply for five British nursing officers, and for permission to train German nurses.

I knew I was treading on eggshells. However, I got permission and I was very lucky. Those five, they were good, many of them went on into the World Health Organisation. We chose people who were health visitors and most of them spoke some German.

The next thing was to train German nurses. I got permission to start a school of nursing in Hanover. We recruited a German matron who had been in the military in Germany, and she was an absolute tower of strength and helped me recruit German nurses. They queued up, because they all wanted jobs. We took them in for a six-week course at a time. It was a success, they were a great success in the camps, and many of them stayed after we left in 1950 when the Germans took over the camps.

After this resounding success, Monica Baly was recruited by the RCN as their south-west area officer. She remained in this post until she retired. In retirement she completed one of the first doctorates in the history of nursing.

Mary Abbott, conscripted into the ATS, Royal Corps of Signals, working on code-breaking, 1939–46

Mary Abbott was not a nurse during the war, but she had a very demanding war working on code-breaking with the Royal Corps of Signals. When she was demobilised, she saw nursing as the one occupation which offered her a definite opportunity to contribute to make life better for people.

I think it was in August 1946 that I was sent back to Britain and demobilised. The war was so devastating for those of us who lived through it that when it was over, our aim was to make life better for everybody.

Mary Abbott's career led her to the World Health Organisation.

I decided that I would like to go to St George's Hospital and I began my training in October 1946. I can only tell you that it is a happy memory for me. The memory of good friends, of really remarkable experiences; but a feeling that we were doing something useful, I think that was probably what motivated us and it gave us courage.

Ever curious and very able, in the post-war world Mary Abbott became involved with nursing on a global platform. She completed her midwifery, and then went to Canada for wider experience. Here she completed a nursing degree. Following work in the Canadian north, she applied for a job with the World Health Organisation (WHO). For the remainder of her career she worked determinedly for nursing and the work of nurses in the WHO throughout the world.

Nurses, nursing and the National Health Service

The National Health Service (NHS) was introduced into Britain with great optimism in 1948.

The nursing and medical staff who had worked so hard to make the EMS schemes work found that some of the suspicions that had existed in the pre-war health service had been smoothed away. Municipal and voluntary hospital staff had found they could work together. Some younger doctors had found that earning a salary could be a more comfortable way of making a living than pursuing outstanding bills from impoverished patients. Most nurses welcomed the new health service. District nurses no longer had the embarrassment of seeking payment from their patients, and they were now in a position to urge those patients to consult their doctor and dentist to seek help with the common but debilitating disorders they suffered from.

To make the new service work, the government had to placate traditional power groups. The most influential of these was the doctors. Compared to their medical colleagues, the nurses posed no threat and, although they were the largest group of employees in the proposed NHS, nurses were not represented on any of the major planning committees convened to design the service. What is more, all the problems that had faced nursing in the first half of the century continued. There were not enough nurses, the heavy domestic work remained and the petty disciplines persisted.

A dramatic illustration of the irritations nurses might expect to confront was reported in the press in November 1948, when 600 student nurses from hospitals in the East End of London threatened to resign. On opening their pay packets they found that their pay had unexpectedly been reduced. The explanation was simple. Following the introduction of the NHS, nurses became eligible to pay National Insurance contributions. In June 1948 there had been agreement between the government and negotiators from the nursing unions and the RCN that nurses should have an increase of £15 per annum as an interim payment. However, this money was not in the November pay packets and the ministry had not informed student nurses that it had been made available.

Some changes were beginning to emerge. A new group of male nurses began to appear. War-time work persuaded some of the male orderlies that nursing could be a satisfying career for them. Those who had obtained certificates in the course of their war-time work could take advantage of a shortened programme of nurse training, something that brought men into a new field of work. They did not usually have to be resident in a nurses' home, enabling them to side-step some of the irritations experienced by female recruits. However, the public still sometimes found it difficult to believe in men as nurses.

David Proctor, student nurse, St Mary's Hospital, Highgate, 1947–9

I'd made enquiries about training to be a nurse because while I was in the services I liked the idea. I used to ask the advice of the QAs I worked with, and they said, 'Well yes, we have male nurses.' But I think most of the male nurses were in mental nursing then and I didn't want to do that because I thought they'd eat me!

So I made enquiries to the London County Council and yes, they were training male nurses. You know, after the war men were coming out from the forces who wanted to do nurse training, so they probably had to fit us in somewhere. So it was St Mary's Hospital, Highgate, for my training.

Arthur Brompton, community staff nurse, c.1945

Arthur Brompton qualified as a Queen's nurse. Even much later in life, he was still in touch with some of his patients.

One of my first district patients had a rectal operation, so it was a big dressing to do and he was told that a district nurse would be calling tomorrow. He once told me, 'I can always remember when you first came to see me. The doorbell went and I said, oh, it's the nurse. I opened the door and there was no nurse there at all, it was a man!

'And you said: "I'm Mr Brompton, I'm the district nurse." I couldn't speak for a moment.'

That happened quite a lot in a way, but I was accepted; I was never, never, never ever turned away.

Unsurprisingly, the NHS had innumerable teething problems. The scale of the task of integrating the scattered provision of health care across the voluntary and local government sectors was daunting. Despite the fact that the mass of expertise held by nurses was consistently undervalued, many senior nurses were instrumental in powering the work of the early NHS. Their loyalty to the fledgling institution was remarkable. The matrons of hospitals were often very competent women and a particularly crucial resource. However, traditional practices in nursing fuelled tension in some situations. The matrons of the major teaching hospitals were accustomed to wielding power within their domain and appointing the next generation of senior nurses without question.

Ivy Scott had been a respected matron of Halifax Royal Infirmary for the entire war. She was, of course, aware of the new National Health Service, and when planning the next phase of her career she discussed her options with Frances Goodall, general secretary of the RCN, and Dame Catherine Watt, chief nurse in the Department of Health. She was appointed to a post in the Ministry of Health, as regional nursing officer for Oxford region in the new NHS. She received very limited guidance or preparation for her new job, where she was particularly involved in inspecting and trying to help those hospitals now included in the NHS that had been Poor Law institutions. She was astonished to discover that some of these institutions were still run by married couples holding 'matron and master' appointments as they had in the old Poor Law days.

Ivy Scott, matron of Royal Halifax Infirmary, 1939–48; regional nurse for Oxford region, Department of Health, 1948

I never had a job description. I made my first effort to make myself known to the regional board and got their permission to visit the hospitals; I got this quite willingly as long as I notified them in advance. Then I went further afield and began introducing myself to the secretaries and the matrons in the region. What I discovered was the shocking state of the chronic sick hospitals when I began to visit them. So much depended on getting on with people.

Kathleen Raven, assistant matron, St Bartholomew's Hospital; matron, Leeds General Infirmary; Chief Nursing Officer, 1958–72

After a very demanding war in the Barts sector, Kathleen Raven decided to branch out and head to Leeds. She went on to a stellar career.

I went back to Barts as assistant matron. From there I went to Leeds in 1948, which Miss Dey, matron of Barts, didn't like very much. When I told her I was going to apply she was furious, furious. She threw her gloves at me and said, 'Get out, get into the provinces, that's the place for you.'

To give her her due, she sent for me to go back and she apologised, and I found out later from my house governor in Leeds that she gave me a most marvellous reference. But she was annoyed.

With her allies on the staff of the Leeds General Infirmary, Kathleen Raven built up a top-class school of nursing and a hospital with a very good reputation.

We built it up, improved the training, got the whole place decorated, got portions sectioned off in the wards for individual patients, we got a new block built. It was really terrific, marvellous. I had a wonderful time there.

Kathleen Raven was involved constructively in nursing politics, and in 1957 she was appointed deputy chief nurse in the Department of Health. A year later she was

Kathleen Raven, one of the most able of post-war nurses.

chief nurse, a post she remained in for fourteen years. In this post she was in a position to influence policy.

I went to the Department [of Health] in '57 after the tremendous things we'd done in Leeds. Don't think I'm talking about me. I had a wonderful staff, absolutely marvellous. Most of them went to be matrons themselves: Budicome went to Cambridge, Addenbrooke's, Jackson went to Liverpool, Harker went to a hospital in Doncaster, and Mary Hall went to the College of Nursing after the Middlesex.

Gertrude Cooper and Doreen Norton both became fascinated by research into nursing. After demobilisation, Gertrude Cooper did not want to return to nurse teaching. She tried several posts; she was matron to the ill-fated Groundnut Scheme* in East Africa; she also worked with the Crown Film Unit and was appointed to teach on a ward sister's course offered by the King's Fund. In 1954 she applied for a post as a nurse researcher. With the support of the National Florence Nightingale Memorial Fund and the Dan Mason Fund, she was involved in several projects. The reports she helped to produce were the first formal modern research into nursing in the UK.

Doreen Norton, student nurse, London County Council Hospitals, 1941–5; nurse researcher

Following her awful experiences as a student nurse, Doreen Norton became fascinated by the care of the elderly. Her curiosity led her to make contact with others who shared her interests. She began applying for research grants and with the support of Professor Exton-Smith, geriatrician at the Whittington Hospital, Highgate, became one of the first nurses to be awarded a substantial research grant.

... In July 1959 we established the first nursing research unit in Britain in a side ward of the [Whittington] Hospital without even a stick of furniture.

---

* A plan to cultivate tracts of what is now Tanzania with peanuts.

Memorials and memories

'... At least 3,076 people in nursing services lost their lives in World War II.'

Nurses themselves wanted to honour the contribution made by colleagues to the tumultuous times that they had lived through. They wanted a visible memorial. In 1946, the *Nursing Mirror* founded the British Empire Nurses War Memorial Fund, later the British Commonwealth Nurses War Memorial Fund, 'to provide a worthy memorial to the nurses, midwives, and auxiliaries of the British Commonwealth and Empire who lost their lives in World War II'. The first part of the memorial was a chapel in Westminster Abbey that was furnished by nurses. This was opened in November 1950 and a roll of honour including 3,000 names was deposited in the chapel. The second part of the memorial was the awarding of travel scholarships to Commonwealth nurses and midwives. These scholarships continued for the next twenty-five years.

Sheena Kilminster, née Craig, sister, PMRAFNS, 1946

Later on in my RAF career, I was very proud indeed to be one of three tall, quite well-built girls [who] were selected from amongst the staff at Halton to represent the whole of the RAF nursing service at the Cenotaph service, the Memorial Remembrance Service, in 1946. That was the year that my brother was killed in Burma, he was killed in March 1946, after the war of course was over. And I was very proud indeed to be one of those three selected and it was a very moving and very interesting experience.

Agnes Barnett, Territorial Army Nursing Service, called up February 1940; served in France, Middle East, Greece, Russia

One thing that I always feel a little bit guilty about, I've got a whole row of medals to show I've been in the army but I think the women who worked in the civilian hospitals at home had a tougher time than I had, because being in a base hospital you were not anywhere near the firing line or the danger area, and you worked hard but then so did everybody else. I wasn't any different, so I did feel a bit of a fraud pinning up my medals on 11 November.

Agnes Barnett's diffidence was typical of her generation, and of her profession. There were countless ordinary people from all walks of life who worked tirelessly and performed extraordinary acts of endurance and courage throughout the war, but nurses have been one of the great overlooked groups. Their contribution to both the British war effort and the rebuilding of the nation in the aftermath of victory was invaluable. The women and men who were interviewed for this project, whose voices still resonate across the years, are the very definition of heroes. We owe them an enormous debt of gratitude.

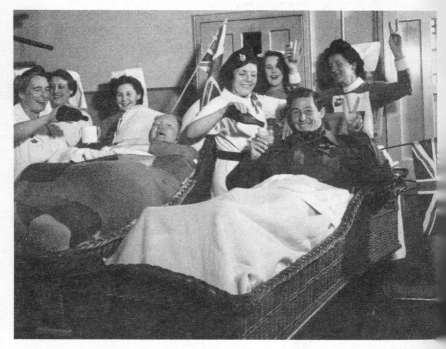

Seriously injured patients in 'spinal carriages' celebrate VE Day with nursing staff in Horley Military Hospital.

Acknowledgements

I wish to thank Hutchinson for commissioning this work and the Royal College of Nursing for supporting the project as it developed. The staff at the archives of the RCN, Fiona Bourne and Anne Cameron, have generously given of their time and helped with many difficulties.

The chapter on the occupation of the Channel Islands owes much to the help offered by Val Garnier, originally of Jersey, who with the support of the Public Health Department wrote a history of the Jersey hospitals to commemorate the fiftieth anniversary of the occupation. Geraldine desForges of Jersey recorded the original interviews for that project and has most generously allowed us to quote from them.

Mrs Peggy Boleat generously permitted us to quote from her account of her life as a patient in war-time. Michael Halliwell offered friendly advice and permitted us to quote from his interview with Betty Thurban.

My editors, Sarah Rigby and Helen Coyle, worked hard to offer very necessary assistance and I thank them heartily for that.

INDEX

All numbers in italics refer to the interview classification codes used at the archives of the Royal College of Nursing.

A

Abbott, Mary *T129,* 286, 297

abortions, 4–5, 127, 276

accommodation for nurses, 4, 17, 18, 50, 104, 107, 224

Addenbrooke's Hospital, 73, 194, 303

Africa, North, 139, 156–7, 214

aftermath of war, 236–7

age of entry, 4, 10, 30, 160

air-raid casualties, 97–8, 98, 108, 136

air-raid sirens, 54, 99–100, 103, 104, 150

Albania, 174, 175

Altschul, Annie Theresa *T/8,* 4–5, 29, 61–2, 68, 71–3, 140, 207–10, 292

ambulances, Green Line buses, 97, 98, 108

America, 296

American soldiers, 148

Americans, 196, 198, 218

amputees, 87–9

analgesia, 124

Anderson, Mary *T/QNI/24,* 131

aprons, 7, 139

Arundel Castle, 180

Ashford, Squandron Leader, 201

Athlone, Earl of, 113

Attlee, Clement, Prime Minister, 238

Australia, 38, 55–6, 60, 296

Australian soldiers, 148

Auxiliary Territorial Service, 76, 168, 196, 204, 292, 297

Aylmer, Sue *T/145,* 8, 40–1, 54, 93, 99–100, 142, 146–7, 147–8, 231

Ayr Hospital, 158

B

baby hoax, 134

badges/medals for nursing, 55, 106, 110, 149

bagpipes, 146

Baker, Betty (née Butlin) *T/CI/1,* 252, 264

Balmain, Isobel *T/75,* 10, 16–7, 193–4

Baly, Monica *T/100,* 35, 93–4, 139, 161–3, 165, 166, 173, 189, 200–1, 295–6

'banana money,' 239

Barnett, Agnes *T/132,* 138–9, 156, 167, 174–7, 206, 294–5, 304–5

Baths, 257

  bed baths, 22, 30, 253

  saline, 186, 189

Batley, Norma *T/128,* 90, 97, 219, 294